M000202838

Bank Loans: Secondary Market and Portfolio Management

Edited by

Frank J. Fabozzi, CFA
Adjunct Professor of Finance
School of Management
Yale University

Published by Frank J. Fabozzi Associates

 © 1998 By Frank J. Fabozzi Associates
New Hope, Pennsylvania

ALL RIGHTS RESERVED. No part of this publication may be reproduced, stored in a retrieval system, or transmitted, in any form or by any means, electronic, mechanical, photocopying, recording, or otherwise without the prior written permission of the publisher and the copyright holder.

This publication is designed to provide accurate and authoritative information in regard to the subject matter covered. It is sold with the understanding that the publisher is not engaged in rendering legal, accounting, or other professional services.

ISBN: 1-883249-44-9

Printed in the United States of America

Table of Contents

Contributing Authors

Mark J. P. Anson   OppenheimerFunds, Inc.
Elliot Asarnow   ING Capital Advisors
Steven Bavaria   Standard & Poor's
William Brennan   Fitch IBCA
Meredith W. Coffey   Loan Pricing Corporation
David Keisman   Portfolio Management Data, LLC
Michael McAdams   ING Capital Advisors
Derek McGirt   Fitch IBCA
Steven Miller   Portfolio Management Data, LLC
Steven D. Oldham   BancAmerica Robertson Stephens
James Roche   Fitch IBCA
Allison A. Taylor   ING Baring (U.S.) Securities, Inc.
and Chairperson of LSTA
Anthony V. Thompson   Goldman, Sachs & Co.
Ronald E. Thompson Jr.   Citicorp Securities, Inc.
Mariarosa Verde   Fitch IBCA
Eva F.J. Yun   Citicorp Securities, Inc.

Chapter 1

The Development of the Leveraged Loan Asset Class

Steven Miller
Principal
Portfolio Management Data, LLC

INTRODUCTION

For those investors that perceive the commercial loan market as the clubby and collegial dinosaur that Ron Chernow eulogized in his book, *The Death of the Banker and the Triumph of Small Investors*, the market may be worth a new look. After five years of steady development, the syndicated leveraged loan market — which broadly encompasses loans of non-investment grade or unrated borrowers priced at 125 basis points over LIBOR or higher — is transforming into an efficient segment of the capital markets. Over this timeframe, the market has developed many of the features normally associated with mature capital markets, including: a liquid secondary market, a large field of competitive underwriting institutions, a broad institutional investor base, securitization vehicles, data/analytic tools, credit ratings, professional managers, third-party providers of back-office functions, and portfolio management disciplines. This is a startling evolution for a financing segment that just 10 years ago was a closed, price-inefficient, bank-only market without any meaningful institutional investor representation.

Increasing liquidity and efficiency has been a boon to issuers, which have enjoyed decreasing credit spreads and underwriting fees as well as greater access to financing. For syndicators and investors, the impact of efficiency has been double-edged. Syndicators have seen underwriting fees decline as more and more new entrants muscled into the market. This has been balanced, however, by increased volume. For investors, the story is similar. Liquidity has meant tighter credit spreads balanced by the ability to better manage portfolios and concentration risk.

The author would like to thank the following individuals for their guidance and invaluable insights in writing this chapter: Tim Cross (LPC), Martin Fridson (Merrill Lynch), David Keisman (PMD), and Martha Klessen (BT Securities Corp.). This chapter is adapted from an article originally published in the July/August 1997 issue of *The Journal of Global High Yield Bond Research*.

The transformation of the syndicated loan market has been spurred by the growing institutional investor interest. Until the last few years, the leveraged loan market was dominated on the underwriting-side by the securities affiliates of a handful of money center banks and, on the investor side, by regional and foreign banks. While securities affiliates of money center banks — led by Bank of America, BT Alex. Brown, Chase Manhattan, Citicorp, J.P. Morgan, and NationsBank — continue to dominate the sell-side of the market, most bulge-bracket securities firms have established beachheads in the market and have begun to capture market share. And, on the buy-side, over 50 institutional investors have entered the market.

This chapter discusses the evolution of the leveraged loan market in recent years and what this evolution means for investors, underwriters, and issuers.

BACKGROUND

Syndications have been a hallmark of the commercial loan market for decades. The syndicated loan market, however, is a fairly new innovation, developed in the mid-1980s as a way to raise senior financing for LBO transactions that were far too large for any one bank to fund.[1] The essential change between syndications and the syndicated loan market is the role of the lead agent. Historically, the lead agent was a representative of the bank group. It negotiated terms and conditions on behalf of the other banks. That role changed dramatically with the development of the syndicated loan market. The lead agent began to act more like an investment bank, viewing the issuer as the client and lenders as investors. The agent now earns its fee by obtaining the best pricing and terms for the issuer.

In recent years, the syndicated loan market has been embraced by the full spectrum of issuers including large investment-grade companies and even middle market borrowers. The reason is that syndicated loans are less expensive and administratively taxing than traditional bilateral lines. The main drawback for issuers in going the syndications route is reduced control over their bank group. Most issuers appear to be willing to sacrifice this control in favor of lower costs and administrative headaches, based on the almost universal use of syndicated loans today. Syndicated loan new-issue volume totaled a record $888 billion in 1996, according to Loan Pricing Corporation (LPC), 550% more than 1987's total and 268% more than 1990's total.[2] And volume seems likely to reach $1 trillion in 1997.

In the 1980s, money center banks led by Bankers Trust (now BT Alex. Brown), Citibank, and Manufacturers Hanover were the primary originators of loans; foreign and regional banks were the primary markets for these loans. The credit crunch of the early 1990s — which was caused by a confluence of factors

---

[1] Dennis McCrary and Jo Ousterhout, "The Development and Future of the Loan Sales Market," *Journal of Applied Corporate Finance* (Fall 1989).

[2] Babak Varzandeh, "Refinancing, M&A Activity Lead to Record Volume; Lenders Get Creative with Structure to Deals," *Gold Sheets* (July 14, 1997).

but primarily a result of the slowing economy which set off a shocking run-up in defaults among speculative grade issuers and real estate developers — laid the groundwork for the transformation of the leveraged loan market to a segment of the capital markets. Here's how:

- *Improved Return Relative to Risk:* Many regional and foreign banks withdrew from the market, making capital scarce. The result was a sharp increase in pricing (relative to risk) which made loans attractive to institutional investors.
- *Introduction of Secondary Liquidity:* When the default rates soared in 1991 and 1992, many banks found themselves with severe concentrations in issuers and industries as well as in real estate. This panicked senior management, regulators, and stockholders. As a result, banks got religion about portfolio management and sought to reduce concentrations by selling off performing and distressed leveraged loans. A number of firms, led by BT Alex. Brown, Bear Stearns, Citibank, Continental Bank, and Goldman Sachs, set up secondary loan trading groups to take advantage of this opportunity. By 1997, roughly 25 dealers actively traded loans and the secondary loan market has blossomed with volume increasing from $8 billion in 1991 to $41 billion in 1996 and $28 billion in just the first six months of 1997, according to LPC.[3]

This combination of higher returns and secondary liquidity helped attract institutional investors into the leveraged loan market. In recent years, the loan investor base has become so robust that issuers have been able to command ever lower pricing, more aggressive credit structures, and looser terms (see "The Impact of Increased Capacity" below). This has left some early institutional entrants and traditional bank lenders pining for the illiquidity premium they were able to extract when there were fewer players competing to underwrite and participate in leveraged loans.

THE LEVERAGED LOAN INVESTOR BASE

Just ten years ago, leveraged loans were anathema to institutional investors. Despite offering collateral protection, covenants, and wide margins, loans were illiquid, prepayable at any time, administratively burdensome, difficult to understand, and offered none of the other features that institutional investors expect such as the ability to access market data and third-party credit ratings. Though almost all loans remain prepayable, most other issues that precluded institutional investment in loans have been removed. As a result, the institutional loan investor base has expanded rapidly, from just 14 institutions in 1993 to roughly 55 during the first half of 1997 (see Exhibit 1).

---

[3] Patrick Sullivan, "Secondary Volume Soars, Bid Levels Rise as Bullish Bankers, Investors Crowd Trading Market," *Gold Sheets* (August 11, 1997).

Exhibit 1: Number of Institutional Loan Investors

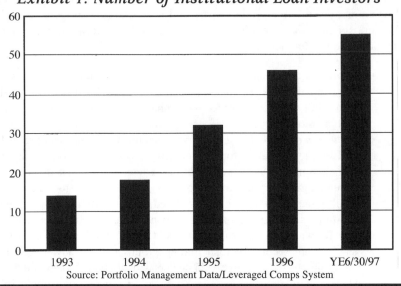

Source: Portfolio Management Data/Leveraged Comps System

Investing in Leveraged Loans

There are three primary ways to invest in loans: direct investment, using a fund manager, or through swaps and derivatives.

Direct Investment

Direct investment is the most straightforward, yet difficult, way to invest. Direct investments in each loan typically require $5 million minimum. To invest directly, an investor needs a portfolio of at least $250 million to attain diversification as well as the critical mass necessary to (1) command the attention of loan underwriters and (2) support a portfolio manager and the back-office necessary to manage and administer the loans.

Investing Through a Fund Manager

Investing using a fund manager offers investors the usual advantages over direct investment. First, the investment minimum is lower ($50 million or $100 million) and there is no administrative burden. Second, fund managers typically have billions of dollars under investment and therefore have access to primary syndications. Third, fund managers can provide diversification without a large amount invested. The cost of hiring a leveraged loan fund manager is roughly 37.5-62.5 basis points per year of amounts under management. Leveraged loan fund managers include: Trust Company of the West, Pilgrim America Group, ING Capital Advisors, Merrill Lynch Asset Management, Chancellor Capital, Oak Hill Securities, Protective Asset Management, Pacific Investment Management Company, Harch Capital, Alliance Capital, Eaton Vance Group, and Cypress Capital.

Derivative/Swaps

The derivatives market for leveraged loans remains in its nascent stages, though the notional amount of leveraged loans swap was estimated at roughly $8-10 billion by the first half of 1997, up from $4 billion in 1996 and $1 billion in 1993. The advantage of derivatives in the loan market, like other markets, is leverage. These products allow investors to leverage their capital five or more times and thereby increase their return on capital — and increase their risk — exponentially. They also require little if any administrative costs.

There are two broad types of leveraged loan derivatives: total rate of return swaps and pooled leveraged loan derivatives.[4] These vehicles are discussed later in this chapter.

Factors Contributing to Growth of
Institutional Loan Investors

The startling growth of institutional loan investors can be attributed to a myriad of factors, including:

- compelling risk/return opportunity
- relatively flat yield curve
- collateral and covenant protection
- growing liquidity
- development of structured products and derivatives
- marketing by syndicators and traders
- increasing use of professional managers
- proliferation of ratings
- data access and research

Compelling Risk/Return Opportunity

Without a compelling risk/return opportunity, the others would obviously be moot. Institutional investors are taking advantage of compelling risk/return opportunity that the loan market offers. To illustrate the risk/return opportunity of bank loans, relative to that of other assets classes, I use index data from January 1992 — the beginning of the secondary loan trading market — through the second quarter of 1997. Exhibit 2 shows that loans have a superior risk-adjusted return, as measured by the Sharpe ratio,[5] than the five other assets classes reviewed: S&P 500, high-yield bonds, corporate bonds, 7- to 10-year Treasuries, and 3- to 5-year Treasuries. The high relative Sharpe ratio is primarily a factor of loans' low price volatility (and, therefore, low risk under capital asset pricing model theory). This low price volatility is caused by the following:[6]

---

[4] Keith Barnish, Steven Miller, and Michael Rushmore, "The New Leveraged Loan Syndications Market," *Journal of Applied Corporate Finance* (Spring 1997).

[5] Defined as return of the asset class less the riskless rate divided by the standard deviation of returns.

[6] Michael Zupon and James Haskins, "NationsBanc Capital Markets, Inc. Leveraged Loan Index — Observations and Index Methodology" (October 21, 1996).

Exhibit 2: Risk-Adjusted Returns — Selected Asset Classes

	Annual Returns	Standard Deviation of Monthly Returns	Sharpe Ratio
S&P 500	13.8%	31.4%	0.30
High-Yield	11.8%	13.0%	0.57
Leveraged Loans	8.0%	4.2%	0.84
Corporate Bonds	7.7%	16.1%	0.21
7-10 year Treasuries	7.1%	19.2%	0.14
3-5 year Treasuries	6.1%	12.4%	0.14

Source: Bloomberg, Merrill Lynch, NationsBanc Capital Markets, Standard & Poor's

Exhibit 3: Correlation Coefficient
January 1, 1992 through June 30, 1997

	S&P 500	High-Yield	Leveraged Loans	Corporate Bonds	7-10 year Treasuries	3-5 year Treasuries
S&P 500	100%	35%	−14%	45%	45%	44%
High-Yield		100%	11%	66%	59%	60%
Leveraged Loans			100%	5%	5%	9%
Corporate Bonds				100%	98%	93%
7-10 year Treasuries					100%	96%
3-5 year Treasuries						100%

Source: Bloomberg, Merrill Lynch, NationsBanc Capital Markets, Standard & Poor's

- *Low interest rate risk:* Loans are floating-rate instruments that are reset every three months to one year. Therefore, they have little of the interest-rate risk associated with fixed-income and equity securities.
- *Low loss risk:* Loans are secured instruments that suffer far less dramatic price deterioration than unsecured corporate debt or equity in a distressed or default situation.
- *Prepayment option:* Borrowers have the option to prepay almost all loans at little or no premium. Therefore, borrowers usually refinance if credit quality improves or market spreads narrow. As a result, loan rarely trade higher than 101%.

Bank loans offer investors an even more important opportunity than high risk-adjusted returns: low correlations (see Exhibit 3) with other securities. The reason, again, is that loans are floating rate and therefore less interest rate sensitive than fixed income securities and equities. These two factors — high risk-adjusted returns and low correlation with equity and fixed-income investments — have made loans a compelling investment opportunity for a growing field of institutional investors.

Relatively Flat Yield Curve

The yield curve has flattened in recent years. The gap between 10-year Treasuries (the base-rate of most high-yield bonds) and 3-month LIBOR (the base rate of most leveraged loans) narrowed from an average of 4.51% in 1991 to just 0.72% during the first half of 1997. This, in turn, has made loans more attractive, relative to high-yield bonds and other fixed-income investments. The growth of retail mutual funds that buy leveraged loans — the *prime funds*, so-named because of their initial promise to return the Prime rate — highlights the effect of a flat yield curve. The assets of these funds grew 164% to $17.4 billion between year-end 1991 and June 30, 1997, according to LPC.[7]

Collateral and Covenant Protection

Leveraged loans are almost always secured by all assets of the borrower or by the capital stock of operating units, and are the senior most obligations in a borrower's capital structure. As a result, the average loss given default for secured leveraged loans was 18%, according to a study of 23 defaulted leveraged loans by LPC.[8] Subordinated bonds, by comparison, suffer an average loss given default of 66.4%, according to Moody's Investors Service.[9] In addition, loans have mandatory prepayment covenants that require prepayments from asset sales, excess cash flow and capital markets issuance. As a result, syndicated leveraged loans are repaid an average of 40% prior to default, according to the LPC study cited above. Unsecured bonds, by contrast, typically have bullet maturities and call protection and, therefore, experience little or no repayments prior to default. This collateral and covenant protection have made loans an attractive investment relatively to unsecured high-yield bonds, particularly for issuers and industries where prospects are uncertain.

Growing Liquidity

Leveraged loans, long-perceived as illiquid assets, have developed an active secondary trading market. By 1997, there were roughly 25 institutions that actively traded loans, and there were two inter-dealer brokers. And, the volume of leveraged loan trading has increased dramatically in recent years, according to LPC (see Exhibit 5 of Chapter 2). The growth of the trading market has removed the illiquidity stigma that kept many institutional investors from entering the market. It also allows leveraged loan investors — both banks and nonbanks — to manage their portfolios. This could help to avoid the concentration risks that exacerbated the credit crunch of the early 1990s.

---

[7] Babak Varzandeh, "Lenders Increase Reliance on Sponsors, Investors As Fight for Market Share Intensifies," *Gold Sheets* (July 28, 1997).

[8] Steven Miller and Christopher Snyder, "Institutional Investment in Leveraged Loans Grows," in John D. Finnerty and Martin S. Fridson (eds.), *The Yearbook of Fixed Income Investing 1995* (Burr Ridge, IL: Irwin Professional Publishing, 1995).

[9] Lea V. Carty and Dana Lieberman, "Historical Default Rates of Corporate Bond Issuers, 1920-1996," *Moody's Investors Service* (January 1997).

Market participants expect the recent formation of the Loan Syndications & Trading Association (LSTA) to further promote secondary liquidity. The LSTA is a trade association that counts among its members nearly every institution that syndicates and trades leveraged loans. It is responsible for developing market convention — as the Emerging Market Trading Association did for emerging markets debt trading. The LSTA has already imposed settlement conventions on the market and instituted a mark-to-market procedure. Just the formation of such an association would have been laughable five years ago. Today, however, the LSTA plays a critical role in making the market more efficient and standard.

Development of Structured Products and Derivatives

Collateralized Loan Obligations The proliferation of collateralized loan obligations (CLOs), securitized pools of leveraged loans, and collateralized debt obligations (CDOs), which buy loans along with fixed-income securities and sometimes equity, has truly been staggering.[10] These vehicles held an estimated $15 billion of leveraged loans by the first half of 1997, up from less than $3 billion in 1994.

By unbundling the risk of pools of assets, securitization structures like CLOs and CDOs attract new money into a market from investors that otherwise would not be buy the underlying assets. CLOs — which obviously must meet rigorous diversification standards — are normally funded by the following three tranches of securities:

	Usual rating	Typical % of liabilities	Estimated spread
Senior tranche	AA	75%	LIBOR+50
Subordinated tranche	BBB	10%	LIBOR+125
Equity residual tranche	NR	15%	

The top two tranches are easy to understand and place because their yield is in line with their credit rating. The equity tranche, which were challenging to place in the early 1990s, have become less so primarily because rating agencies have a more positive view of loan loss. Until 1995, the rating agencies employed draconian loss-given-default assumptions for loans. Under this view, which was based on a severe lack of empirical data, the agencies simply notched loans up one or two ratings places from the rating of subordinated, unsecured bonds of the same issuer (from B− to B+, for example). This reduced default probability of loans by several percentage points but did not address the vastly superior recovery prospects of loans. Today, as discussed below, rating agencies give far more credit for the covenant and collateral protection of leveraged loans and, therefore, employ a more favorable loss-given-default assumption. As a result, underwriters can structure CLOs with less equity today than they could several years ago. This greater leverage, of course, means higher nominal equity returns.

---

[10] For a further discussion, see Chapters 8 and 9.

Exhibit 4: Example of CLO Structures

Size of CLO ($MM) $100.00
Average LIBOR Spread of Assets L+250
Estimated LIBOR   6.25%

	Rating	Size of Tranche	Estimated Spread
Senior Tranche	AA	75	L+50
Subordinated Tranche	BBB	10	L+125
Equity Residual Tranche	NR	15	
Total		100	

Income To Equity Residual Tranche ($MM)	
Total Income	8.75
Interest to Senior Tranche	5.06
Interest to Subordinated Tranche	0.75
Management Fee	0.50
Income To Equity	2.44
Return on Investment	16.3%

Return on Equity Tranche (Adjusted for Default/Loss Rates)

	Average Recovery		
One Year Default Rate	40%	29%	18%
3.0%	8.3%	10.5%	12.7%
3.9%	5.9%	8.8%	11.6%
4.9%	3.2%	6.8%	10.4%

In bold are the average Moody's 1-year Default Rate and average senior secured bank loan recovery rate.

Exhibit 4 shows that the equity tranche of a CLO would produce a nominal return (without adjusting for default and loss) of 16%, based on the structure outlined above. The risk-adjusted return is 8.8%, using an average 3.9%, 1-year default rate for speculative grade bonds and an average 28.8% loss-given-default rate for secured loans reported by Moody's Investor Service. The risk-adjusted return, using the same default rate and LPC's 18% loss given default rate for loans, is 11.6%.

Derivatives There are two primary derivative structures in the leveraged loan market: total rate of return swaps and pooled leveraged loan derivative structures. These vehicles have attracted hedge funds, insurance companies and other institutional investors into the loan market by offering the ability to leverage their capital — and thereby increase their return and their risk.

1. Total Rate of Return Swaps: These are far and away the most common type of loan derivative. These instruments enable an investor to purchase the returns associated with a loan or a basket of loans in exchange for a fee. The fee can take the form of the spread on a loan to finance the derivative or could be an upfront fee built into the deal. Appaloosa and Shenkman Capital Management are among the hedge funds that actively purchase loan swaps, according to market sources. Hedge funds are an ideal candidate for loan swaps because they require little administration and can be leveraged up as much as the selling institution will allow.

Take, for example, a recent 3-year swap on a $10 million piece of River-wood International's Term Loan B, as described by one loan trader. Under the swap, the buyer put up $1 million of collateral, which was put in Treasuries. The seller provided a $10 million loan backed by this collateral. The buyer receives the return of Riverwood's Term Loan B — 300 basis points over LIBOR — plus any gains or losses from loan's closing value of slightly over par. In exchange, the seller receives the LIBOR rate plus 75 basis points (bp) on a $10 million loan. The buyer would normally borrow at roughly 12.5-25 bp over LIBOR, meaning a fee to the seller of 50-62.5 basis points. In addition to the fee, the buyer assumes total exposure to loss on the entire $10 million amount. The swap amortizes by scheduled and unscheduled repayments and there is an undisclosed break-up fee.

The buyer's return over Treasuries on its capital — assuming, of course, no default — is 22.5%, as well as the Treasury rate. However, a 10% decline in the loan's value wipes out the buyer's entire capital position.

2. Pooled Leveraged Loan Derivatives: Pooled leveraged loan derivatives, though still in the nascent stages of development, may have the most appeal to institutional investors, particularly those not already in the loan market. The reason is simple: they offer leverage, diversification and compelling risk/return — if you believe the risk these vehicle's ratings imply. Chase Securities is the primary purveyor of this product, according to market sources, with its Chase Secured Loan Trust Note (CSLTN). By the first half of 1997, there were four such products in the market: KZH-Soliel (run by SunAmerica Investments), KZH-ING (run by ING Capital Advisors), KZH Holdings III (run by Oppenheimer), and KZH-Crescent (run by Trust Company of the West). BT Alex. Brown has a similar offering called "High-Yield Loan Notes." Insurance companies are the primary buyers of these derivatives, according to market sources. For insurance companies, they are attractive because they offer investment grade ratings and, therefore, require lower capital reserves under the NAIC's rating scale than loans purchased in the cash market.

Pooled leveraged loan derivatives like CSLTN are fairly complex vehicles that usually: (1) carry an investment grade rating and (2) limits an investor's downside to its capital contribution while allowing the ability to leverage its capital up to seven times. Here's how a CSLTN-like structure works, (according to market participants):

An investor puts its capital into a trust for a predetermined period. The trust invests in Treasury securities which are used as collateral to purchase leveraged loan assets. In most cases, the collateral is leveraged between three and five times (meaning three to five dollars of leveraged loan assets purchased for every dollar of collateral). For example, an investor could invest $10 million in the trust. The $10 million is invested in Treasuries and used as collateral for a $50 million loan to purchase leveraged loan assets. The higher the leverage, of course, the higher the potential return as well as risk. If the amount used to finance the loans ($50 million less the value of the loans) is less than the collateral amount, the trust automatically unwinds and the investment is lost.

Exhibit 5: Potential Returns on a 3-Year Leveraged Loan Derivative, Based on Default Rates and Leverage

Annual Default Rate	Annual Loss Rate *	Leverage					
		2×	3×	4×	5×	6×	7×
1.00%	0.18%	9.68%	11.29%	12.93%	14.58%	16.26%	17.95%
2.00%	0.36%	9.31%	10.74%	12.18%	13.63%	15.10%	16.59%
3.00%	0.54%	8.94%	10.18%	11.43%	12.69%	13.96%	15.24%
3.93%	**0.71%**	**8.60%**	**9.66%**	**10.74%**	**11.82%**	**12.90%**	**14.00%**
5.00%	0.90%	8.21%	9.07%	9.94%	10.82%	11.70%	12.58%
6.00%	1.08%	7.85%	8.53%	9.21%	9.89%	10.58%	11.27%
7.00%	1.26%	7.48%	7.98%	8.47%	8.97%	9.47%	9.97%

Assumptions

3-year Treasury	6.50%
Average return of loans	2.50%
Fee (paid by the investor)	0.75%
Average loss given default*	18.0%

Moody's 1-year default rate for speculative grade issues in bold.

Quarterly compounding

* Based on a Loan Pricing Corp. study of 23 defaulted syndicated leveraged loans.

The trust pays a rate of roughly 75 bp over LIBOR to finance its purchase of leveraged loan assets. In return, the trust receives the rate paid on the loans (typically LIBOR+225) along with any gains or losses on the loans. It also receives the income generated by the collateral (either Treasuries or a LIBOR equivalent). In effect, therefore, the investor — who owns the trust — receives a base rate on its investment (either Treasuries or LIBOR) plus whatever return the leverage loan assets generate over the LIB+75. As leverage increases, the returns can become extremely attractive, particularly if an investor believes default rates will stay low (see Exhibit 5).

Marketing by Syndicators and Traders

Marketing is a significant factor in the growth of any market. Most people are now familiar with the maxim that equities, over time, are the best investment. This conclusion, based on the S&P 500 and other indexes, has been pushed relentlessly by brokers and purveyors of mutual funds over the past 10 years. On a far less grand scale, syndicators and traders have developed market benchmarks that allow potential investors to gauge leveraged loan returns. By 1997, there were five published leveraged loan indexes available from the following players: BT Alex. Brown, Citibank, Goldman Sachs/Loan Pricing Corporation, Lehman Brothers, and NationsBank. As illustrated above, these indexes provided the empirical data necessary to make a compelling case for loans as an asset class on a risk-adjusted return basis.

Increasing Use of Professional Managers

The growing field of professional managers has allowed many insurance companies and other institutional investors to invest in the syndicated loan market without going through the expense of hiring a portfolio manager and administrative staff to manage their portfolio. Also, fund managers, by wielding billions of dollars to invest, are able to command attention in primary syndications that a single investor with a $100 million or $200 million portfolio simply can't. As noted earlier, the price of hiring a fund manager is roughly 37.5-62.5 basis points per year of assets under management. By 1997, there are four primary managers of insurance company money: Trust Company of the West, Chancellor Capital, Cypress Capital, and ING Capital Advisors. Of the 23 insurance companies that invested in the leveraged loan market at June 30, 1997, 13 did so through a non-captive fund manager, according to Portfolio Management Data (PMD).

Proliferation of Ratings

Leveraged loan ratings are a fairly new innovation. Until 1995, the rating agencies effectively ignored this fairly arcane market. Banks, after all, had large and costly infrastructure designed to evaluate credit risk. In recent years, however, the market has become more dynamic, with a growing field of institutional investors that do not have the staff or wherewithal to evaluate each loan the way most banks do. As a result, rating agencies have embraced the market, offering loan ratings that incorporate not just default probability but loss-given-default expectations. For loan investors, of course, expected loss-given-default can be an even more important factor than default probability.

By the first half of 1997, Moody's Investors Service and Standard & Poor's had rated the vast majority of large, syndicated leveraged loans. These ratings promote transparency and thereby make loans more attractive to investors. As a result, a growing number of issuers and underwriters are incorporating bank loan ratings — which provide a disinterested risk assessment and a credit write-up — into the loan syndications and structuring process. A recent loan syndicated by J.P. Morgan for Bethlehem Steel, for example, had pricing tied to the borrower's bank loan, rather than corporate credit, rating.

Data Access and Research

An article in the August 6, 1997 issue of American Banker quotes Bob Woods, the recently hired head of loan syndications at Societe Generale, as saying that access to information is the major difference he has observed in the loan market since the late 1980s.[11] Since that time, the syndicated loan market has attracted a cottage industry of information providers — including Bloomberg, Euromoney, Intralinks, KMV, LPC, and SDC.

---

[11] Omri Ben-Amos, "French Bank Finds U.S. Syndications Chief at Citi," *American Banker* (August 6, 1997).

Syndicated loan data services have gone a long way toward leveling the playing field by allowing information to be more equitably distributed. Until recently, the large syndicating banks had a virtual hammer-lock on market information simply because they did so many deals and had the staff necessary to research and compile data. Today, information services allow most market participants to efficiently access, compile, and analyze market data. While the large syndicating banks and active investors continue to have an edge — as they do in every market — this edge is not nearly as formidable as it once was.

Research is another new facet of the loan market that market players expect to add transparency and thereby attract a growing field of investors. Bank of America was the first firm to commit a dedicated staff to publish industry- and issuer-specific "Street" research on loans. Bank of America has been followed by Bank of Boston, Bank of Montreal, BZW, and Citibank in setting up loan research groups.

THE IMPACT OF INCREASED CAPACITY

The previous section explains why institutional investors have been entering the leveraged loan market in unprecedented numbers. This section explores the impact of this growing investor base on the market.

The first and most obvious consequence of more investors is ever-larger deal capacity. Total capacity of the syndicated loan market to absorb a single leveraged loan increased 36%, to $3.8 billion, between 1996 and 1997, according to a study by PMD.[12] This increase in deal capacity far outstripped the 5.6% increase in leveraged loan volume reported by LPC during the first half of 1997 (see Exhibit 11 of Chapter 2). So, despite the rapid increase in leveraged loan volume in recent years, there is an overhang in deal capacity which has led to lower pricing and less conservative structures.

Pricing

Both credit spreads and upfront fees have compressed in recent years as issuers take advantage of strong demand to extract more and more favorable terms. In talking about pricing, the market is divided into pro rata tranches and institutional tranches (see Exhibit 6). *Pro rata tranches* comprise revolving credits and amortizing term loans and are syndicated primarily to banks. These tranches usually run five to seven years. *Institutional tranches* comprise back-end loaded term loans named in alphabet series (e.g., B term loan, C term loan, D term loan) and are syndicated primarily to institutional investors. These tranches are generally priced at a 25 to 100 basis point premium to pro rata tranches because they run longer in tenor, usually 7 to 10 years.

---

[12] This study looked at loans with pro forma Debt/EBITDA of 4.00× or greater and excluded such brand-name borrowers as Westinghouse and Norfolk Southern.

Exhibit 6: Syndicated Leveraged Loan Characteristics

Leveraged credits are typically divided into tranches, with longer-dated instruments carved out for institutional investors. These "B," "C," or "D" term loans have back-end loaded maturities and are priced incrementally higher than amortizing bank term loans.

Ranking: Senior, secured instruments which, at times, have pari passu public or private debt.

Stated Maturity & Average Life

	Average Life	Final Maturity
Revolving Credit	Bullet Maturity	5-7 years
Amortizing TL	3-5 years	5-7 years
TL B	5-7 years	6-8 years
TL C	6-7.5 years	7-8.5 years
TL D	7-8.5 years	8-9.5 years

Typical Pricing (Spread over LIBOR)

Single B/B- (senior unsecured rating)	
Revolving Credit	175-300
Amortizing TL	175-300
TL B	200-350
TL C	225-375
TL D	300-400
BB-/B+ (Senior unsecured rating)	125-162.5*
BB+/BB (Senior unsecured rating)	50-112.5*

* Typically, loans to these companies do not have B/C/D tranches.

Pricing Options

Borrowers tend to use a loan's fixed-rate, LIBOR option, which is reset every one to 12 months at the borrower's option. A short-term, Prime option is also available. This is almost always a more costly alternative and, therefore, is used mainly for overnight or short-term borrowings.

Covenants   Tight financial compliance is required. The loans usually have at least one coverage and one leverage covenant, both set tightly to projections. The borrowers ability to take on more debt, sell assets, pay dividends or make investments is restricted.

Voting Rights

Issue	Typical Consent
Amendments/waivers/consents	51-67%
Material collateral release	100% on most loans; 51%-85% on loans for some large corporate and equity sponsors.
Interim amortization	51-100%
Final maturity	100%
Rate reduction	100%
Tranche voting	Any changes that affect an individual tranche usually require the approval of 51% of the affected lenders.

Typical Mandatory Prepayments

The borrower must repay the loans from a variety of sources including

Excess cash flow	50-75% *
Asset sale proceeds	Typically 100% of non-reinvested proceeds
Equity proceeds	0-100% *
Debt proceeds	Typically 100%

* Prepayments from these sources are often reduced or waived if the borrower achieves a pre-defined performance test.

Optional Prepayments   The borrower is always allowed to prepay, usually without penalty.

Interest Payments   Quarterly

Upfront Fees

Upfront fees — which are paid to lenders at close of syndication — are the syndicated loan market's version of discounts in the bond market. Upfront fees are set by commitment (with larger commitments receiving a larger upfront fee — e.g., 0.25% for $25 million dollar commitments and 0.10% for $10 million commitments) and paid on allocations (e.g., if an institution commits $25 million and is scaled back to $15 million it would receive 0.25% on $15 million). Upfront fees have compressed significantly in recent years for both pro rata and institutional commitments. (See Exhibit 22 of Chapter 2.)

- *Pro Rata Tranches:* On average, fees paid at the lowest commitment tier for pro rata commitments have declined from 1.00% in 1992 and 1993 to 0.34% during the first half of 1997, according to PMD.
- *Institutional Tranches:* Compression in the institutional segment has been even more pronounced, as more and more investors enter the market. Since syndicators began to set fees differently for institutional and pro rata tranches in 1995, fees for institutional commitments declined to 0.27% during the first half of 1997, from 0.625% in 1995. And, in a possible sign of things to come, BT Alex. Brown's August 1997 syndication of a $1.245 billion loan backing Goodman Manufacturing Company's acquisition of Raytheon Appliance Inc. offered no upfront fees on $460 million of institutional term loans.[13]

Spreads

The story is much the same with credit spreads.

- *Pro Rata Tranches:* Until recently, the LIBOR plus 250 basis point pricing point was a bulwark for new highly leveraged loans — those with Debt/EBITDA of five times or higher, out of the box. Despite all the compression in the investment grade and near-investment grade market from 1991 to 1995, it wasn't until late 1996 that pricing for the highly leveraged loans began to slip. The first large loan to break the model was a $650 million credit led by Bank of America, Merrill Lynch, and NationsBank that backed Kohlberg, Kravis & Roberts' leveraged buyout of Spalding & Evenflo Companies. It was priced at LIB+225, based on the strength of the sponsor, a large equity contribution (which totaled 35% of total sources), and Spalding's long and successful history as a seasoned leveraged borrower. Exhibit 7 shows that spread compression in the leveraged market has been most pronounced for near-investment grade loans — those with Debt/EBITDA of 3.00× to 3.99×, out of the box. This is because demand has been the strongest in

---

[13] Beth Harmen, "Late-Breaking News — Goodman Manufacturing," *Gold Sheets* (August 4, 1997).

the near-investment grade segment. Spread compression has been more gradual for highly leveraged loans (those with Debt/EBITDA ratios of 5.00× or higher) with more and more deals — particularly those with strong corporate or equity sponsors and stories — priced at LIB+225, rather than LIB+250.

- *Institutional Tranches:* Institutional lenders were able to resist pricing declines that affected most segments of the syndicated loan market between 1992 and 1995 because there were so few players in the market. That, as stated earlier, is no longer the case. Exhibit 8 shows that, since 1995, the average pricing of new institutional term loans with starting Debt/EBITDA of 5.00× to 6.00× declined from LIB+334 to LIB+293 as a result of increased demand for paper. Another form of pricing compression is the increasing use of pricing grids — which allow pricing to step down as an issuer's performance improves — on institutional tranches. These grids, long a staple of pro rata tranches, were seen rarely on institutional tranches prior to 1996. During the first half of 1997, 41% of institutional term loans were tied to pricing grids, according to PMD.

Credit Structures

With diminishing credit spreads and more aggressive structures, the clear question is: Are lenders repeating the excesses of the 1980s? The answer just as clearly is no.

Exhibit 7: LIBOR Spread of Leveraged Loans by Initial Pro Forma Debt/EBITDA Ratio

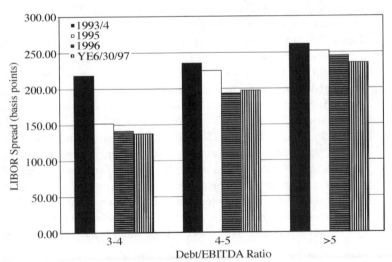

Exhibit 8: Pricing of New Institutional Term Loans with Debt/EBITDA Multiples of 5.00× to 6.00×

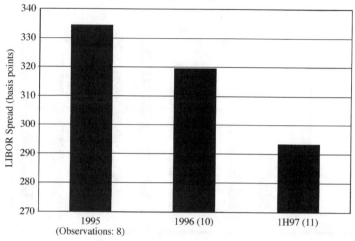

Though overall debt multiples have expanded since the credit crunch of the early 1990s, they are nowhere near the stratospheric levels seen in the late 1980s (see Exhibit 16 in Chapter 2). And, more important, the average equity contributed to new leveraged buyouts has remained at roughly 25% of total sources throughout the 1990s, far above the single-digit contributions that were common in the late 1980s (see Exhibit 9). Perhaps the riskiest type of loan common in the late 1980s — the asset sale bridge — is rarely seen today. In fact, the $7.5 billion acquisition loan led by Chase/Chemical and J.P. Morgan that backed Westinghouse's 1995 acquisition of CBS is the exception that proves the rule. The loan included a $2.5 billion asset sales bridge loan. It is telling that only a borrower with the clout and massive market capitalization of Westinghouse can obtain a syndicated asset sales bridge loan.

While lenders are clearly not repeating the excesses of the 1980s, this is not to say that they aren't taking new risks. The increase in bank debt/EBITDA multiples shown in Exhibit 16 of Chapter 2 is one such risk. There have been a number of cash flow-based deals in recent years financed solely with bank debt and equity. Several of these deals, namely London Fog and Camelot Music, have met with disastrous results when the borrowers defaulted — because without subordinated debt in the capital structure banks have little protection again loss given default. London Fog and Camelot, both syndicated by Chemical Bank, were originally structured with a tranche of subordinated debt which was abandoned in favor of more bank debt when the bonds proved too difficult to place. Since their respective defaults, London Fog and Camelot's bank debt had initial distressed trading levels of 20-40 cents on the dollar. This is far below the trading levels of 60-80 cents on the dollar normally seen for defaulted loans that are senior to a significant tranche of subordinated debt.

Exhibit 9: Equity Contribution to LBOs, as a Percent of Total Source

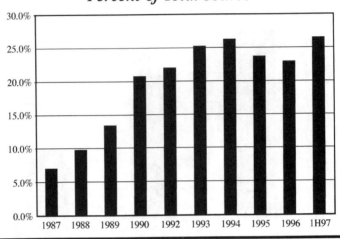

Covenants

By 1997, issuers were unquestionably able to negotiate more flexible agreements than they could just two or three years before — with bigger acquisition baskets and performance triggers that reduce or even waive mandatory prepayments from cash flow and equity. And, supermajority voting is appearing on a small but growing number of deals, where as little as 51% of lenders are required to approve collateral release and amortization changes — provisions where full votes were, until recently, a sacrosanct right. In fact, the percent of all leveraged loans backed by an equity sponsor that has supermajority collateral release voting increased to 12.6% during the first half of 1997, from 6.9% in 1995, according to PMD.

While lenders are accepting more and more flexible structures, particularly if the borrower achieves specified performance targets, financial compliance covenants in the vast majority of deals remains tight. And, all highly leveraged loans are still secured by either all assets or, in the case of loans backed by the strongest sponsors, like KKR and Investcorp, capital stock of operating subsidiaries. Therefore, leveraged loan investors are generally more concerned about diminishing return and more aggressive credit statistics than covenant deterioration.

Rapid Refinancing

Strong investor demand is encouraging issuers to refinance loans — which are prepayable at any time with little or (in most cases) no prepayment premium — at reduced pricing, longer tenors, and less restrictive covenants. And, a recent LPC study found that they are doing so with greater and greater urgency.[14] Of all insti-

---

[14] Babak Varzandeh, "Rapid Refinancings Gather Momentum, Leaving Investors Between Rock and Hard Place," *Gold Sheets* (May 26, 1997).

tutional term loans syndicated in 1996, 36% were refinanced within one year, up from 15% of those loans syndicated in 1992. Rapid refinancing is another form of pricing compression that is likely to accelerate as the market becomes increasingly efficient and underwriters compete vociferously for business.

RECENT TRENDS

Convergence has been the dominant theme on both the sell- and buy-side of the leveraged finance market in the late 1990s.

Sell-Side

Nearly all of the bulge bracket investment banks entered or stepped up their efforts in the leveraged loan market since 1995. Between 1995 and the first half of 1997, in fact, investment banks have increased their share of lead agent positions for leveraged loans backed by equity sponsors — the most coveted segment of the leveraged loan market — from just 2% to 18%, according to LPC.[15] At the same time, market leader Chase/Chemical's share of this segment has declined from an astonishing 32% to 20%. These firms are, in part, responding to the in-roads made by commercial banks, through their section 20 affiliates, into the high-yield bond and M&A advisory markets. These section 20 affiliates, which include BA Securities, BT Securities, Chase Securities, CIBC/Wood Gundy, J.P. Morgan Securities, and NationsBanc Capital Markets, have made major strides into the high-yield bond market and ranked among the top 15 high-yield bond managers during the first half of 1997, according to SDC.

Money center banks and bulge-bracket investment banks are able to offer one-stop shopping capabilities — loans and bonds — to leveraged issuers. The transformation of leverage finance into an increasingly seamless market is having a profound influence on the way deals are executed and placed. First and foremost, the underwriters can look across the loan and bond markets to provide the best, and most cost-effective, execution. Second, underwriters are developing products that appeal to both high-yield bond and institutional loan investors.

The first such product was institutional term loans bundled with prepayment premiums. Loans traditionally did not have such premiums, which made them less attractive to institutional investors which usually expect some form of prepayment protection. In recent years, however, underwriters have offered issuers the option to include modest upfront fees on institutional loans in exchange for a concession on the credit spread. Goldman Sachs was the first firm to formalize this effort with its Amortization Extended Loans (Axels) which included prepayment fees usually in the range of 1.5-3.0% in year one declining incrementally in year two and three and waived entirely in year four. These loans are not wide

---

[15] Varzandeh, "Lenders Increase Reliance on Sponsors, Investors As Fight for Market Share Intensifies."

spread yet, representing only 11 of the 214 institutional term loan tracked in PMD's Leveraged Comps System (LCS) in 1996 and the first half of 1997. However, they may gain momentum as issuers use the prepayment premium to reduce credit spreads. For the institutional term loans tracked in LCS with prepayment premiums, the average credit spread was roughly 15 basis points less than those with prepayment fees.[16]

A more recent product innovation is so-called "hybrid" loans. These products are like bonds because they have few or no compliance covenants and often carry prepayment penalties. They are like loans in that hybrids are secured instruments that do not have call protection. Between the time BT Alex. Brown introduced the first hybrid loan in March 1997 — a $135 million term loan for Huntsman Specialty Group — and September of that year, there were seven hybrid loans syndicated with a total volume of nearly a billion dollars. (See Exhibit 10.) Hybrid loans for Refraco Inc and Playtex Inc were publicly filed, meaning some of the terms are available.

Refraco

The Refraco loan, led by BT Alex. Brown, backed the acquisition of Hepworth Refractories Ltd. by the company's Adience Inc. unit. It was syndicated in conjunction with a $130 million credit for Adience which comprised a $35 million 6-year revolving credit, a $50 million 6-year amortizing term loan, and a $45 million 8-year institutional term loan. The hybrid has several significant differences from the Adience loan:

- *Longer Tenor:* It runs 10 years.
- *Prepayment Penalty:* It carries a prepayment penalty (3.0% in year one, 1.0% in year two, and 0.5% in year three). There is no prepayment penalty on the Adience loan.
- *Higher Spread:* It is priced at LIB+375, compared to LIB+250 on the Adience revolver and amortizing term loan and LIB+300 on the institutional term loan.
- *Looser Covenants:* It has just one financial compliance covenant (a debt/ EBITDA test), compared to four covenants on the Adience loan (fixed charge coverage, debt/EBITDA, interest coverage, and EBITDA). And, the debt/EBITDA covenant is looser in the hybrid than the Adience loan.
- *Security:* The hybrid is a holding company loan that is secured by capital stock of Refraco and $30 million of stock of Superior TeleCom (a company owned by Refraco's parent, Alpine Group). The Adience loan is secured by all operating company assets.

---

[16] The credit spread is measured relative to the pro rata tranches of the same transaction. Without prepayment fees, the credit spread of institutional term loans is, on average, 48 basis points. With prepayment fees, it is 33 basis points.

Exhibit 10: Characteristics of Hybrid Term Loans

Issuer	Date	Amount	Lead Agents	Spread	Term	Prepayment Fees		
						Year 1	Year 2	Year 3
Adience Inc	Apr-97	$60.00	BT Alex. Brown	L+375	8.5	3.00%	1.00%	0.50%
Dayton Superior Corp	Nov-97	$100.00	Donaldson Lufkin Jenrette/BT Alex. Brown/BankAmerica	L+275	8.0	2.00%	1.00%	0.50%
Huntsman Specialty Chemicals Corp	Mar-97	$135.00	BT Alex. Brown	L+350	10.0	3.00%	1.50%	0.75%
Pioneer Americas Acquisition Corp	Jun-97	$100.00	Donaldson Lufkin Jenrette/ BankAmerica/Salomon	L+250	9.5	3.00%	2.00%	1.00%
Playtex Inc	Jul-97	$150.00	Donaldson Lufkin Jenrette	L+150	6.5	3.00%	2.00%	1.00%
SC Intern'l Services	Sep-97	$160.00	JP Morgan/BT Alex. Brown	L+150	7.8	No Prepayment Fees		
Total Renal Care	Oct-97	$200.00	Bank of New York/Donaldson Lufkin Jenrette	NA	10.0	1.50%	0.75%	
Total		$905.00						

Playtex

Unlike the Refraco hybrid described above, the Playtex hybrid — led by Donaldson Lufkin Jenrette — is secured on a pari passu, ratable basis with the company's credit agreement. The Playtex hybrid was syndicated with a $170 million credit agreement for Playtex that comprised a $75 million revolving credit; a $55 million term loan, and a $40 million acquisition facility. All three of these facilities run six years and are priced at LIB+125. The hybrid differs from Playtex credit agreement in the following ways:

- *Longer Tenor:* It runs 6.5 years.
- *Prepayment Penalty:* It carries a prepayment penalty (3.0% in year one, 2.0% in year two and 1.0% in year three). There is no prepayment penalty on the credit agreement.
- *Higher Spread:* It is priced higher at LIB+150, compared to LIB+125 on credit agreement facilities.
- *Looser Covenants:* It has no compliance covenants. The credit agreement has three such covenants (cash flow coverage, debt/EBITDA, and capital expenditures). If the credit agreement is paid off, therefore, the hybrid lenders are left without compliance covenants.

The Playtex loan was also unusual, and may indicate future directions, because DLJ syndicated it much like a bond, according to LPC's Gold Sheets.[17] The loan was priced to market rather than the normal syndicated loan market convention of setting pricing first (usually with a healthy dose of market talk and feedback) and then placing the loan to investors.

Buy-Side

The buy-side of the market has seen a rash of relative-value players that look across the balance sheet of leveraged issuers to identify the best value. These players include (1) mutual funds, like Eaton Vance Group's Senior Debt Portfolio and Merrill Lynch Asset Management's Senior High-Income Portfolio, (2) collateralized debt obligations, including vehicles from Oak Hill Securities and Trust Company of the West, and (3) traditional high-yield investors including insurance companies.

Relative value investors have a significant advantage over investors that are limited to only leveraged loans or high-yield. The reason is that relative-value investors can take a point of view on an issuer or industry and act accordingly either by buying the loans or the bonds. If, for instance, the issuer's prospects seem positive, the relative-value investor may choose to invest in the issuer's bonds, which have call protection and offer a higher yield. If prospects are less certain, the investor may choose to invest in the issuer's loan to take advantage of collateral and covenants.[18]

---

[17] Beth Harmen, "Late-Breaking News — Playtex," *Gold Sheets* (July 14, 1997).
[18] Barnish, Miller, and Rushmore, "The New Leveraged Loan Syndications Market."

CONCLUSION

Despite the rapid increase in institutional involvement, leveraged loans remain the largest untapped source of high-yield paper. Of the estimated $200 billion of leveraged loans outstanding, only $40-$50 billion is in the hands of nonbank investors. In the next few years, institutional involvement seems poised for significant growth given the compelling risk/return opportunity of leveraged loans and rapid development of the market. Already, demand from investors is so ravenous that many loans — even those without prepayment premiums — are trading as 101% of par. And, many institutional investors are stepping up for amortizing term loans and even revolving credits, tranches they avoided in the past when demand for paper was less robust. This demand will undoubtedly provide issuers with (1) ever greater access to senior financing to support acquisitions, recapitalizations, and new technologies like personal communications systems and satellite technology and (2) the ability to negotiate ever lower credit spreads and upfront fees as well as more flexible credit terms.

Chapter 2

The Leveraged
Bank Loan Market

Steven D. Oldham, CFA
Senior Associate and Loan Research Analyst
BancAmerica Robertson Stephens

INTRODUCTION

The leveraged bank loan market offers an attractive combination of flexibility and efficiency, structure, and pricing that continues to attract leveraged loan issuers and investors alike. A continuous syndication bull market has thrived since 1992, and the leveraged bank loan marketplace continues to enjoy excellent liquidity and acceptable risk/return profile, despite the structure and pricing erosion caused by fierce competition. The following trends drive the continuing evolution of the leveraged bank loan market:

- Traditional pockets of debt capital are melding into one large capital pool, as new funds continue to pour into the leveraged loan market. Indeed, the leveraged loan syndication process is evolving from a private placement-type model to a bond-type model.
- Relative value drives the leveraged loan market pricing and structure, with the convergence and integration of bank loan and bond originators and investors causing pricing in one market to affect the other.
- The dramatic increase in new institutional loan investors has transformed leveraged loan market demand and made possible a variety of innovative bond-like structures.
- Heavy competition for loan paper has fueled more aggressive pricing and structure, although credit statistics remain more conservative than in the late 1980s.
- The leveraged loan bull market still has plenty of room to run. Equity sponsor fund raising continues to increase, additional institutional investors enter the market, and originating banks are accelerating the speed of innovation.

Exhibit 1: Leveraged Bank Loans:
Total and Leveraged Loan Volume, 1988–1H97

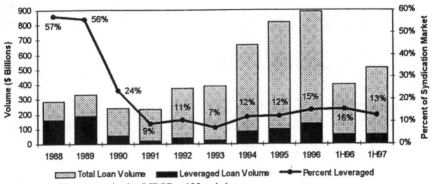

Note: Leveraged loans are priced at LIBOR + 125 and above.
Source: BancAmerica Robertson Stephens and Loan Pricing Corporation.

Market convention defines leveraged loans as noninvestment grade and unrated credits priced at the London Interbank Offer Rate (LIBOR) + 125 to 225 basis points and highly leveraged transactions (HLTs) as LIBOR + 225 and above. Corporations and financial sponsors turn to the loan syndications market to finance acquisitions, leveraged recapitalizations, divestitures, and spin-offs. Exhibit 1 illustrates the robust leveraged lending market, fueled by this transaction activity.

RELATIVE VALUE

The capital and loan markets are converging, driven by commercial banks expanding beyond traditional roles, by investment banks adding lending capabilities, and by investors who assess the relative returns from bank and bond investment vehicles. Despite robust growth in leveraged bank loan market issuance, investment supply is well short of demand from banks and institutional investors. The flood of liquidity into the leveraged loan sector has not only overwhelmed the supply of new leveraged loans, but also has fundamentally changed the way leveraged loans are structured and priced. Agent banks must closely consider bond returns when structuring and pricing leveraged loans to ensure the interest of both issuers and investors.

Comparing fixed-rate bonds and floating-rate loans involves assessing the trade-offs associated with each investment vehicle. Loans offer a senior secured position in the capital structure, offset by the borrower's option to prepay at any time, but the value of these embedded provisions can only be estimated at origination. While the reduced risk in the loan's senior secured status will result in a lower yield than that of an unsecured high yield bond, the severity of the discount is determined by the cost of the issuer's prepayment option, as defined in the credit agreement of the loan. Estimating refinancing risk is an important step for leveraged bank loan investors, especially those who purchase loans in the secondary market. Despite nominal maturities of 7–10 years, Exhibit 2 shows that institutional tranches are outstanding an average of only 18 months, with fully three-quarters of B/C/D term loans repaid within three years.

The strong economy has enabled many debt-laden borrowers to rapidly delever and issue subsequent financings without institutional term loans. Even when the business fundamentals and credit profile of a company are not meaningfully changed, the excessive loan market liquidity has enabled the issuer to refinance at lower spreads. With money returning almost as fast as institutions can reinvest it, market participants are very hungry for new opportunities. In some cases, institutional investors remained in refinanced deals, despite lower spreads, due to the lack of alternatives and their familiarity with the credit. Call protection for issuers in such an environment can prove quite valuable.

Primary Market Volatility

As originators have developed the capability to underwrite entire financing structures, they provide issuers the opportunity to survey the leveraged loan and high yield bond markets in search of the optimal combination of debt capitalization. It has been common in 1997 for the issuer and the underwriter to adjust the sizes of the loan and bond tranches prior to closing to obtain better terms for the issuer. The resulting dynamic is that indicative pricing for the institutional loan tranches directly reflect *public* bond market pricing. Examples include:

- *Packard BioScience* The $265 million credit backing Stonington Partners' leveraged buyout of Packard BioScience changed as market reception for the bonds was better than anticipated. $50 million was added to the high yield bond offering, while A and C term loans were dropped, and the total senior debt portion was reduced from $140 million to $115 million.
- *Del Monte Corporation* The institutional term loan B tranche was increased in the financing for the acquisition of Del Monte Corporation by Texas Pacific Group, after the high yield bond market became less attractive to the issuer on a relative value basis.

Exhibit 2: Cumulative Repayment Rate of Institutional Term Loans Since 1992

Year	Percent Repaid
1	27
2	63
3	76
4	87

Source: Loan Pricing Corporation.

• *Pioneer Americas* Pioneer Americas' $300 million term loan/bond financing for the company's acquisition of an Occidental Chemical's chlor-akali plant offered two investments with equal seniority and collateral, and similar covenants: a $200 million, 10 year 144-A bond and a $100 million, 9.5 year term loan. The bond was not callable for five years, with three years of declining call premiums thereafter. The term loan offered call premiums of 3%, 2%, and 1% in years 3, 2, and 1, respectively, but whose LIBOR spread was set after, and consistent with, the fixed-rate bond pricing.

LEVERAGED BANK LOAN INVESTORS

Institutional Investors

With low risk per unit of return, bank loans have become an important asset class for insurance companies, hedge funds, collateralized loan obligations (CLOs), and prime funds. Investors are drawn to bank loans' low duration which protects against the threat of rising interest rates. In addition, Moody's average recovery rates for bank loans during default reach 71% of par, more than double the average subordinated bond recovery rate of 34%.[1] The relatively stable total return for the bank loan asset class is particularly attractive to investors in the current environment. With the migration of investors to the loan market, the increased liquidity has fueled the dramatic changes in this assets class. In the first half 1997, 55 institutions participated in the leveraged loan market, a 70% increase over the January 1996 level.[2] The growing institutional investor sector has increased its influence on the primary leveraged loan market, which is highlighted in Exhibit 3. As issuers and agents target these relatively new, influential players, the loan market is forced to comply with bond market pricing through the mechanism of relative value.

The recent popularity of collateralized debt obligations (CDOs) have also contributed to the rapid growth in the loan market investor base. CDOs are structured investment vehicles which hold a well-diversified portfolio of loans and high yield bonds, funded by investment grade securities and equity. The traditional barrier to creating CDOs was selling the equity portion of the financing structure, which has been made easier due to low default rates. According to Fitch Investors Service, over $11.25 billion of CDOs were issued during the first half of 1997, matching the full year record 1996 level.

Beginning in the early 1990s, the bank loan market began to offer institutional tranche structures, matching both investor and issuer needs for funded, low-amortization capital. Institutional tranches are the B/C/D term loans that, while equal with the traditional bank revolver and term loan in seniority, feature longer

---

[1] Lea V. Carty and Dana Lieberman, "Defaulted Bank Loan Recoveries," *Moody's Investors Service* (November 1996).
[2] For a discussion of the institutional investor base, see Chapter 1.

maturities, with little or no mandatory prepayments. The structures fit well with leveraged issuers' desire for amortization relief, especially with leveraged build-up companies, where the borrower's ability to reinvest available cash flow is important. Agent banks have taken advantage of the growing institutional investor base by structuring increasingly larger portions of leveraged financing with institutional tranches. Volume of institutional term loans has grown since 1992 at an average compounded annual rate of 75%, as shown in Exhibit 4.

Exhibit 3: Leveraged Loan Investors: Primary Market Share, 1994–2Q97

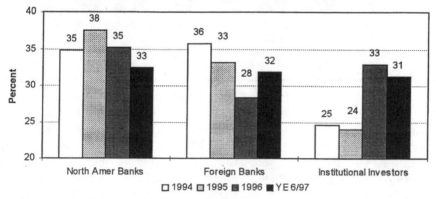

Excludes money center banks and all agent commitments.
Source: Portfolio Management Data LLC.

Exhibit 4: Leveraged Bank Loans: Term Loan B/C/D Volume, 1992–1996

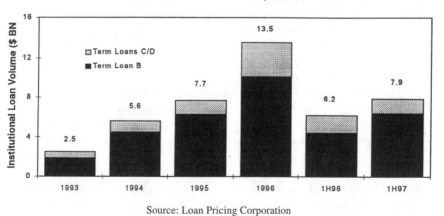

Source: Loan Pricing Corporation

Exhibit 5: Leveraged Bank Loans: Secondary Trading Volume, 1991–1996

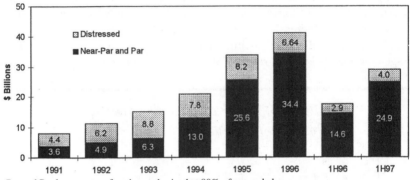

Near-Par and Par loans are performing and priced at 80% of par and above.
Distressed loans are non-performing and priced below 80% of par.
Source: Loan Pricing Corporation

Bank Loan Trading

The emergence and rapid growth of the bank loan secondary market has had a signif-icant effect on all the players in the marketplace. Overwhelmingly, loan trading involves noninvestment grade loans, where LIBOR spreads are in excess of 125 basis points. Total secondary trading volume reached $41 billion in 1996, marking the fifth consecutive year of growth. Exhibit 5 details the remarkable expansion in secondary loan trading. Par volume (trades of performing bank loans priced at 80% of par and above) accounted for 84% of total secondary volume and is a driving force behind the portfolio risk management revolution in the leveraged bank loan market.

Loan trading provides liquidity for the distribution infrastructure of the leveraged bank loan market that serves a constituency of institutional investors, commercial and investment banks, and loan dealers and brokers. The existence of a liquid secondary bank loan market lowers asset class risk, alters investors' view of acceptable credit risk over the loan term, and results in lower pricing for issu-ers. For investors, this creates the following new opportunities:

- to adjust holdings and manage portfolio risks through asset granularity and distribution of credit exposures;
- to provide a constant flow of information on market expectations;
- to use credit-based derivatives (such as bank loan options, total rate of return swaps, and credit default swaps) which require mark-to-market pricing;
- to arbitrage market inefficiencies and exploit superior credit expertise.

Bank Loan Ratings

Introduced in 1995, bank loan ratings mark another characteristic of the conver-gence between the loan syndication and bond markets. Loan ratings should facilitate important changes in the market, such as asset class analysis and active portfolio management. Especially for investors who must use only public information, bank loan ratings will make the private bank loan market more transparent, increasing the speed of investment analysis, and therefore more liquid.

AGENT INSTITUTIONS

Competition for leveraged finance continues to grow as providers of capital-raising expertise increasingly supply a broader menu of financial products. Over 20 commercial banking Section 20 subsidiaries have begun to make inroads into the high yield bond market, and every bulge bracket investment bank has staffed a loan syndication desk. Commercial banks' Section 20 affiliates participated in a record 58% of total high-yield bond issuances in 1996, and represented 9 of the top 20 high yield bond underwriters.

Commercial Banks

The extended liquidity cycle should significantly affect the commercial banks in future years. As investment grade lending margins continue to fall, additional yield-seeking banks are targeting the leveraged lending sector for spreads that are accretive to their return on assets. The incremental competition for leveraged paper will put pressure on profitability in the leveraged bank loan market, making volume the primary lever for profitability.

Investment Banks

Investment banks initiated their activity in the bank loan market in the early 1990s, responding to commercial banking competition in the high yield bond market. These new entrants have increased their commitment of capital and other resources in an effort to develop underwriting, distribution, and trading capabilities. The first wave of investment banks' involvement in bank loans began on the trading side, then followed with origination. Subsequently, all major investment banks now staff loan syndication desks. While investment banks captured only 5% of the leveraged agent-only league table volume in 1996 with a collective $13.9 billion in transactions, the annual total was triple the 1995 level.

LEVERAGED ISSUERS

Leveraged merger and acquisition activity is the lifeblood of the leveraged bank loan market. Not only are the fees higher, but also is the likelihood of repeat loan business. M&A activity exploded in 1995 and 1996, ignited by both corporate and financial sponsors. Drivers of demand include consolidation within industries (such as insurance, healthcare, and media and communications, including leveraged build-up strategies) and spin-offs and divestitures, which increase focus on specific industries. The combination of favorable equity markets, interest rates and economic activity have paved the way for higher M&A activity. Returns increase as the appreciated stock market provides generous financing and exit market valuations.

Bank loans today play a reduced role in total merger and acquisition activity than in the late 1980s, due to the high level of corporate acquisition activity and the frequent use of stock as a source of financing. Exhibits 6 and 7 allow for a comparison between the current environment and the late 1980s. Merger and acquisition loans totaled 70% of total M&A transaction volume in 1989, versus only 25% in 1996. Similarly, 71% of these M&A loans were leveraged in 1989, compared to only 30% in 1996.

Exhibit 6: M&A Transaction and Loan Volume, 1Q94–2Q97

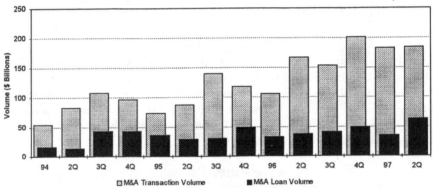

Source: BancAmerica Robertson Stephens, Securities Data Co. and Loan Pricing Corporation.

Exhibit 7: M&A Transaction and Loan Volume, 1987–1Q97

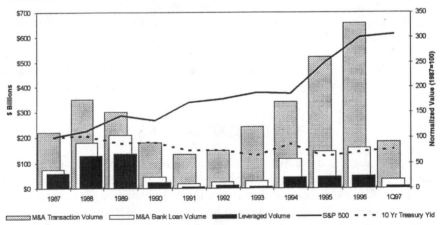

Note: Announced M&A deals with US targets.
Source: BancAmerica Robertson Stephens, Securities Data Co. and Loan Pricing Corporation.

Exhibit 8: Mergers & Acquisitions: EBIT Purchase Multiples, 1988–February 1997

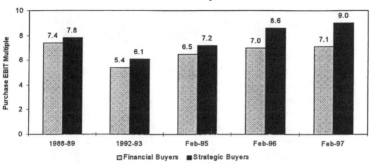

Note: Purchase multiple = Price/Earnings before Interest and taxes (EBIT)

Source: *Buyouts Newsletter*

The rapid rise in stock-based transactions has increased purchase multiples paid by strategic (corporate) buyers. The most recent survey conducted by *Buyouts Newsletter* indicated that strategic buyers were paying 9.0 times earnings before interest and taxes (EBIT), up 150% from the 1992–93 low of 6.1× as shown in Exhibit 8.[3]

Financial sponsors often have been unwilling to bid at the levels characterized by strategic buyers. Sponsors typically do not benefit from operational synergies unless they acquire through an existing portfolio company, and are at a high risk of losing to a strategic bidder. Financial sponsors, on average, pay 7.1× EBIT, up from 5.4× in 1992–93, but essentially unchanged over the years 1995 and 1996. Notably, the differential paid between financial and corporate sponsors has widened to 1.9× EBIT from 0.4× at the previous peak in 1988–1989.

Industry Activity in the Leveraged Loan Market

The media industry was easily the largest source of leveraged loan volume in 1996 as recent deregulation in the broadcasting industry translated into substantial M&A activity in both television and radio. Cable system operators and rural system operators (RSOs) were active in the first half of 1996, as they refinanced existing credits on more favorable terms. Exhibit 9 shows the relative participation in the leveraged loan market by industry, 1996 compared to 1987-1989.

Other active industries included general manufacturing (largely on the strength of sponsored LBOs including KKR's Spalding & Evenflo and Joseph Littlejohn & Levy's Hayes Wheels) and chemicals, metals, mining, and energy. Consolidation within healthcare and telecommunications (primarily paging and cellular) was also a strong source of leveraged loan volume in 1996. Despite numerous defaults among retail borrowers during the first half of 1996, the retail sector generated more than $10 billion of new leveraged volume last year, with the $3.7 billion K-Mart credit accounting for over a third of this total.

---

[3] *Buyouts Newsletter*, February 21, 1997.

Exhibit 9: Leveraged Loan Volume by Industry Group, 1996 versus 1987–1989

1996 Industry Group	Volume ($BN)	No. of Deals	PCT. Vol.
Media	$20.7	72	15
Manufacturing	13.3	84	10
Chemicals, Metals, Mining, & Energy	12.9	83	9
Telecommunications	10.8	34	8
Healthcare	10.7	59	8
Retailing	10.2	48	7
Entertainment & Leisure	8.7	58	6
Services	8.4	49	6
Food & Beverage	7.4	45	5
Real Estate	6.9	52	5
Forest Products	6.9	18	5
Financial Services	4.8	26	4
Printing & Publishing	4.5	20	3
Aerospace, Defense, & Transportation	3.6	28	3
Computers & Electronics	3.5	35	3
Construction & Building Materials	3.2	26	2
Total	136.6	737	100
1987-1989 Industry Group	Volume ($BN)	No. of Deals	PCT. Vol.
Food & Beverage	61.1	61	17
Aerospace, Defense, & Transportation	48.0	44	13
Manufacturing	41.8	122	12
Chemicals, Metals, Mining, & Energy	32.7	92	9
Forest Products	25.3	18	7
Retailing	23.8	56	7
Media	21.0	74	6
Construction & Building Materials	20.3	27	6
Services	17.0	60	5
Printing & Publishing	15.2	25	4
Healthcare	14.8	27	4
Computers & Electronics	14.4	40	4
Entertainment & Leisure	11.3	31	3
Telecommunications	8.4	26	2
Financial Services	3.8	23	1
Real Estate	2.0	16	1
Total	360.6	745	100

Source: BancAmerica Robertson Stephens and Loan Pricing Corporation.

Exhibit 10: Leveraged Spin-Off Activity, 1993–1996

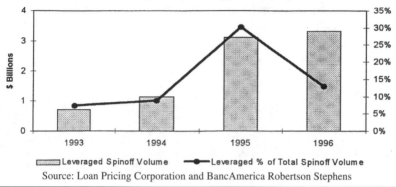

Leveraged Spinoff Volume   ●Leveraged % of Total Spinoff Volume

Source: Loan Pricing Corporation and BancAmerica Robertson Stephens

Spin-Offs and Divestitures

Divestitures and spin-offs have been very popular in the 1990s; increased efficiency and the stock market's favorable view of easy to analyze "pure play" companies are reasons behind the trend. The syndicated bank loan market has proven to be an attractive capital raising alternative for companies seeking to enhance shareholder value by spinning off companies as separate entities. Spin-off related loan activity reached record levels in 1996, with volume of $25.5 billion, over double the total recorded for 1995.

Spin-offs have gained acceptance because relationship banks, which already know the management and the business, wish to establish a relationship and maintain existing ancillary business with the new company. Examples include the $2.25 billion bank financing for Millenium Chemicals' spin-off from Hanson Plc, the $1.5 billion credit backing Allegiance's spin-off from Baxter and the $215 million loan for Earthgrains spin-off from Anheuser Busch.

Leveraged spin-off volume, illustrated in Exhibit 10, increased in 1996 to $3.3 billion, triple the 1994 level. Leveraged loan volume represented a high of 30% of total spin-off loan activity in 1995, though that percentage fell to 13% the following year, due to the massive investment grade Lucent Technologies spin-off from AT&T in 1996.

FINANCIAL SPONSORS

The leveraged bank loan market is heavily focused on sponsors. From the loan origination perspective, financial buyers are valued clients which require a full complement of capital-raising products in order to invest equity capital efficiently, often require fully committed financing to make an acquisition bid, and represent the potential for multiple transactions. Leveraged loan investors recognize the value of a strong sponsor, including experience with the operating and financial strategies necessary in a leveraged environment, the ability to invest additional capital for growth or in stressed deal situations, and often possess significant knowledge of, and experience in, the industries in which they invest.

Exhibit 11: Leveraged Bank Loans:
Sponsored Loan Volume, 1Q94–2Q97

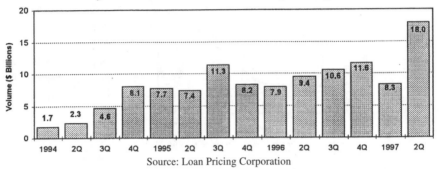

Source: Loan Pricing Corporation

Exhibit 12: Buyout Fund Raising and
Fund Closes by Quarter, 1Q93–2Q97

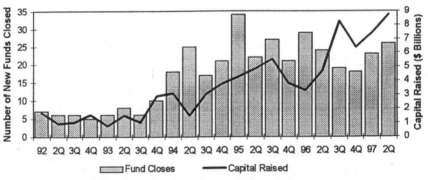

Source: BancAmerica Robertson Stephens and *Buyouts*.

Financial sponsor activity depends on three factors — investment funding, available debt financing, and cost-effective acquisition opportunities. The first two factors, raising equity and debt capital, could hardly be more accommodating. As shown in Exhibit 11, sponsored loan volume over the 12 months ended June 1997 reached $48.5 billion, 32% above the year-ago period.

Sponsor equity fund raising also has been remarkable, as represented by the line in Exhibit 12. Buyout firms raised a record $31.4 billion over the 12 months ended June 1997 versus $22.6 billion in calendar 1996, itself a 21% increase from 1995. Much of the growth comes from pension funds, whose increased comfort with "alternative investments" has resulted in a larger allocation of pension assets to equity sponsor fund raising. With much of equity sponsor funds raised in 1996 uninvested, or in the form of "dry powder," as well as a significant portion of the money raised over the past four years also uninvested, the private equity market has significant capacity and a strong desire to put that capacity to work. With increased competitive pressure for acquisitions, sponsors have adapted their strategies to allow for a wider selection of industries, combined buyout efforts with other sponsors, or targeted smaller transaction sizes.

With 30% of overall leveraged market, sponsors have a large impact on the market's aggressiveness in pushing precedents in debt multiples and structural flexibility. Equity sponsor influence is also remarkably concentrated. Collectively, KKR's $5.7 billion fund, DLJ Merchant Banking Partners' $3 billion fund and Hicks, Muse, Tate & Furst's $1 billion fund together accounted for 43% of all buyout funds raised in 1996. Exhibit 13 lists the sponsors with the largest new issue loan volume, and Exhibit 14 highlights the importance of bank debt in a typical LBO capital structure. From the financial sponsors' perspective, bank financing is available quickly, and provides a cost effective, flexible source of capital. Further, banks are willing to provide bridge financing and raise various forms of financing in the public and private markets, thereby providing "one-stop" financing solutions.

Exhibit 13: Most Active Equity Sponsors, 1994–1H97

Year	Rank	Equity Sponsor	Loan Volume ($MM)	# of Deals
1H97	1	Hicks, Muse, Tate & Furst	$2,028	8
	2	Kohlberg Kravis Roberts & Co.	$1,915	4
	3	Texas Pacific Group	$930	2
	4	MacAndrews & Forbes	$750	1
	5	Joseph Littlejohn & Levy	$741	1
1996	1	Hicks, Muse, Tate & Furst	$2,345	8
	2	Kohlberg Kravis Roberts & Co.	$1,784	3
	3	Texas Pacific Group	$1,700	2
	4	Forstman Little & Co.	$1,550	2
	5	Bain Capital	$1,535	7
1995	1	Hicks, Muse, Tate & Furst	$1,662	6
	2	Yucaipa Companies	$1,455	3
	3	Kohlberg Kravis Roberts & Co.	$1,318	5
	4	Corporate Advisors	$1,200	1
	5	Hellman & Friedman Capital Partners	$1,190	2
1994	1	Kohlberg Kravis Roberts & Co.	$2,075	1
	2	Forstman Little & Co.	$1,814	2
	3	MacAndrews & Forbes	$1,551	4
	4	Zell/Chilmark Partners	$805	1
	5	Clayton, Dubilier & Rice	$730	2

New loans, including M&A, LBO, and build-ups.
Source: Loan Pricing Corporation.

Exhibit 14: General Industry LBOs: Financing Sources as a Percent of Total, 1995–1996

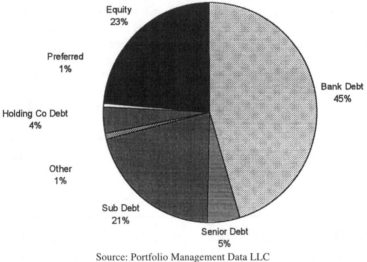

Equity
23%

Preferred
1%

Holding Co Debt
4%

Other
1%

Sub Debt
21%

Bank Debt
45%

Senior Debt
5%

Source: Portfolio Management Data LLC

Industry Activity in the Sponsored Loan Market

Manufacturing and food and beverages were the most popular industries for leveraged buyouts in the late 1980s, accounting for roughly 50% of all sponsored deal activity from 1987 through 1989. The stable, predictable cash flows and low costs of financial distress characteristic of these industries made them good candidates for the traditional LBO structure. The resulting strategy was to lever the company to gain ownership, sell any nonstrategic assets and then operate it privately to amortize the debt. While these industry segments continue to be attractive to buyout shops, intense competition from both strategic and other financial buyers has forced sponsors to look outside of traditional LBO industries and strategies. (See Exhibit 15 for a comparison of loan concentration by industry between the current market and the late 1980s.)

Clearly, the distribution of sponsor-favored industries has broadened in recent years. Specifically, media, healthcare, and various service companies have become prime equity sponsor targets as the fragmented nature of these industries encouraged the popular "leveraged build-up" strategy. In such cases, the sponsor purchased an original platform company (with above-normal equity commitments) with the intention of making numerous add-on acquisitions of smaller companies within the industry. Credit facilities for these build-up companies typically include highly structured acquisition baskets or acquisition revolvers, with availability dependent on the borrower achieving certain performance hurdles.

Exhibit 15: Sponsored Loan Volume by Industry Group, 1996 versus 1987–1989

1996 Industry Group	Volume ($BN)	No. of Deals	PCT. Vol.
Manufacturing	7.5	43	18
Food & Beverage	5.5	21	13
Forest Products	4.3	8	10
Services	3.9	20	9
Healthcare	3.4	23	8
Chemicals, Metals, Mining, & Energy	3.0	16	7
Printing & Publishing	2.9	10	7
Media	2.6	14	6
Financial Services	2.0	9	5
Construction & Building Materials	2.0	8	5
Entertainment & Leisure	1.9	14	4
Computers & Electronics	1.3	9	3
Aerospace, Defense, & Transportation	1.2	7	3
Retailing	0.9	4	2
Telecommunications	0.5	2	1
Real Estate	0.3	3	1
Total	43.1	211	100
1987-1989 Industry Group	**Volume ($BN)**	**No. of Deals**	**PCT. Vol.**
Food & Beverage	35.6	15	34
Manufacturing	16.7	27	16
Construction & Building Materials	10.0	7	10
Printing & Publishing	7.8	8	7
Chemicals, Metals, Mining, & Energy	7.5	9	7
Services	7.1	6	7
Forest Products	5.4	5	5
Computers & Electronics	3.7	4	4
Entertainment & Leisure	3.7	6	4
Aerospace, Defense, & Transportation	3.2	7	3
Retailing	2.1	8	2
Media	0.5	1	0
Healthcare	0.4	1	0
Telecommunications	0.2	2	0
Financial Services	0.2	1	0
Real Estate	0.2	1	0
Total	104.4	108	100

Source: BancAmerica Robertson Stephens and Loan Pricing Corporation.

LEVERAGED LOAN STRUCTURE

Hybrid Tranches

A small subset of loan structures have appeared in the leveraged loan market that provide broad implications for the leveraged sector. Hybrids, or "covenant light" term loans, blur the differences between bonds and loans in security, call premiums, and pricing conventions. These innovative bond-like term loans help agent institutions provide an integrated financing package for issuers. Hybrid term loans have been used as a substitute for public securities for a client that wished to remain a privately reporting entity. For example, Huntsman Specialty Chemical completely replaced a contemplated $135 million bond offering with a unique 10-year term loan D tranche priced at LIBOR + 350 basis points. Relative to the high yield debt, the tranche offered second lien security rights, and a more flexible covenant package and call provisions. In response to the previously discussed primary loan market volatility, innovative hybrid term loan structures have been used to explicitly link high yield bond rates (set by the market) to leveraged loan spreads (traditionally set by the agent banks). The hybrid loan "cushion" effectively reduces the underwriters' risk and investor frustration with shifting loan metrics.

Drivers of Senior Debt Sizing

Bank loans are traditionally the cheapest, most flexible debt available to equity sponsors, and they desire the maximum available senior financing. The nature of the constantly-changing bank market allows for no absolute parameters on senior debt availability, although the following benchmarks drive the relative sizing of most leveraged facilities for general industrial borrowers as follows:

Benchmark	Level	Definition
Total Leverage	5.0-6.5	Total Debt/EBITDA
Senior Leverage	3.5-4.5	Senior Debt/EBITDA
Interest Coverage	1.5-2.5	EBITDA/Interest
Senior Capitalization	40-50%	Senior Debt/Total Capitalization
Total Capitalization	65-80%	Total Debt/Total Capitalization
Tenor	5-10 yrs.	—
EBITDA = Earnings before interest, taxes, depreciation and amortization.		

A number of other factors can influence the bank loan market's appetite for a given credit, whether or not it tests the limits of the relevant benchmarks. Industry dynamics, sponsorship, collateral value, bank relationships, and the company "story" (synergies, asset sales, market position, and turnaround potential) are influential to the success of a loan syndication.

Exhibit 16: Highly Leveraged Loans: Average Debt Multiple, 1987–1H1997

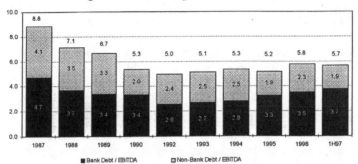

Criteria: HLTs - Pre 1996 L+250 and above, 1996 after L+225 and above. Insufficient data for 1991.
Source: Portfolio Management Data LLC.

Leverage Ratio

As shown in Exhibit 16, average proforma debt/EBITDA of general industrial HLT loans reached 5.7× in the first half of 1997, aggressive relative to the tight credit environment of 1992, but rather benign when viewed against 1980s leverage levels. The high demand for leveraged loan investments has raised fears of deteriorating credit quality among loan market observers as agent banks compete for underwriting mandates. Indeed, we have seen an incremental rise in leverage ratios.

Offsetting concern about the rise in debt multiples in highly leveraged transactions has been the relatively large amount of equity that sponsors have contributed to LBOs. Equity contributions to LBOs have fluctuated around 25% since 1992, a clear shift from the 1980s nadir, when equity percentages reached average lows of 7%–10% of the capital structure.[4]

While credit structures reflect market changes, the pressure on credit structures is a function of other market forces including:

- Tremendous growth in market capitalization supporting the senior debt,
- Highly liquid debt and equity capital markets which provide a secondary source of repayment,
- The tendency for non-bank institutional investors to provide the longer-dated senior financing for leveraged capital structures, and
- The current annualized corporate default rate of 1.6% for 1997 is well below the 3.6% historical average.

Tenor

The average tenor of various tranches of leveraged bank loans has increased since 1995, as the leveraged market has moved beyond the old 5-year standard. Average maturity by bank tranche is shown in Exhibit 17. Term loan A credit facilities have

---

[4] For a discussion of equity contributions to LBOs, see Chapter 1.

been extended as leveraged loan investors provide additional flexibility in their response to the loss of product to institutional investors. (See Exhibit 18 for an illustration of the interplay between bank revolvers and term loans and institutional term loan tranches in maturity extension.) The average tenor of the institutional tranches also has been extended as the market becomes more aggressive. In part, the extension in the average tenor of institutional tranches reflects the low cash flow volatility in the industries, such as media, which were more active in 1996.

Performance Triggers

A growing number of covenants are tied to performance measures, which, once a grid level is reached, may reduce or waive restrictions on the company. Excess cash flow percentages, discretionary investment limits, and change of control provisions are examples of covenants that are structured in this way. Agent banks, especially those with underwriting exposure, are better able to insist on strong initial covenant levels to protect against the downside, while easing restrictions if the company performs at or above their operating plan.

Exhibit 17: Leveraged Bank Loans: Average Tenor, 1996

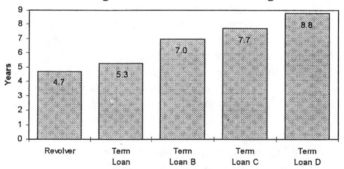

Source: BancAmerica Robertson Stephens and Loan Pricing Corporation.

Exhibit 18: Leveraged Loans: Average Maturity, 1987–1H97

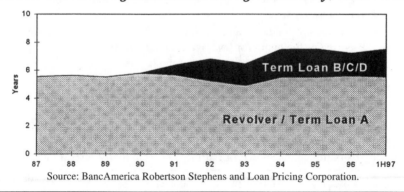

Source: BancAmerica Robertson Stephens and Loan Pricing Corporation.

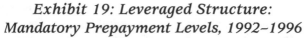

Exhibit 19: Leveraged Structure:
Mandatory Prepayment Levels, 1992–1996

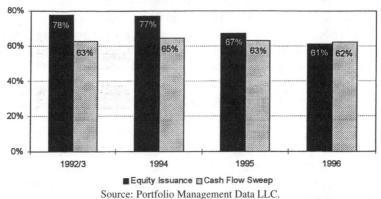

■ Equity Issuance ⊠ Cash Flow Sweep
Source: Portfolio Management Data LLC.

Voting Thresholds — Required Lenders

A simple majority vote of the lending group usually is sufficient for changes in non-money terms such as financial covenants, while unanimous support is traditionally required for interest rate changes. Class-specific votes for mandatory prepayment adjustments are often specified to protect the interests of the smaller tranche lenders.

Secondary trading can quickly change the population of a lending group to a much wider universe, possibly limiting sponsors' influence on any changes. In response, well-established equity sponsors have increasingly negotiated to move from unanimous voting requirements to supermajority (67–80%) thresholds for certain "money" issues, such as release of collateral and changes in interim amortization. However, KKR's Kindercare Learning Centers transaction (January 1997), pushed even further and required just 50.1% of revolver and term loan B lenders to release collateral.

Mandatory Prepayments

Leveraged loans are structured to require borrowers to prepay loans with funds from asset sales, debt/equity issuance, or excess cash flow. Normally, 100% of the funds raised from asset sales, insurance settlements or new debt must be prepaid, while an average of 60% of equity issuance proceeds must go toward the loan. Excess cash flow prepayments (cash flow sweeps) are initially set at 50-75%, though liquidity pressure on the marketplace has forced many agent banks to go with the lower end of the scale. The recent downward drift in mandatory prepayment levels is shown in Exhibit 19. Performance triggers, when reached, reduce or waive the cash flow sweep requirement. For example, American Radio's excess cash flow and equity issuance required prepayments are waived if the company's debt/cash flow ratio falls below certain hurdles.

The prepayments proceeds are distributed on a pro-rata basis to the different tranches of the loan, although the institutional B/C/D term loans are usually given a right of refusal to the runoff. Prepayments that are refused can be distributed to the Term Loan A or shared with the company. In today's liquid market, B/C/D lenders will tend to waive prepayments, even in poorly-performing credits. Over 80% of Riverwood International's institutional tranche investors waived their share of the prepayment proceeds of the company's 1996 asset sales.

Other Structuring Issues
Loan Assignments

Assignments are usually freely allowed within the lender group or among affiliates with no minimums, but may require a minimum of $5-10 million to outside assignees. An eligible assignee is generally defined as a commercial bank, financial institution, or "accredited investor," where consent (not to be unreasonably withheld) is required from both the issuer and the agent.

The relative standardization of assignment language still leaves room for the borrower to manage its bank group through unusual restrictions. I&M Rail Link and Jacor Communications are examples. I&M Rail requires an assigning lender (who wishes to sell a portion of the loan to an investor outside the bank group) to give the current holders of the loan right of first refusal at the offer price. Jacor Communications requires each assigning lender to give the company four days notice prior to sending Jacor's corporate and financial information to prospective purchasers.

Acquisition Baskets

Due to the popularity of the leveraged build-up strategy, banks carefully structure limits on discretionary investments. Covenants can restrict purchases to within the same industry or take the form of dollar limits. Examples are aggregate levels over the life of the loan, annual investment amounts, or per-transaction restrictions. Acquisition limits also may be increased by some fraction of the cumulative excess cash flow generated by the borrower.

Change of Control

The change of control covenant is one of the most negotiated provisions in a sponsored deal. The covenant plays a pivotal role in enforcing the loan investor market's preference for ownership stability. Sponsors, on the other hand, want flexibility to harvest their equity investments and will continue to press for more lenient language in the credit agreement. In the sponsored-deal bank loan market, we observe four methods that lenders use to structure a change in control covenant, which in default would enable the investors to accelerate the bank facilities: (1) percent ownership by the equity sponsor group, (2) sponsor maintenance of board control, (3) third-party ownership limits, and (4) sponsor principal continuity. These covenants may also include provisions that reduce control change restrictions through performance triggers and public equity offerings.

Exhibit 20: Normalized LIBOR Spread by Rating Grade, 1Q92–2Q97

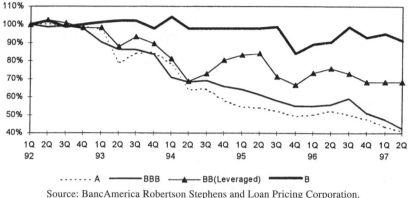

Source: BancAmerica Robertson Stephens and Loan Pricing Corporation.

LEVERAGED LOAN PRICING

LIBOR Spreads

The heavy liquidity in the leveraged bank loan market has had remarkably muted affect on B rated LIBOR spreads, relative to the rest of the credit spectrum. Exhibit 20 shows the declining price trend in the bank loan market. While we have seen erosion in the BB (near-investment grade) spreads over the past five years, average bank loan spreads for B rated issuers (on Revolver/Term Loan A tranches) have remained close to 250 basis points. Spreads, on fully-leveraged transactions with debt/ EBITDA ratios in excess of five times, can range from 275 basis points for an aggressive debt multiple or low coverage transaction, to 225 basis points for an influential sponsored deal. Institutional B/C/D tranches typically offer an additional 25 to 50 basis points spread for tenors that extend an extra 6 to 12 months.

The pricing grid in Exhibit 21 shows average all-in pricing for debt multiples 5–5.5 times EBITDA reached LIBOR + 235, down from 245 basis points in 1996.[5] It is interesting to note the changing dispersion in market spreads. There is relatively little variation in spreads at the highest levels of leverage, while more variation exists at the lower end of the grids.

LIBOR spreads are typically locked in for the first 3 to 6 months of a bank loan, after which the spread normally will float according to a pricing grid. Grids allow for automatic adjustments of loan spreads if a performance measure, such as a leverage ratio or rating level, moves beyond a step on the grid. Normally, only the revolving and term loan A portions of the loan would feature performance pricing. Recently, however, some institutional B tranches have included stepdowns in pricing, though they are limited in the number of steps and often include a floor level.

---

[5] For information on the average pro rata spread, see Chapter 1.

Exhibit 21: Pro Rata Leveraged Loans: Pricing Grids by Tier, Six Months Ended April 1997

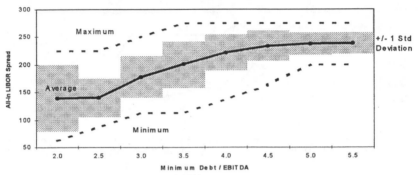

ProRata includes Revolver and Term Loan A facilities.
Source: Portfolio Management Data LLC.

Exhibit 22: Highly Leveraged Bank Loans: Average Upfront Fee of Acquisition-Related Highly Leveraged Loans by Pro Rata and Institutional Tranches 1992, Year Ended 9/30/97

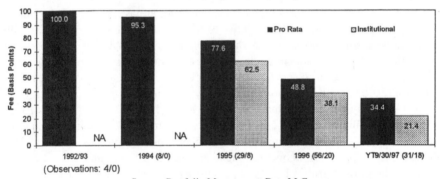

Source: Portfolio Management Data LLC.

Upfront Fees

The second important source of return for high yield bank loan investors is the difference from par for which the loan is acquired. In the primary market, upfront fees, or discounts to par, may be offered. Fees are higher for larger commitments in the primary distribution, and, because many leveraged credits trade above par in the secondary market, can greatly affect returns on investment.

As shown in Exhibit 22, competitive pressures on the leveraged loan marketplace have had their greatest effect on upfront fees. In 1995, upfronts for retail commitments ($10 to 15 million) averaged a full percentage point. Fees dropped in 1993 to 80 basis points and fell dramatically in 1996 to 45 basis points. By the second quarter of 1997, the decline had continued to approximately 34 basis points.

CONCLUSION

There are essentially two trends in today's leveraged loan market — rapid volume growth and loan-bond market convergence. Increased M&A activity and rapid loan refinancing have boosted leveraged loan issuance volume. More significantly, however, the dramatic increase in new institutional investor demand has forced the leveraged loan market to more closely track public bond market pricing and made possible a variety of innovative bond-like loan structures. These bond-like term loans represent the next step of the relative value transformation of the loan market into a component of the public debt markets.

Chapter 3

Evolving Role of Credit Ratings for Bank Loans

Steven Bavaria
Director — Corporate Ratings
Standard & Poor's

INTRODUCTION

An important sign of the evolution of the syndicated loan market into a "real" securities market has been the emergence of credit ratings on the loans themselves. This reflects an increasing sophistication in the understanding and use of ratings by investors, issuers, and their bankers. It also demonstrates how the relationship between a rating agency like Standard & Poor's and its corporate clients has evolved. Where companies once may have perceived the credit rating exercise as a passive, one-way dialogue, many now use their rating agency relationship as a source of ongoing strategic insight into how they are and will be perceived by the market, and how to influence that perception. This chapter will trace the background for this, describing the changes in both the bank loan market and the credit rating business that have helped to foster these developments.

TRANSPARENCY AND EFFICIENCY IN CREDIT MARKETS

Many of the recent developments in the bank loan market[1] involve the introduction of steps that make the market more efficient and transparent. Efficiency in a financial market context generally requires there be lots of issuers, investors, and intermediaries, clear-cut roles for each, standardized instruments, well-understood trading, pricing and transfer protocols, and universally available information about the deal and, if a debt instrument, about the credit of the borrower. (See Exhibit 1.) The latter feature — universally available information — is often called "transparency." Efficient market theories which hold that capital markets absorb information about individual securities and incorporate it into their prices on an ongoing basis always assume transparency as a necessary prerequisite.

---

[1] Much of this discussion also applies to the private placement market, where the establishment of SEC Rule 144A fostered the rise of an efficient securities market in what was previously a smaller, less efficient (albeit more profitable for investors) buy-and-hold market in unregistered corporate debt.

49

In recent years speakers at many conferences have talked about the increasing efficiency in the loan market as though its coming were an unmixed blessing, but in reality there have been both winners and losers. Traditionally the bank loan market has been *inefficient*, by securities market standards, although someone writing about it several years ago would probably have described it as a "relationship market," rather than calling it "inefficient."

The traditional bank loan involved a relationship between the borrower and the bank, which both originated and structured the loan and played the role of investor by holding it in its own portfolio. The primary value that the banker brought to the transaction was credit expertise. The expertise might include unique knowledge about that particular borrower, as well as, in some cases, specialty knowledge about the industry (movies, cable, ships, project finance, etc.). As a result, banks often developed their own niches, and would concentrate their loan marketing in their areas of expertise.[2] The more complex and difficult an industry, the fewer the number of bankers that had the necessary expertise to lend to it safely. As a result, specialty lending of one sort or another was more lucrative than "plain vanilla" corporate lending. It was precisely the lack of transparency — the fact that there was *not* universal knowledge among lenders about how to finance power plants, or liquid natural gas carriers, or the movie industry, etc. — that made these niches more profitable to the banks that were knowledgeable about them.

Exhibit 1: Efficient and Inefficient Markets

Characteristics of Efficient Markets
- Widespread, easily available information (transparency)
- Numerous investors
- Clearly established roles for issuers, intermediaries and investors
- Secondary trading
- Established protocols for trading and distribution
- Standardized instruments
- Credit ratings and independent research available
- Competitive pricing, with comparable deal pricing information widely available

Characteristics of Inefficient Markets
- Information confidential or closely held
- Investors have relationship with or specialized knowledge about borrower
- Buy-and-hold portfolio lenders, minimal secondary trading
- Individually tailored transactions
- No credit ratings or third-party research
- Negotiated pricing that reflects specialized nature of each deal

---

[2] This often resulted in concentrations in their loan portfolios as well, which, until recently when banks began applying "portfolio theory" techniques to their loan portfolios, was only deemed a problem if the particular specialty niche experienced widespread defaults (e.g., the real estate or oil and gas lending experience of many banks in the 1980s)

As long as most banks continued to see themselves primarily as relationship lenders whose major compensation for the lending relationship was the interest on the loan, then they had little interest in the market becoming more efficient, if "efficient" meant opening up their specialty areas to more participants and making their unique credit analysis techniques widely available to all. Efficiency would have benefited the borrowers and the new lenders that it allowed into the business, but not the existing bankers.[3]

A good example of this has been the project finance market. For many years the project finance market was considered a specialty credit market dominated by a few highly experienced banks, insurance companies, and other lenders. This small group of lenders possessed the expertise to do the highly complex and difficult credit analysis involved in financing complex ventures — cogeneration facilities, mining projects, etc. — whose structure usually involved multiple, overlapping risks that were hard to assess and quantify, as opposed to straightforward corporate credit risks. Because of the complicated nature of these deals and the relatively few investors that understood how to do them, the borrowing cost on project financing tended to be relatively high. Several years ago, however, Standard & Poor's began rating project finance-related debt and published detailed articles on the risks involved and how to analyze them. As a result, many more investors who previously might have avoided project finance as too complicated and, therefore, too risky, were able to become more knowledgeable about and, ultimately, comfortable with the credit risk, and began buying project finance debt. The increased *transparency* in the market led to a greater supply of potential capital for project finance deals, and resulted in borrowing costs falling to levels more consistent with that of other bonds of similar credit rating.[4] Obviously there is now a more *efficient* market in project finance debt — more investors, more transparency of information, tighter pricing — but the efficiency has not benefited everybody. Issuers who can borrow more cheaply and from a wider investor base are better off. So are the investors who are now empowered to participate in a new market previously closed to them. But the small group of bankers and other financiers who used to dominate project finance lending and who benefited from having specialized expertise that was not widely available have seen their lending margins cut.

ROLE OF AGENT BANKS: AGENTS FOR WHOM?

Until recently, the lead or "agent" bank in a loan syndication has been, essentially, an agent for the other commercial bank lenders, not for the borrower. This was dif-

---

[3] Even existing lenders will benefit from the additional liquidity and growth of secondary loan and credit derivatives markets, which will facilitate their use of portfolio theory in managing their own loan portfolios, especially in reducing industry concentrations.

[4] There may still be a slight "complexity premium" for deals that are more complicated than straight corporate debt that is similarly rated, reflecting (1) the additional analytical work in evaluating a more complicated credit structure and (2) the fact that, even with credit ratings on project finance deals, there will always be some investors that choose to avoid more complex deals.

ferent from the role played by an investment banker who underwrote a stock, bond, or other security issue for a corporate client. The investment banker is the agent for the issuing client, and, as such, has an incentive to get the issuer the best deal possible, in terms of pricing and other terms of the transaction. The investment banker is also an *intermediary* between the issuer (the corporate borrower) and the investors, who may be institutional investors or individuals. The agent bank in a commercial bank syndication, by contrast, performed both the roles of intermediary and investor, and had an incentive to get the best terms possible for itself and the other bank lenders.[5] Only in recent years has there emerged a clear distinction between the role of the agent bank in syndicated loan transactions and that of the investors (lenders).

Changes in the roles of banks participating in the loan market are among a number of developments that have occurred, all of which have had a reinforcing effect on each other, on the increased efficiency of the market, and, ultimately, on the increased demand for credit ratings on bank loans. These changes are:

- the rise of a group of large syndicating banks primarily focused on earning fees for leading deals, rather than on earning spread income by holding the loans on their books
- the entry of new non-bank institutional investors as buyers of loans
- the entry of investment banks (i.e. non-commercial banks) into the syndicated loan underwriting market
- the separation of the loan underwriting function from the loan portfolio management function within major commercial banks
- the widespread introduction of portfolio theory to the management of bank loan portfolios
- the growth of a large secondary trading market for syndicated bank loans
- the rise of credit derivatives as a way to transfer credit risk from one investor to another without having to transfer ownership of the underlying loan

The result of the interaction of all these trends is a new set of players, behaviors, and opportunities in the syndicated loan market. Commercial banks now are able to separate the business of originating and syndicating loans from their traditional business of lending money at a spread over their cost of funds. Those banks whose business is now driven primarily by the desire to earn fees as a syndicator have every incentive to push spreads on loans as low as the market will bear if that is what it takes to obtain mandates from corporate clients, even if it means that the returns on the loans they underwrite would no longer be attractive to themselves as lenders. Similarly, banks whose relationships with certain industries allow them to originate more of those companies' syndicated loans than they would want to hold

---

[5] In reality the difference is not quite as clear as it might appear. Investment bankers' incentive to get the best possible deal for their issuing clients is tempered by their need to protect their own reputations with investors to whom they need to sell future deals. Commercial bankers' desire to obtain the best deal for themselves and other lenders is tempered by their need to maintain a long-term relationship with the client and obtain repeat business.

in their portfolio can use the secondary market or the credit derivatives market to balance their portfolio from a credit standpoint, without jeopardizing their good relationships and ability to do future business with those borrowers.

Non-commercial banks have opportunities they previously did not have. Institutional investors can now consider bank loans as an investment alternative, and can buy them either in primary syndication or in the secondary market. Investment bankers can leverage off their existing bond underwriting capabilities to offer clients "one stop shopping," the ability to tap the loan or bond markets, or both, in a single transaction with the same underwriter. (Large commercial banks, most of whom now have securities affiliates, can offer their clients the same option.)

BANK LOAN RATINGS

One result of all these developments, which we have grouped under the general heading of the loan market becoming more *efficient*, is to make credit ratings on loans virtually inevitable. As long as the bank originating a loan was also primarily an investor in the deal, and especially if the other lenders were also banks, there was neither a *need* nor an *incentive* for obtaining a credit rating on most transactions. Who would need a rating if all the investors are banks staffed by professional credit people who have relationships with the borrowers? Why would the banks want one if it had the effect of making a complex credit more obvious and understandable to other potential lenders, who could then compete with the existing lenders and drive down pricing?

However, once the loan market takes on the characteristics of a more efficient market, these dynamics change. A large syndicating bank is driven by the desire to win mandates from borrowers and earn fees, in competition with other syndicators. That requires them to convince the borrower that they will strive to obtain the best terms available in the market, irrespective of whether the resulting loan is one the syndicator would ideally want to buy for its own portfolio. Getting the best terms means reaching the largest possible investor universe, and that means going beyond the banks that are already familiar with the issuer or the industry.

Credit ratings provide information, analysis, and an objective opinion on the credit to investors, including new ones who previously may not have been familiar with the credit. Institutional investors (especially mutual funds), limited partnerships, and other investors that do not have large professional credit staffs (like banks do) are more likely to consider investing in loans if they have ratings. Indeed, such institutional investors are accustomed to seeing credit ratings on the other debt securities they buy, and need ratings on loans so they can compare them with other securities already in their portfolio or that they may be considering. Since deals are priced at the margin, a deal that can be sold to a broader set of potential investors because it is rated will likely command more attractive pricing than the same deal if it is unrated and can only be sold to a more limited universe of lenders.

Exhibit 2: Company's Liability Structure

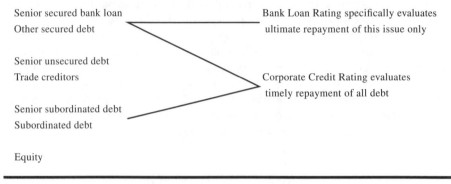

Senior secured bank loan
Other secured debt

Senior unsecured debt
Trade creditors

Senior subordinated debt
Subordinated debt

Equity

Bank Loan Rating specifically evaluates
ultimate repayment of this issue only

Corporate Credit Rating evaluates
timely repayment of all debt

BEYOND THE CORPORATE CREDIT

A credit rating is an objective, third-party opinion on the likelihood of financial performance. It can apply to a company (or other entity) as a whole, or it can apply to a specific debt instrument. This is an important distinction, especially in the bank loan market, since many loans are secured or have structural features that give bank lenders a preferred position in bankruptcy to that of other creditors. That may be reflected, in some cases, in the bank loan being assigned a rating higher than the borrower's corporate credit rating.

The *corporate credit rating* describes the overall likelihood of a company meeting its financial obligations. (See Exhibit 2.) It does not differentiate among specific obligations as to whether they are senior or junior to one another, secured or unsecured, etc. It is the baseline rating that refers to the creditworthiness of the overall entity (e.g., "XYZ Co. is a single-A company"). Particular classes of creditors enhance their position in the event of default or bankruptcy by obtaining a security interest in certain assets of the company. Since credit can be a zero-sum game, the preference usually comes at the expense of some other class of creditors, whose position becomes junior or "subordinated" to that of the creditors whose position is secured. Ratings on specific debt issues may be notched up or down from the company's corporate credit rating to reflect whether the holder of that issue is substantially advantaged or disadvantaged vis a vis other creditors of the company in the event of a default. Bank loans that are well secured, which is typically the case in leveraged loans (i.e., secured loans to borrowers rated BB and below), may be rated higher than the borrower's corporate rating, if Standard & Poor's believes that the security provides adequate protection to bank lenders in a projected post-default workout scenario. Likewise, subordinated debt or unsecured debt whose repayment prospects are adversely affected by their position in the capital structure may be notched down from the corporate credit rating.

LOAN RATINGS IN THE MARKET

Standard & Poor's began rating bank loans in 1995. Volume was small at first, primarily because the loan market was booming and issuers and their bankers felt that ratings were unnecessary to the successful completion of a deal, given the huge demand for bank loans by banks and other investors. By midyear 1996, S&P's loan rating total had only grown to 30. By the end of 1997, it was over 600.

This rapid growth reflects the combination of all the factors previously discussed, which have created the necessary preconditions for a rated market, with an aggressive marketing of ratings to issuers, bankers, and investors in the loan market by Standard & Poor's and the other rating agencies. Investors who are accustomed to using ratings and the additional insight they provide have been in favor of bank loan ratings from the beginning. Bankers and issuers have moved through several attitudinal phases, starting initially with "reluctance" or even "resistance" to loan ratings when they were first introduced, moving through "open-mindedness" to "acquiescence" and finally, in increasing numbers, to "enthusiasm."

The initial reluctance or resistance reflected many bankers' belief, which was communicated to their clients, that ratings would cost more, delay the deal, and be unnecessary, given the strong demand for loans to begin with. Many bankers also believed, but did not communicate to their clients, that ratings might depress credit spreads, which were already at historically low levels. As Standard & Poor's continued to promote loan ratings directly to its corporate clients, many of them realized that, despite the fact that they may have been happy with the terms of their existing bank loan, having a rating that expanded the list of potential investors in their loan, or validated the worth of the collateral and structure of the deal, could only help them.

This view was confirmed when a number of companies began pegging the pricing on their loans to their bank loan ratings. For a long time many loan agreements had tied the loan price to the borrower's corporate credit rating, so that as the company's credit quality, as reflected in the rating, moved up or down, the pricing on the loan followed suit. Once this practice became established, companies began to see that if their loan pricing was going to be based on a rating, it made more sense and in many cases saved them money to have it be the rating on the loan itself, rather than just the rating on the company. The rating on the loan, unlike the company rating, incorporated the effect of collateral, covenants, and other protective features unique to the loan, and therefore might often be higher than the corporate rating. On a pricing grid, that could mean a lower interest rate. Increasingly loans are being priced on this basis. As word spreads among corporate CFOs of the advantages of pricing their loans off bank loan ratings, the practice is expected to grow rapidly.

RELATIONS WITH RATING AGENCIES

While the use of bank loan ratings in the syndicated loan market reflects the various developments discussed already, it also demonstrates the changes in the credit ratings business in recent years. Credit ratings have been a prerequisite in the issuance of public bonds for decades. But in recent years companies have begun to look to rating agencies for broader, more strategic insight into their business, rather than just for a rating on specific bond issues. This reflects, at least in part, companies' recognition that their credit quality is the largest single factor in determining what their financing options are. What capital markets are open to a company, on what terms, and at what price all depends on what its credit quality is.

Companies of all sizes have been going global — to sell products, to source raw materials, and to raise capital. At the same time, the use of derivative products, hedging techniques, and other capital market products in the day-to-day management of most companies' business has multiplied. As a result, even relatively small companies find themselves continually needing to present themselves to new business and financial customers and counterparties to whom they may formerly have been unknown. This has created a tremendous demand for corporate credit ratings from companies that may have no public debt outstanding, and previously would not have expected to have a relationship with a rating agency. Since 1992, Standard & Poor's, for example, has developed hundreds of such corporate relationships, all with companies that realized that knowing exactly what their credit quality was, and why, was valuable strategic information.

Seeing the credit rating as a *strategic tool*, rather than just a static description, is leading corporations to additional creative uses of their rating relationships. Using specialized ratings, as we have seen in the bank loan market, to broaden the potential investor base for their debt and improve their credit terms is just a first step for many companies. There has also been a big increase in corporate clients approaching rating agencies *prior* to making decisions about mergers, divestitures, restructurings or other strategic actions, in order to learn what impact the move would have on its credit rating.

CONCLUSION

The bank loan market is the last major financial market to become *disintermediated*, where the providers of capital (the investors), the users of capital (the issuers or borrowers), and the intermediaries (the agents or underwriters) are now finally three identifiably separate groups, with their own unique interests and objectives. Disintermediated markets, by their nature, are more efficient than markets where some of the roles of investor, issuer and intermediary are merged, as was previously the case in the traditional bank loan market. Such markets require transparency of information, especially with regard to credit quality, which is the single most important variable in a debt market. The rapid growth in the use of credit ratings in the bank loan market is the logical result of this, and as the bank loan market expands and converges with other debt markets, we should expect to see even more attention paid to ratings and other analytical tools and techniques that allow credit instruments — old ones, new ones, and those not yet in existence — to be evaluated, compared and contrasted across markets and borders.

Chapter 4

Bank Loan Ratings

James Roche
Analyst
Fitch IBCA

William Brennan
Analyst
Fitch IBCA

Derek McGirt
Analyst
Fitch IBCA

Mariarosa Verde
Analyst
Fitch IBCA

INTRODUCTION

Rating agency focus on secured bank loans as an asset class has intensified measurably over the past few years. The unique investment features of bank loans have attracted non-traditional investors into the asset class, including insurance companies, prime rate and hedge funds, and managers of increasingly prominent collateralized bond and loan obligations. Because many of these newer institutional investors are ratings sensitive, external ratings of broadly syndicated bank facilities have grown in importance. Demand for external ratings of bank loans has been further stimulated by technological changes improving primary and secondary trading activity and convergence of the leveraged loan market with the high-yield bond market, which has expedited investor cross-over activity.

What distinguishes the ratings process relating to this asset class from other ratable corporate securities is treatment of security and other credit enhancements, such as structural priority. In this chapter, the key findings and general rating process of Fitch IBCA, Inc. are presented for perspective. Highlighted in the chapter are the distinction in historical recovery experience between bank loans and various grades of unsecured indebtedness, analytical techniques applied to capture this distinction, and documentary issues that are unique to the asset class.

57

Exhibit 1: Average Recovery by Selected Industry

	Avg. Price
Building/Materials/Construction	112
Energy	106
Department Stores	102
Health Care	96
Financial/Real Estate	83
Supermarket/Convenience/Drug Store	83
Paper & Forest Products	79
Apparel/Textiles	78
Apparel Retailers	74
Discount Department Stores	70
Computers/Electronics	63
Specialty Retailers	57
Average	82

Exhibit 2: Time in Distress for U.S. Bank Loans

<12 mos.	16
12-24 Mos.	26
24-36 Mos.	8
36-48 Mos.	4
>48 Mos.	3

Exhibit 3: Distressed Borrowers -
Relative Pricing of Capital Structure Securities
(% of Par)

Issuer	Date	Bank Debt	Senior Subordinated Debt	Subordinated Debt
R. H. Macy Co., Inc.	Dec-94	117.75	66.00	28.50
Petrolane Inc.	Dec-94	99.25	36.00	--
Interco Inc.	Aug-92	93.00	19.00	6.00

* Emergence from Chapter 11 Bankruptcy.
Source: Loan Pricing Corp. and Interactive Data Corp.

BANK LOAN RECOVERY FINDINGS

To illustrate the role security plays in distinguishing ratings of secured bank loans and other unsecured debt securities, the following summary of an October 1997 study by Fitch IBCA is presented. In its study, Fitch IBCA reviewed 60 distressed widely syndicated secured bank loans aggregating $25 billion. (Exhibits 1, 2, and 3 provide some major results of the study.) The following was observed:

• Distressed bank loans recovered 82%, while senior subordinated debt of the same issuers recovered 42%, and subordinated debt recovered 39%.

- Recoveries correlated to industry factors. Companies with low levels of hard assets, high levels of assets pledged to other financing sources, or obsolescence risk tended to recover less. Companies with solid business franchise and high quality plant or property had much higher recovery values.
- There were benefits of security, covenants, and collateral contained in well structured bank lending agreements.
- The average period that a loan remained in distress was 19 months.
- There is a moderate correlation between distressed bank debt prices and movements in the stock market.

The study examined trading prices of broadly syndicated bank loans, using data provided by Loan Pricing Corp., over a 6-year period ended June 1997. Given the development of the secondary market for performing and nonperforming loans, trading prices at the end of a restructuring or bankruptcy proceeding can be considered a proxy for the ultimate realization of value.

From a rating perspective, the appropriate notching — the rating differential between loans and bonds — will ultimately rely on differentiations in recovery expectations. As loan ratings are still in their infancy, Fitch IBCA's study supplies critical analytic data to support notching criteria.

The study's results are also important because syndicated bank loans are increasingly being pledged to collateralized loan obligations (CLOs) and collateralized bond obligations (CBOs). Rating these structured transactions requires underlying ratings on loans in the portfolios, as well as stress tests to model these transactions. Important inputs to the model include recovery rates of defaulted loans, and length of workout or default.

Fitch IBCA's study of the distressed securities market compared recoveries on distressed loan debt to the distressed bond debt of the same issuer. A variety of industries are represented in the sample. The recovery rate is derived from the last price listed for each security (bank debt and bonds) as the borrower emerged from distressed status. Fitch IBCA's analysis included comparing the last available price for each of the 60 companies' bank debt, e.g., senior unsecured, senior subordinated, and/or subordinated. Available prices for the senior unsecured debt were insufficient to estimate a statistically significant recovery rate. Fitch IBCA believes these prices are more reflective of ultimate value realization than previous bond studies that consider bond prices one month subsequent to bankruptcy. Given investors' high return expectations for defaulted debt, prices near the point of bankruptcy are generally much lower than final values of emergence from bankruptcy.

Ultimate recovery of bank loans can vary significantly across industries. The average recovery of all 60 distressed loans in the study was 82%. However, by excluding the three industries with the lowest recoveries, (specialty retailers, computers/electronics, and discount department stores) from this calculation, the average increased to 89%. While general economic conditions can impact ultimate recovery, the unique characteristics of each company and industry are the primary determinants.

The retail sector was represented by 18 of the 60 companies in the study, and was divided into four subcategories: discount department stores, apparel retailers, specialty retailers, and department stores. Specialty retailers, in particular, have been adversely affected by changes in demographics such as decreasing traffic in shopping malls, and in fashion trends. These industry trends have impeded revenue growth and margin improvements, thus limiting the enterprise value of these borrowers. In such cases, a greater percentage of the recovery may come in the form of equity or liquidation becomes more of a consideration. In a liquidation scenario, however, retailers generally do not have significant assets to support bank debt; facilities are usually leased and or receivables are pledged as part of a separate financing program.

Not only do competitive pressures impact the enterprise value of apparel retailers, inventory is also subject to shifts in style causing this type of collateral to lose value in a relatively short period of time. For retail credits, items effecting enterprise value, including operating performance and business/industry outlook, are key considerations in assessing ultimate recovery. Large retailers such as Federated Department Stores, Inc., and Macy's, experienced higher than average recoveries because of their ability to retain value as a going concern. The ability of these entities to position themselves as providers of quality merchandise allowed each to maintain higher operating margins, resulting in more robust cash flows.

A number of correlation studies were performed to test the theory that the size of the borrower, as measured by sales, significantly influenced the ultimate recovery of distressed credits. The study found that absolute size is not the sole determinant of recovery. As in the case of the retailers, a variety of characteristics contribute to the asset quality and/or franchise value of the borrower and are significant in the determination of ultimate recovery.

Broadly syndicated bank loans that become distressed are typically reorganized instead of liquidated. The size of these credits allow the borrower to more easily absorb expenses associated with operating in a distressed environment (e.g., legal, advisory) and large borrowers are more likely to maintain franchise value.

As discussed in greater detail later in this chapter, once a credit becomes distressed, investors will value it based upon tangible assets and franchise value. A strong equity market enhances the value of most companies and their constituent parts, as the equity component of enterprise value is augmented. This improves the prospects and quality of recovery for distressed companies. A higher valuation implies a greater value for subsidiaries contemplated for sale and minimizes the amount of equity distributed in lieu of debt in a reorganization scenario.

Fitch IBCA studied the relationship between the weekly prices of the secured bank debt issues in the study's sample and the DJIA. Exhibit 4 illustrates the distribution of correlation coefficients between the DJIA and each of the 60 domestic distressed bank debt issues since 1990. Approximately two thirds of the observations had a correlation coefficient of 0.5 or higher, supporting a positive relationship between the movements in the equity market and bank debt recovery.

Exhibit 4: Correlation Between Bank Loan Prices and DJIA

Correlation Coefficient	# of Loans *
<(0.5)	6
(0.5) - 0.0	4
0.0 - 0.5	11
>0.5	36

* Out of 57 Loans
DJIA - Dow Jones Industrial Average

These findings suggest that the highest bank debt recoveries would occur during periods of growth in the equity market. Robust equity markets provide a useful backdrop for selling off divisions, reorganizing, or restructuring.

GENERAL RATING PROCESS

At the onset of an explicit loan rating engagement, rating agencies are normally provided with a transaction memorandum that outlines the operational and financial history of a borrower and describes its position within the primary markets served. If the company is an issuer of public securities, additional resources (such as security prospectuses, equity and fixed income research reports, and peer comparisons) may be available. These materials and other information pertinent to the understanding of the company's background and its primary industries are reviewed in preparation for a due diligence meeting with management.

A formal face-to-face due diligence meeting with management of the borrowing entity is scheduled as early in the process as possible. This meeting is considered the most important source of information regarding the issuer's financial, organization, and operational goals. Discussion at these meetings centers the current and proposed financial structure, financial policies, profitability, cash flow generating ability, and organization structure.

Shortly after the due diligence meeting, an indication is provided to management as to what rating will be recommended to the rating committee. In this follow-up discussion, the analyst's view of the company's positive traits and rating concerns are addressed. The analyst's recommendation is a major consideration impacting the rating committee's decision, given his or her direct involvement in the due diligence process.

Generally within one week of the due diligence meeting, and subject to the receipt of all required information, a committee comprised of senior analysts will meet to determine the appropriate bank loan rating level. Both qualitative and quantitative factors are weighed and balanced to arrive at the appropriate rating.

Exhibit 5: Default Frequency (%)*

Rating Category	Default Frequency
AAA	1.00
AA	1.50
A	1.55
BBB+	3.35
BBB	4.25
BBB-	7.75
BB+	11.25
BB	14.50
BB-	21.00
B	33.25

* 10-year period

Though Fitch IBCA ratings are prospective in nature, they are reviewed periodically and when a financing or material event occurs. In addition to ongoing dialogue in the normal course, any material events reviewed are specifically addressed with management. If an event occurs that may affect a company's bank loan rating, the rating is place on alert, with an indication of whether the change is likely to be positive or negative. When necessary, the analyst will convene a rating committee to decide on the appropriate change. Because Fitch IBCA ratings are prospective, changes are not made to prevailing ratings unless the event or trend is considered to be fundamental and likely to persist for a significant period of time.

LOAN RATING METHODOLOGY

Unlike rating public bonds, Fitch IBCA's approach to rating secured bank debt relies on post-default recoveries as much as the possibility of default. Integrating the analysis of the possibility of default (default frequency) with that of a post-default recovery (loss severity) derives the "expected loss." The expected loss represents the credit loss a lender can expect on a loan and is calculated by multiplying the default frequency by the loss severity. Ideally, there should be a direct correlation between a lender's expected loss and the credit spread it charges a borrower.

Default Frequency

Fitch IBCA defines default frequency as the probability, measured as a percentage, that an issuer will not be able to pay the interest or principal related to a specific loan in a timely manner. Each ratings category has a corresponding default frequency based on studies measuring the payment default history of publicly traded bonds (see Exhibit 5). For example, many studies have shown that a BB bond has a 14.5% 10-year default probability, or 1.45% annually. This means that over a 10-year period, there is a 14.5% chance that a BB bond will default with respect to the timely payment of interest and principal. According to these same studies, a BBB bond has a 4.25% chance of defaulting over a 10-year period.

A Fitch IBCA public bond rating, and related default frequency, are based primarily on the analysis of a borrower's competitive position, financial profile, management, industry outlook, capital structure, and cash flow characteristics.

This type of analysis is commonly referred to as traditional ratings analysis. Little consideration is given to whether the borrower will ultimately recover all or a portion of the outstanding loan, foregone interest, and related costs at some point in the future. The difference between a Fitch IBCA public bond rating and a rating on a secured bank facility is that the bank loan ratings incorporate loss severity as well as the probability of default in making timely payment of interest and principal.

Default frequency is determined simply by assigning an unsecured rating to a bank loan using the traditional ratings analysis. The default frequency may be adjusted to reflect effective paydown provisions that serve to shorten the duration of a loan.

The process for determining a secured bank loan's default frequency is the same as the one used to determine a rating and related default frequency for a unsecured public bond. The secured bank loan rating, however, requires two additional steps to arrive at a rating based on ultimate recovery — the determination of loss severity and the calculation of an expected loss percentage.

Loss Severity

Loss severity represents the estimated loss a lender can expect to encounter when a loan defaults. A loss could result from the restructuring of a loan or an eventual sale of a business or assets at a price insufficient to recover all principal, interests, and costs.

Fitch IBCA applies collateral valuation, simulated default scenario, priority claims table, loss severity, and expected loss percentage — to quantify an issuer's loss severity. Once a secured bank loan's loss severity is determined, it is multiplied by its default frequency to arrive at its expected loss percentage and corresponding rating.

Step 1 – Collateral Valuation

A collateral valuation is performed to assess whether there is enough asset coverage to protect secured bank lenders against loss and allow bank lenders to continue to accrue post-petition interest (which is allowed under the U.S. bankruptcy code, assuming lenders can demonstrate that there is adequate coverage). To the extent collateral asset values do not exceed the loan balance, the lenders would not be allowed to accrue post-petition interest.

The review of collateral involves a comprehensive assessment of the overall quality of the assets pledged as security. When evaluating collateral packages, Fitch IBCA focuses on the asset's ability to maintain its value over time, especially in a post-default scenario. Special attention is given to the liquidity of a particular asset pledged as collateral, as well as the historical price and value volatility associated with specific collateral types.

Step 2 – Simulated Default Scenario

To quantify loss severity, Fitch IBCA employs an analytical process beginning with a simulated default scenario. To simulate a default scenario, Fitch IBCA first decides which default scenario is more likely — liquidation or reorganization. A liquidation scenario would most likely be used in a situation where a company had a relatively simple capital structure, liquid assets pledged as collateral, and a relatively weak business outlook. In a situation where a company has a good business whose risk of default would most likely arise from high leverage, Fitch IBCA would assume the company would be reorganized and not liquidated. As a result, the potential value of the enterprise as a whole would be available to satisfy all relevant claims, including the amount of outstanding bank debt.

Step 3 – Priority Claims Table

Next, a strict priority claims table is constructed to determine what percentage of the bank loan would be covered by asset value after considering priority claims and outlays used to preserve the value of the secured claim. Fitch IBCA may apportion a small percentage of recovery to unsecured creditors given that it may be required to facilitate a consensual reorganization.

Step 4 – Loss Severity

Once the distribution of collateral is complete, the present value of the projected recovery is calculated. The present value of this expected recovery is then subtracted from 100% to determine the bank loan's loss severity.

Step 5 – Expected Loss Percentage

The expected loss percentage is calculated by multiplying the issuer's default frequency by loss severity. Once the expected loss percentage is determined, the secured bank loan is assigned a corresponding letter rating. (See Exhibit 6.)

Exhibit 6: Rating Categories

Expected Loss Percentage	Rating Equivalent
≤ 1%	A– through AAA
> 1% and ≤ 2%	BBB–, BBB, BBB+
> 2% and ≤ 5%	BB–, BB, BB+
> 5% and ≤ 10%	B–, B, B+
> 10% and ≤ 20%	CCC, CC
> 20%	C–, DDD, DD, D

NOTCHING

The foundation for rating bank loans is a "default" rating which reflects an issuer's ability to meet scheduled debt service requirements associated with the pro forma total debt capitalization. This default rating is then adjusted through a notching process that captures the floor recovery expected to be generated by liquidating the underlying collateral, restructuring the capitalization or reorganizing the company. Because the downside recovery outcome is generally much different in liquidation versus reorganization scenarios, a critical component of the analysis is determining which method of resolving a potential default is most probable given the company's profile.

The determination of whether recovery of principal or interest will most likely result from a liquidation or a reorganization is made on a case-by-case basis. Typically, liquidation candidates represent companies that are reporting deteriorating financial results and have products or services that are either obsolete or commodity-like. On the hand, reorganization candidates are normally companies that provide unique products or services that have had difficulty fulfilling their debt obligations due to leverage or operational issues believed to be reparable.

When it is determined the probable downside scenario facing a debt issuer is a liquidation, the analysis normally boils down to collateral analysis. In deriving its floor recovery assessment in these cases, Fitch IBCA will first rely on whatever appraisals may be available and on what basis and by whom they were prepared. The three largest asset categories — accounts receivable, inventory, and fixed assets — clearly require different treatment. Receivable analysis tends to focus on credit quality of the counterparties, average age of outstanding receivables, and economic conditions affecting the industries in which major counterparties operate. Inventory analysis is centered on obsolescence risk, work-in-process exposure, exposure to special purpose categories, and the quality of the manufacturing, distribution or retail channels finished goods are sold into. Fixed asset analysis is dependent on issues such as industry, capacity, and special purpose nature of the underlying plants or plant assets.

The leveraged loan market tends to be characterized as a reorganization market, in which defaults are dealt with either in out-of-court settlements or in Chapter 11 reorganizations. Chapter 7 liquidations have been infrequent in these markets. Favored candidates for leveraged loans are those with historically stable financial track records, leading market share positions, diversified customer bases or defensible manufacturing or service capabilities. Since most reorganizations of this nature are based on an entity's enterprise value at the time of default, Fitch IBCA uses multi-scenario forecasting to determine the probable range of outcomes in a default scenario. Fitch IBCA defines enterprise value as the purchase price a company could garner from informed buyers in a given market. Contributing inputs to this analysis are data observed from publicly disclosed acquisitions occurring within an issuer's market during the past economic cycle.

When utilizing enterprise values to gauge downside recovery expectations, Fitch IBCA estimates a stressed EBITDA run rate after its review if the risks facing the issuer and conditions affecting the market it serves. To this stressed EBITDA a conservative purchase multiple is applied, based on the range of purchase multiples paid for similar enterprises throughout at least one business cycle. In determining the distressed EBITDA level, Fitch IBCA considers the level of expected earnings volatility demonstrated by the company through the last economic cycle and whether cost saving opportunities earmarked are intuitive. A substantial discount is applied to the pro forma EBITDA run rate to account for the effect a less advantageous economic climate might have on the company as well as the prospective nature of cost saving estimates. Stressed cash flow multiples are used to reflect the fact that reorganizations tend to occur at a time when an issuer's prospects may be viewed less favorably than other participants, that may be less levered.

The estimated downside enterprise value is then compared to the senior secured credit facility commitment to determine an implied recovery level. The number of notches to be added to the senior unsecured (default) rating incorporates Fitch IBCA's findings from its syndicated bank loan recovery study (October 1997) as its foundation, whereby bank loans recovered 82% while junior debt of the same issuer recovered 42%. Where full recovery is not anticipated, Fitch IBCA recognizes that a recovery scenario consistent with the study findings does indeed warrant a higher rating than for junior securities in the same capital structure. Where full recovery is foreseen, the magnitude of the notching from the default rating will be determined by the level of coverage of interest accrued during distressed period. The ultimate notching determination is based on the relative recovery differential anticipated between the different securities in the capital structure.

LEGAL DUE DILIGENCE

A chief component of the bank loan rating process is documentation review. The crux of this review is to determine if the loan agreements and related documentation contain certain provisions or features that either enhance the bank lender's position vis-à-vis an issuer's other creditors, provide secondary sources of loan repayment or, in some cases, weaken the lender's position relative to other creditors. Four broad areas account for the bulk of Fitch IBCA's analysis: support provisions and agreements, covenants, structural considerations, and unique features.

Support

The most tangible source of secondary loan repayment, absent timely receipt of scheduled principal and interest from free cash flow, is collateral liquidation. A key focus of Fitch IBCA's collateral analysis is the nature of the pledged security, which is assessed after asking the following questions: Are hard, tangible assets pledged or is the security in the form of capital stock or intangible assets, such as intellectual property? Is the support rather in the form of secured guarantees or third-party assets? In addition to evaluating the nature of the underlying collateral, Fitch IBCA reviews security and pledge agreements to ensure that there are no material exclusions from the expected collateral pool, that the assets have been properly perfected and to determine whether the lender's position is a first or second priority.

Guarantees offer a secondary source of repayment. Fitch IBCA considers the type of guarantees offered relative to what is adequate and customary for the given transaction. For example, when the loan is to a holding company that has multiple subsidiaries, Fitch IBCA considers whether the loan documents include upstream guarantees to support the holding company obligations. Secured upstream guarantees from operating subsidiaries help to mitigate the risk of implied structural subordination.

Covenants

Historically, a distinguishing characteristic of the non-investment grade bank loan market has been that loan agreements contain more restrictive and comprehensive covenant packages than similar documentation underlying other debt securities. Properly drafted financial covenants provide advance warning of deteriorating performance and afford senior creditors sufficient time to evaluate their respective rights and remedies during periods when the debt issuer's performance is worse than expected. Fitch IBCA assesses the reasonableness of financial covenants in the context of financial projections submitted by management as well as against covenant packages for loan agreements for comparable debt issuers.

Affirmative and negative non-financial covenants are also reviewed for reasonableness and for their ability to limit or control risk from increasing in the future. The more material non-financial covenants, often referred to as *negative covenants*, include debt incurrence limitations (both existing and prospective), restrictions on distributions outside of mandatory debt payments, and limitations on capital expenditures. Clearly, analysis of such covenants is issuer and industry specific, as factors such as cyclicality and growth prospects must be considered.

Structural Considerations

Given that high recovery rates associated with bank loans largely result from their legal priority, it is important to assess the borrower's position within the organizational structure of the corporate entity to which it is a part. Most fundamental is whether the borrower is an operating subsidiary or a holding company. Holding company debt is often structurally subordinated to direct obligations of its subsidiaries, particularly in situations where upstream guarantees have not been provided by the operating subsidiaries. More favorable ratings consideration is afforded bank debt that is closely tied to actual operating cash flows and assets. Issuing secured bank debt at the operating company level limits the possibility of structural subordination and allows lenders a first priority claim on the entity's assets and cash flows.

In addition to evaluating the legal structure of the borrowing entity, Fitch IBCA reviews intercreditor and subordination agreements affecting the interrelationship between the senior bank group and other creditors of the borrowing entity or any affiliated entities. Of particular note is whether cross-default agreements exist that place junior securities in default once a bank loan covenant has been tripped and what type of standstill provisions exist that hold junior or unsecured creditors in abeyance while the senior bank group contemplates its action plan regarding covenant defaults.

Unique Features

Documentary review has become an increasingly important component of the analysis of non-investment grade debt issuers. One byproduct of the demand/supply imbalance that has developed in the non-investment grade loan market in recent years, as well as its convergence with the high-yield bond market, is that basic terms and conditions relating to an increasing number of debt issuances have deteriorated. Within the past 18 months, several broadly syndicated bank loan transactions have been brought to market stripped of important support features. These transactions have been commonly referred to as "covenant lite" or "hybrid" loans because they lack conventional levels of covenants, security or other protective features, and thus represent a cross between traditional senior loans and unsecured high-yield bonds.

Among the newer loan innovations are those that (1) have been stripped of certain or all financial covenants, (2) incorporate standstill provisions for certain senior secured tranches, (3) have diminished event of default provisions, and (4) either dilute the collateral pool for the entire senior loan facility or for a particular tranche within it. In some cases, these structures call for collateral to be shared equally between the bank group and bond holders. In other cases, the senior loan is tranched such that a portion of the loan is secured by a first lien of the primary operating assets and another portion is secured by a second lien on the same collateral. In yet other cases, none of the operating assets are liened but the capital stock is pledged. The rating implication of these innovations is that certain bank loans, or tranches thereof, may qualify for lower ratings than if the features were not diluted. A lower rating recognizes the fact that hybrid lenders might have less ability to pursue remedies to cure a default and may absorb any shortfalls in recovery proceeds.

CONCLUSION

As the bank loan asset class increasingly evolves into a capital market solution, with respect to trading, optionality and investor coverage, the demand for external ratings on bank loans has strengthened. Unlike other ratable asset classes, secured bank loans have covenant packages, priority claims on assets or stock, and other credit enhancements that serve to improve average principal recovery and lower downside risk. Accurate assessment of these characteristics requires analytical techniques regarding collateral and market valuation that must accompany a fundamental analysis of the underlying business.

Chapter 5

The Impact of
Subordination on Loan Loss

David Keisman
Principal
Portfolio Management Data, LLC

Steven Miller
Principal
Portfolio Management Data, LLC

INTRODUCTION

The flood of institutional investors into the leveraged loan market has transformed leveraged lending from a traditional bank-only segment to a full-fledged member of the capital markets. The growth of the institutional loan investor base in recent years has been striking. By year-end 1997, their ranks swelled to 64, up from 13 at the end of 1993[1] as these investors became, for the first time, the largest discrete market for highly leveraged loans. Institutional loan investors — which include hedge funds, insurance companies, mutual funds and securitization vehicles — have been drawn into the market for a variety of reasons that are described in Chapter 1. Among the first and foremost of these is the collateral protection and seniority offered by loans which limits loss-given-default for loan investors and, which it has been assumed, offers a competitive or even superior risk-adjusted return versus other asset classes.

The convergence of the leveraged loan and high-yield debt market described in Chapter 1, however, has added complexity to investors' job of evaluating credit risk. Traditional product definitions are becoming blurred as arrangers develop new hybrid and institutional term loan products that take a "Chinese menu" approach to covenants and security. Traditionally an investor would need to cross the Rubicon to go from senior secured bank debt to senior unsecured notes to subordinated bonds. Today, hybrid loans and crossover products make the distinctions more ambiguous and make it harder for an investor to know which factors to focus on when trying to determine which product offers the best trade-off between risk and return.

---

[1] See Exhibit 1 in Chapter 1.

PMD would like to thank Leo Brand and Reza Bahar for their help and guidance in compiling the data used in this study.

Exhibit 1: Issuers Included in Study

Issuer	Earliest Default Date (if different from Chapter 11)	Chapter 11 Date	Date of Emergence	Time in Default (Years)
Allied Stores Corp.		January 15, 1990	February 1992	2.06
CDK/Kendall Co.	May 1, 1990	May 20, 1992	July 1992	0.13
Charter Medical Corp.	February 15, 1991	June 2, 1992	July 1992	1.43
Federated Department Stores Inc.		January 15, 1990	February 1992	2.06
Grand Union Co.	January 15, 1995	January 25, 1995	June 1995	0.41
Insilco Corp.		January 14, 1991	April 1993	2.22
Interco Inc.	June 15, 1990	January 24, 1991	August 1992	2.14
Revco DS Inc.	June 15, 1988	July 28, 1988	June 1992	3.85
RH Macy & Co.		January 27, 1992	December 1994	2.90
Southland Corp.	June 15, 1990	October 24, 1990	March 1991	0.72
USG Corp.	January 15, 1991	March 17, 1993	May 1993	2.31
Average				1.84

These two factors, the evolution of the market into a capital market with traditional institutional investors and the convergence of the leveraged loan and high-yield markets, reinforce the need to refine information allowing for an accurate assessment of the total return of the leveraged loan market and to compare these returns to those of other asset classes. An important component in this assessment is the loss-given-default of leveraged loans. This chapter abstracts a study by Portfolio Management Data (PMD) that explores the loss-given-default experience of 10 of the largest leveraged transaction defaults of the late 1980s and early 1990s drawn from Standard & Poor's default study (see Exhibit 1).[2] The PMD study presents average recovery levels for five traditional debt products — bank debt, senior secured notes, senior unsecured bonds, senior subordinated bonds, and junior subordinated bonds. It then takes this analysis one step further by comparing loss suffered on a particular instrument with the amount of debt subordinated to that instrument.

SUMMARY OF FINDINGS

It is no surprise that subordination plays an important role in loss-given-default. However, it remains an area that is largely unexplored because most studies report recoveries only by class of debt. The study abstracted in this chapter is a first indication of how subordination affects loss-given-default across types of instruments for the largest, most liquid high-yield transactions. PMD believes that this analysis will be an increasingly important factor in making loss-given-default assumptions for pricing and credit-risk models given: (1) the rapid convergence between leveraged loan and high-yield bonds market, blurring the distinction between traditional product classes and (2) the movement away from subordinated debt toward senior unsecured bonds that ensued after the high-yield market collapsed in the early 1990s and continues today.

---

[2] A description of the transactions studied is provided in the appendix to this chapter.

Exhibit 2: Present Value of Bank Debt, Senior Unsecured Debt, and Senior Subordinated Debt Recovery Versus Subordination

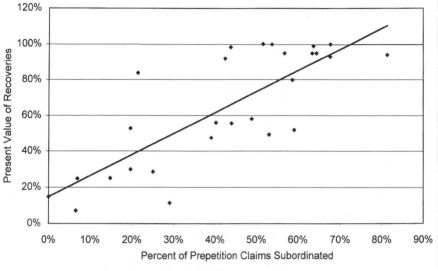

OBSERVATIONS

The two main observations of this analysis are as follows. First, higher subordination results in higher recovery. This analysis is intuitive but important: As the cushion of subordination increases the recovery for a particularly piece of debt tends to increase. As shown in Exhibits 2 through 5, this is true within a class of debt (i.e., bank debt or senior subordinated notes) or throughout the entire universe of debt instruments reviewed regardless of class.

Second, subordination is a better indicator of recovery than class for the large, most liquid deals reviewed in this study. Exhibits 6 and 7 show the average recovery and one standard deviation around this average by class of security and amount of subordination, respectively. It is striking that the standard deviations are far tighter and more consistent when viewing recoveries by subordination than by class of security. This is particularly true for subordinated instruments. For instance, the average recovery of the nine senior subordinated bonds reviewed in this study was 36%. The standard deviation around this average is 26%. Therefore, one standard deviation is fully 69% of the average. Similarly, the average recovery for the five senior unsecured notes reviewed was 67% compared with a standard deviation equal to 31% of this average. Viewing the data by subordination, in contrast, shows that the standard deviation in the three ranges of subordination used — 50% or more, 25%-49% and less than 25% — is never more than 20% of the average.

Exhibit 3: Present Value of Bank Debt Recovery Versus Subordination

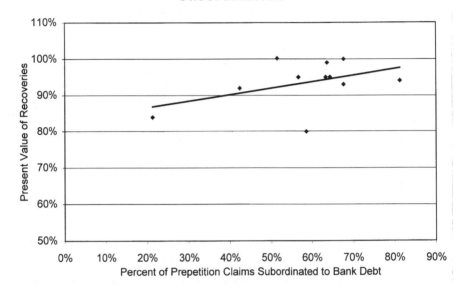

Exhibit 4: Present Value of Senior Subordinated Debt Recovery Versus Subordination

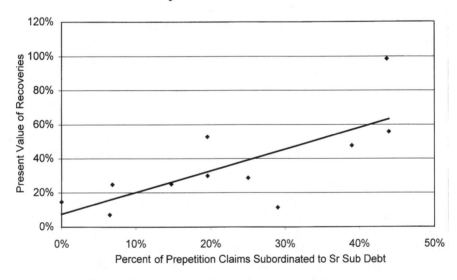

Exhibit 5: Present Value of Junior Subordinated Debt Recovery Versus Amount Senior to the Debt

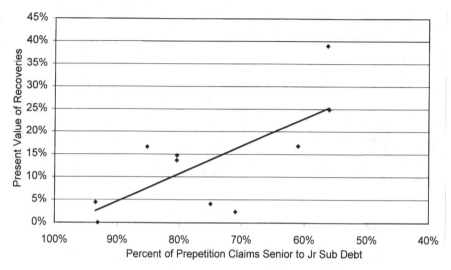

Exhibit 6: Average and Standard Deviation of Recoveries by Type of Debt

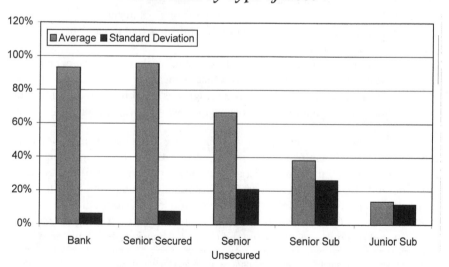

Exhibit 7: Average and Standard Deviation of Recoveries by Subordination Level

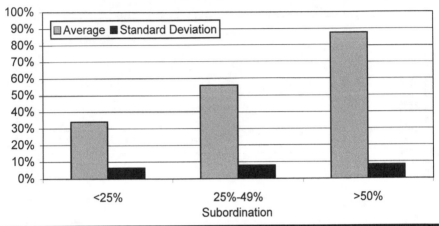

INCLUSION CRITERIA AND METHODOLOGY

PMD selected the ten bankruptcies analyzed in this study based on the following criteria:

- Large, highly liquid leveraged transactions of at least $950 million.
- Bank debt was a large percentage of the original financing.
- A capital structure with at least four of the five traditional debt classes.
- Defaults within the past ten years
- Readily available information on the original deals, on reasons for default, and on trading prices of the post-emergence debt and equity issued to creditors
- Transactions in which excess leverage was the primary reason for default rather than litigation, questionable management practices or outright fraud.

PMD obtained source data for the study from bankruptcy documents (reorganization and disclosure statements), Securities & Exchange Commission filings, press articles, press releases, and previous studies,[3] as well as Standard & Poor's default studies. PMD reviewed bankruptcy documents and SEC filings for the principal and interest claims of each creditor class. Nominal recoveries for each debt issue were calculated from the post-emergence trading prices of the new debt and/or equity received for the claim.[4] If markets for these new instru-

---

[3] Steven Miller and Christopher Snyder, "Institutional Investment in Leveraged Loans Grows," in John D. Finnerty and Martin S. Fridson (eds.), *The Yearbook of Fixed Income Investing 1995* (Burr Ridge, Ill: Irwin Professional Publishing, 1996).

[4] Post-emergence trading prices are based on information from New Generation Research, Bloomberg, and articles written at the time of emergence.

ments did not exist at the time of emergence, then PMD discounted back, at the rate of the original pre-default instrument, from the date that the instruments did ultimately trade to the date of emergence.

PMD employed post-emergence prices — rather than the distressed prices for the original debt either immediately after default or immediately prior to emergence — because systemic factors influence the trading price of debt issues in default. Not the least of these factors was the severe liquidity crisis of the early 1990s when only a few vulture funds were purchasing distressed debt and banks and other holders were highly motivated sellers. PMD felt that this supply/demand imbalance might distort the value of this debt whereas this distortion would not be included in post-emergence debt. Also, the complexity of the settlements, which often involved a combination of cash, several new classes of debt, new stock, and new warrants, made the valuations difficult before post-emergence trading of the settlement pieces commenced. And, post-emergence trading prices will be a consistent valuation approach as PMD expands this study to smaller, less liquid issues that did not typically have reported trading prices during default or bankruptcy.

ASSUMPTIONS

In this study, PMD employed the following assumptions:

- PMD excluded debt specifically tied to an asset from the study, including industrial revenue bonds, mortgages, and purchase money debt. The recovery rate of such debt is highly dependent on the value of the underlying asset. As a result, the amount of subordination does not influence recoveries.
- If PMD could not determine the default date for a specific debt issue, then the date was set at the earliest default date of any related issue of debt. Because most debt in a borrower's capital structure are subject to cross-default covenants and therefore default simultaneously, the effect on present value calculations is negligible.
- If the debt was listed as "Unimpaired," recoveries are assumed to be 100 cents on the dollar because all interest and principal payments were made on a contractual basis. This also ensures that present value of recoveries for this debt would also be 100 cents on the dollar. Note that only two specific debt issues in the study were unimpaired and both of these were the most senior and fully secured in their respective capital structure.
- PMD excluded unimpaired debt from the analysis of settlement by debt class (Exhibits 8) because unimpaired classes, by definition, receive no new settlement.

Exhibit 8: Sample Breakdown of
Settlement for Bank Creditors

	New Debt	Stock/Warrants	Cash
Settlement for Bank Creditors (%)	89	5	6
Settlement for Senior Secured Creditors (%)	87	6	7
Settlement for Senior Unsecured Creditors (%)	27	43	30
Settlement for Senior Subordinated Creditors (%)	36	61	3
Settlement for Junior Subordinated Creditors (%)	36	62	2

- PMD excluded pre-petition common and preferred stock from subordination amounts because, for the issuers reviewed, this equity had either insignificant or no economic value at emergence.
- The dates of default (if different from the date of bankruptcy), bankruptcy and emergence are based on information from reorganization documents, news articles, and Standard & Poor's data.

APPENDIX

TRANSACTIONS STUDIED

The following descriptions of the transactions in the study based on information from Reorganization documents, SEC filings, news articles, Standard & Poor's releases and press releases.

Department store operators *Allied Stores Corporation* and *Federated Department Stores, Inc.* were taken private by Campeau Corporation in October 1986 and May 1988, respectively, for a combined price of over $10 billion. As a result of the large amount of debt, the combined companies started experiencing a liquidity crisis almost immediately after the $6.6 billion Federated purchase, which was won in an auction with R.H. Macy and Co. The aggressive cash flow projections used to value the Federated purchase proved unrealistic and by mid-1989, Campeau had negotiated an emergency loan from Olympia & York and had entered into discussions with its bank group. The inability to refinance its debt coupled with concerns about suppliers withholding shipments led Federated to file for bankruptcy protection on January 15, 1990. It emerged as a public company in February 1992.

Charter Medical Corp. is an operator of psychiatric hospitals. While it had originally focused on both psychiatric and general hospitals, by the mid-1980s it had restructured to focus mainly on psychiatric facilities. It was taken private by WAF Acquisition Corp, which was formed by Charter's management and the family of William A. Fickling, in September 1988. The company incurred over $1.6 billion in LBO debt at the beginning of an industry-wide reduction in demand for psychiatric inpatient services, a corresponding demand for more out-patient care and the emergence of third-party payer efforts, mainly by insurance companies, to control rising mental health expenses. Nonetheless, Charter continued to build inpatient facilities. As a consequence, revenues decreased but costs were not sufficiently controlled. In January 1991 the company announced that it was preparing an exchange offer to restructure its outstanding debt and that it would not pay interest on its public debt in February. In October 1992, it reached a deal with its bank group and with the steering committees for its noteholders to pursue a pre-packaged Chapter 11 filing which was made on June 2, 1992. Charter emerged as a public company in July 1992.

Grand Union Company, a supermarket chain which had 306 stores primarily in the Northeast, was acquired by Salomon Brothers Inc., Miller Tabak & Hirsch and Co. for $1.2 billion in 1989. In July 1992, it completed a $1.3 billion recapitalization, which included the public offering of $850 million in debt and a new $310 million bank credit agreement, as well as the sale of zero-coupon notes by Grand Union Capital, the parent of Grand Union Company. The interest burden from the additional debt left the company unable to weather the problems caused by a weak economy in the Northeast United States and competitive pressures. In November 1994, Grand Union announced that by early 1995 cash from operations would not meet cash interest payments. After missing a January interest payment on its public debt, the company presented a restructuring proposal to its creditor groups and filed a pre-packaged bankruptcy reorganization on January 25, 1995. It emerged as a public company in June 1995.

Insilco Corporation, a diversified manufacturer whose subsidiaries included Rolodex, Taylor Textbook Publishing Co. and Red Devil paint, was taken private in October 1986 in a $1.1 billion LBO that topped an announced $742 million management buyout. The deal's sponsor, INR Holdings Inc., a company owned by Texas Investors Cyril Wagner Jr. and Jack E. Brown, believed that expansion of existing businesses coupled with cost reductions were achievable and would make the transaction a success. A weakening economy both reduced demand for many of the company's products and decreased the potential purchase price of assets offered for sale. This, coupled with the debt burden led Insilco to file a plan in May 1990 with the SEC to swap about $488 million of debt for new debt, cash and convertible preferred stock. The swap was never completed and on January 14, 1991 the company declared Chapter 11. It emerged as a public company in April 1993.

City Capital Associates made a hostile bid in 1988 for *Interco, Inc.*, a diversified manufacturer and retailer of furniture, footwear and apparel. To avoid this bid, Interco implemented a major restructuring and recapitalization program starting in November 1988. The recapitalization, which included a special dividend to shareholder totaling approximately $1.4 billion in cash and more than $1.3 billion in new debt, left the company highly leveraged. The company expected to repay the debt through the sale of non-core businesses and through increased efficiencies resulting in stronger operating cash flow. The debt burden proved too high and Interco restructured its bank agreement in March 1990. It also announced that it would not make the June 15 interest payments on its senior subordinated debentures and junior payment-in-kind subordinated debentures. It attempted to restructure this debt in May 1990 outside of bankruptcy and when the restructuring failed, a Chapter 11 petition was filed on January 24, 1991. Interco emerged in August 1992.

CDK Holding, controlled by Clayton and Dubilier acquired the *Kendall Co.* from Colgate-Palmolive in October 1988 for roughly $960 million. It was, at that time, Clayton and Dubilier's largest LBO. Kendall manufactures and markets disposable medical supplies to hospitals and alternate-site health care facilities and sells health-care products to pharmacies and other retail outlets. It also manufactures and markets adhesive products and tapes for health-care and other applications. The company planned to service debt from the LBO with cash flow from operations but results from operations never reached forecast levels for a variety of reasons including declining sales in several divisions, the recession and increased expenses resulting from a voluntary recall in the institutional health-care products unit. By May 1989, the bank facility was increased to fund working capital needs and in May 1991 Kendall missed an interest payment on its debentures. Kendall started negotiating a restructuring agreement with its banks and institutional debtholders in April 1991. CDK/Kendall filed a pre-packaged bankruptcy agreement on May 20, 1992 and emerged as a public company in July 1992.

Revco DS, Inc., a drugstore chain, was taken private in a $1.3 billion LBO by the company's chairman and founder in December 1988. Cash flow projections proved overly ambitious as the proxy statement predicted sales growth of 50% in the year-to-May 1988 versus actual sales growth of only around 5%. By 1988, cash flow was less than needed to meet interest obligations and the company announced that it would probably not be able to make a June interest payment prompting the holders of more than 25% of Revco's 13.125% senior subordinated debentures to accelerate the maturity date on the principal of the issue. Revco, the first big 1980s LBO to go bust, declared Chapter 11 on July 28, 1988. Both Revco and its creditors submitted reorganization plans and two rival drugstore chains bid for Revco, further delaying its emergence from bankruptcy. Revco finally emerged as a public company in June 1992.

R.H. Macy & Co., Inc., a national department store retailer, was taken private in July 1986 in a $3.5 billion LBO by a group of investors led by current and former management. Macy subsequently acquired the I. Magnin and Bullock's divisions of Federated in May 1988 for an additional $1.04 billion. A weak retailing environment, particularly in the Northeast, coupled with a recession caused sales to decline significantly reducing cash flow. While Macy retained enough liquidity to meet its short-term obligations, substantial concerns remained about its long-term financial position. Several efforts were instituted to reduce debt including the sale of its credit card operations to GE Capital and the buyback of debt at a discount using the proceeds from more than $200 million of new equity. Nonetheless, confidence in the company was undermined by continued losses and delayed payments to trade creditors. After unsuccessful attempts to restructure its debt or to find an equity infusion, Macy filed for Chapter 11 on January 27, 1992. Federated Department Stores, recently out of bankruptcy, acquired a position in Macy by purchasing a debt claim from Prudential Insurance and ultimately acquired the company in December 1994.

Southland Corporation is a convenience stores operator. To avoid a hostile takeover, Southland was taken private in December 1987 in a $4.9 billion LBO by JT Acquisition, which was controlled by members of the founding Thompson family. Due to the timing of the deal, just after the October stock market crash, the high-yield bond market was very volatile and it took the deal's arrangers, Goldman Sachs and Salomon Brothers, three attempts to raise $1.5 billion in expensive long-term debt. Operating earnings fell short of forecasts and the company was required to sell major assets such as its 50% stake in Citgo Petroleum Corp, its Chief Auto Parts chain, and more than 900 of its shops, in addition to those scheduled for disposition. Restrictions in the credit agreement limited the level of capital expenditures at a time of new competition from (1) grocery stores and discount stores with increased hours of operation as well as from (2) gasoline retailers that were experimenting with their own on-site convenience stores. In addition, the company concluded that it did not have the cash flow to meet scheduled amortization payments. In March 1990 Southland announced that it had signed a definitive agreement with Ito-Yokado and 7-Eleven Japan Co Ltd. to buy new a 75% interest in Southland common stock for $400 million. The stock purchase was contingent on a successful restructuring of Southland's outstanding public debt and preferred stock. In June 1990, Southland was kept by its bank group from making interest payments on some of its notes and accelerated negotiations with its bondholders. After these negotiations were successfully completed, the company filed a pre-packaged reorganization on October 24, 1990 and emerged on March 5, 1991.

Desert Partners L.P made a hostile bid in 1988 for *USG Corp.*, a manufacturer of building materials. To avoid this bid, USG borrowed heavily to finance a special $1.92 billion dividend to shareholders. USG planned to accelerate the paydown of its now $3.1 billion in debt by trimming capital expenditures, by reducing its workforce, and by selling assets. Debt was reduced to approximately $2.4 billion before an extended softness in gypsum markets, reflecting the adverse economic conditions in the building industry and excess capacity in the gypsum sector, reduced earnings to a point where USG could no longer service its debt through operations. USG defaulted on a December 1990 principal payment to its bank group, precluding interest payments due January 1991 on its public debt. A proposed financial restructuring aimed at keeping the company out of bankruptcy court was unsuccessful. After lengthy negotiations with its bank group and bondholders, USG filed a pre-packaged reorganization on March 17, 1993. USG emerged in May 1993.

Chapter 6

Market Standards for Loan Trading in the Secondary Market

Allison A. Taylor
Senior Vice President
ING Baring (U.S.) Securities, Inc.
and Chairperson of LSTA

INTRODUCTION

The volume of secondary loan trading exploded in the 1990s. Between 1991 and 1997, volume grew almost 600%. In 1991, a total of $8 billion (face amount) of loans traded in the secondary market, according to Loan Pricing Corporation. In 1997, secondary volume grew to a total of $62 billion (face amount). This dramatic growth is shown in Exhibit 1.

Exhibit 1: Secondary Loan Trading Volume
($ in Billions)

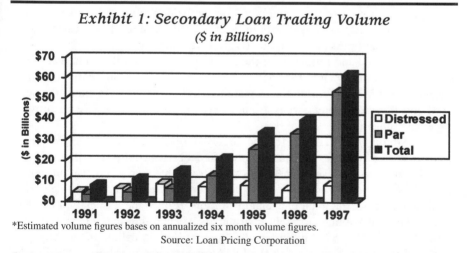

*Estimated volume figures bases on annualized six month volume figures.
Source: Loan Pricing Corporation

The author would like to thank the following individuals for their guidance and assistance in writing this chapter: Stephen Blauner (Milbank Tweed Hadley and McCloy), Tim Cross (LPC), and Natalie Lowe (LSTA).

There are many reasons why the secondary loan trading volume grew at such an exponential rate. The syndicated new-issue loan market also grew over the same time period, although not as quickly. In 1997, volume reached $1.1 trillion, according to LPC. This represents a 374% increase from a total of $234 billion in 1991. Additionally, during the early 1990s, default rates soared. Consequently, many banks felt the need to reduce their exposure to these distressed loans and sold them into a young and developing secondary loan trading market. As can be seen in Exhibit 1, the volume of distressed loans in the secondary market was greater than that of the par loan volume until 1994. Furthermore, the investors for loans that yield Libor + 150 or higher have changed extensively since the mid-1980s. During the mid-1980s investors of loans were largely banks, savings and loans, finance companies, and sometimes insurance companies. Today, mutual funds for both loans and bonds, pension funds, many insurance companies, and collateral loan obligation trusts are major investors in loans as an asset class.

As a result of this growth of secondary loan trading volume, it became quite evident that standards were needed for trading loans in the secondary market. Because loans are not securities, the trading of loans is (not regulated by a legal authority such as the Securities and Exchange Commission. Consequently, in order for market standards to exist, the "marketplace" needed to create the standards itself.

In July 1995, a questionnaire was distributed to 15 major international financial institutions asking if they believed a standard settlement period was needed for loan trades. All 15 institutions responded unanimously — *yes*! In December 1995, this same group of loan traders pooled their resources in order to form an Association in an effort to develop standard settlement and operational procedures, market practices, and other mechanisms to trade the increasing volume of par and distressed bank debt more efficiently. As a result, the Loan Syndications and Trading Association, Inc. (LSTA) was formed.

The need and formation of the LSTA was not dissimilar from that of the International Swap Dealers Association (ISDA), or the Emerging Markets Traders Association (EMTA). Prior to the formation of ISDA, swaps were cumbersome to trade and illiquid. Today, swaps are not only highly liquid, but are an actively traded instrument.

Similarly, EMTA was formed largely in response to the trading opportunities created by the Mexican and Venezuelan debt reschedulings under the Brady Plan. In an effort to develop mechanisms to trade the nearly U.S. $50 billion of new debt securities issued under these plans more efficiently, a group of debt traders from major international financial institutions formed the Association in 1990. Today, the total volumes for debt instruments of emerging markets instruments have risen from U.S. $734 billion in 1992 to over U.S. $5 trillion in 1997.

Prior to the formation of the LSTA, many trade disputes occurred in the marketplace. The buyer of a loan never knew when settlement would occur. Counterparties would often argue about who would receive a paydown on a loan between trade date and settlement date. Counterparties would often argue about who would pay the assignment fee to the agent. Counterparties often argued about breakfunding costs. In the past, counterparties could end up in a trade dispute over a variety of issues. Today, as a result of the efforts of the LSTA to develop standard terms and conditions for loan trading, a buyer and a seller are *not* likely to end up in a trade dispute with each other.

From an original membership of 15 institutions, the LSTA has grown today to a total of 70 members. Members include commercial banks, investment banks, mutual funds, CLO fund managers, buy-side institutions, sell-side institutions, law firms, accounting firms, brokers, and many others. Within these institutions one is likely to see the following type of people attending an LSTA meeting: loan traders, syndicators, commercial lending officers, portfolio managers, and work out officers.

Through the efforts and many long hours of donated time of its members, standards for trading loans have been created. The Association's main goal is to promote the orderly development of a "fair, efficient, liquid, and professional trading market for commercial loans and other similar private debt." It is a not-for-profit association.

As of the print of this book, the LSTA consisted of 28 founding members, 18 full members and 24 affiliate members. Founding members are leading commercial banks and dealers, and institutions that have been and will continue to be instrumental in developing the Association, its agenda, and initiatives. Full members are institutions that directly or through affiliates, trade bank debt or invest in bank loans for their own account, such as dealers, commercial and investment banks, funds, and insurance companies. The affiliate member organizations have general interest in the market and include law firms, brokers, consultants, and advisors.

The LSTA undertakes a variety of activities including:

- producing standard trading documentation (including standard confirmations and option agreements)
- establishing recognized market practices
- publishing a code of conduct for the trading of bank debt and commercial credits
- publishing month-end prices
- operating a multilateral netting facility for loan assets
- organizing an arbitration panel and arbitration procedures to resolve price disputes
- establishing a forum for market participants to discuss important developments and relevant information

Since its inception, the LSTA has developed and distributed numerous standardized documents and proposed uniform market practices in the secondary loan market. In order to accomplish its goals, the LSTA formed the following committees: Settlement, Mark-to-Market, Distressed Debt, Syndications, Options, and the Lawyers Committee. The Association's committees have been successful in identifying and analyzing several significant issues impacting the loan trading market that will be the subject of standardized forms and recommended practices.

It is important to remember that all procedures and forms are recommendations of the LSTA. The LSTA is not a regulatory authority. It has no authority to compel the use of any of its forms by any market participant. *The buyer and seller of a loan always have the opportunity to make modifications to the recommended forms and closing procedures.* It is also important to remember that the terms discussed throughout this chapter have generally been accepted by the marketplace. Should a buyer or seller wish to trade on terms different from those identified in this chapter, the buyer or seller should specify the changes from standard market practices *prior* to consummating a trade. This will insure that the buyer and seller understand and agree on the terms of the trade and will help prevent any trade dispute in the future.

It is also important to remember that procedures and recommendations discussed throughout this chapter were the recommendations of the LSTA at the time of print of this book. All forms and procedures recommended by the LSTA can and do change from time to time. Anyone following the procedures described throughout this chapter should verify their current status with the LSTA.

The LSTA has refrained from officially defining the difference between "par/near par loans" and "distressed loans." What may seem to be a distressed loan to one counterparty may be considered a par/near par loan to another counterparty. The trade confirmation for par/near par loans is quite different from the distressed trade confirmation. These differences are outlined later in this chapter and *will* affect the price of a loan. The LSTA procedures leave it to the counterparties to specify whether a particular loan asset is being traded as a par/near par loan or as a distressed loan. Because many loans fall into a "gray area" it is essential that the parties specify prior to orally concluding a trade the basis on which the loan is being traded. Counterparties that clarify their understanding of a loan upfront will avoid any trade disputes or possible failed trades in the future.

PAR/NEAR PAR LOANS

The Establishment of Standard Settlement Procedures (*T*+10) for *Par/Near Par Loans*

The most significant accomplishment of LSTA since its inception has been the establishment of standard settlement procedures, otherwise known as *T+10 for Par Loans* (settlement date = trade date + 10 business days). This convention was formally introduced by LSTA in December 1995 and was quickly adopted by the loan trading marketplace. Appendix I is the standard *LSTA Par/Near Par Trade Confirmation* as most recently modified in October 1997. Prior to using the document, the reader should verify with the LSTA its current status.

As the reader will see, the Confirmation incorporates Standard Terms and Conditions, which are quite extensive. Listed below is a brief summary of the significant terms of the standard confirmation for par/near par loans. For simplicity sake, the list is divided into issues that are *more* likely to affect the price of a loan and issues that are *less* likely to affect the price of a loan. Following this brief description is a more detailed report on the *Settlement Process; Interest Payments and Fee; Delayed Settlement Compensation/Funding Costs; Failed Trades Payments; Close-Out Procedures; and the Arbitration Procedures.*

Standard Terms that are More Likely to Affect the Economic Price of a Loan

1. Buyer and Seller agree to settle the trade within 10 business days (*T*+10).

2. Buyer and Seller agree that if the trade has not settled in 10 business day, the Seller will pay the Buyer delay compensation, as described later, beginning on *T* + 11.

3. Buyer and Seller agree that no breakfunding compensation shall be paid.

4. Buyer and Seller agree to close the trade as an Assignment rather than a Participation.

5. If Buyer and Seller agree that the loan will "Settle Without Accrued Interest," such accrued amounts are not paid by Buyer to Seller on the settlement date; rather, Buyer pays such amounts to Seller only when Buyer is actually paid; provided, that if the loan goes into default such accrued amounts (whenever paid) will belong to the Buyer.

6. Buyer and Seller agree to split the Assignment Fee (sometimes known as the Novation Fee or the Transfer Fee).

7. Permanent Commitment reductions and permanent repayments of principal occurring between trade date and settlement date shall be for the account of the Buyer.

8. Amendment or other fees (other than commitment fees or facility fees) paid between trade date and settlement date shall be for the account of the Buyer.

9. All interest and commitment, facility and letter of credit, and other similar fees are based on contractual rates, as set forth in the credit agreement.

10. Buyer and Seller agree to Buy-in/Sell-out procedures, as detailed later in this chapter, should settlement not occur on the Settlement Date specified in the Confirmation. *These procedures differ depending on which counterparty fails to perform.*

11. Buyer and Seller agree that Settlement Date for "When Issued" Trades shall be no later than 10 business days after the signing of the credit agreement.

Standard Terms that are Less Likely to Affect the Economic Price of a Loan

1. The Seller will prepare the confirmation and any related transaction documents, and will obtain any necessary consents.
2. Buyer and Seller each bear its own costs and expenses.
3. The Seller agrees to provide the Buyer with the Credit Agreement and related documents if requested.
4. Buyer and Seller are presumed to be acting as principals (as opposed to agents).
5. The Buyer represents to the Seller that it is sophisticated, that it has the information it deems necessary to make an informed decision, and that it has made its own credit decision without reliance on the Seller.
6. Buyer and Seller agree to keep the terms of the trade confidential.
7. Buyer and Seller agree to be legally bound to the trade upon oral agreement.
8. A facsimile of a counterpart will suffice in the absence of an original counterpart.
9. Syndicate Confidential Information — Buyer and Seller make various representations to each other regarding disclosure of information made available by the borrower to the lending syndicate that are detailed later in this chapter under the title of *Syndicate and Borrow Confidential Information.*

Assignment versus Participation

In an *assignment*, the buyer becomes the direct lender of record and is entitled to all voting privileges of the other lenders of record. Assignments are recorded on the books of the agent, whose consent for such transfer is generally required. Additionally, the consent of the issuer/borrower is generally required.

In a *participation*, the form of transfer is generally transparent to the issuer/borrower. The buyer becomes a participant in a share of the assignee's loan. Most participants do not have full voting rights. Generally participants have the right to vote on terms concerning maturity, amortization, coupon and fees, release of collateral, or forgiveness of debt. Usually participations are made without recourse to the assignee and is considered to be a full sale for accounting and regulatory purposes.

Settlement Process

For loan purchase and sale transactions, the closing process begins after a Seller and Buyer have agreed, usually by telephone, on the terms of the purchase or sale. Within 24 hours of verbal agreement, the Seller provides a written confirmation by fax to the Buyer in the standard form developed and approved by the LSTA. This confirmation is reviewed, signed and returned by fax to the Seller by the Buyer *within 48 hours* of receipt by the Buyer.

Exhibit 2: T + 10 Settlement Process

T+1	Confirmation Letter is prepared and signed by Seller (within 24 hours of trade) and faxed to Buyer.
T+2	Buyer faxes signed confirmation to Seller.
T+3	Seller prepares and faxes Assignment Agreement to Buyer.
T+4	Buyer faxes signed Assignment Agreement to Seller.
T+5-6	Seller faxes Assignment Agreement (signed by both Buyer and Seller) to Agent(s) and Company (if consent is required). Seller calls Agent to set the closing date.
T+10	Seller prepares and faxes Funding Memo to Buyer; transaction settles (delivery and payment).

Following the receipt of the signed confirmation, the Seller prepares the documentation, usually in the form of an assignment agreement but, depending upon the terms of the transaction, alternatively in the form of a participation agreement. The draft documents are faxed to the Buyer. The Buyer reviews the draft documents, negotiates as necessary with the Seller and, when agreement on the documentation has been reached, signs the agreements. Any consents which are required to be obtained, whether from the borrower, the agent or a letter of credit issuing bank, *are the responsibility of the Seller.*

When the documentation has been signed, including evidence of all required consents, the Seller prepares and sends by fax to the Buyer a standard form of funding memorandum, which also serves as a final, written agreement on all aspects of the remittances between the two parties. The standard terms provide for the two parties to split equally any assignment, processing, or recordation fees.

The LSTA has received many requests for a timeline illustrating the T+10 settlement process. For that reason, Exhibit 2 is provided which shows a timeline of how someone in the loan closing area can achieve a T+10 settlement.

Interest Payments and Fees

Settled Without Accrued Interest

In late 1997, the "Interest Payments and Fees" section of the LSTA Par/Near Par Trade Confirmation was revised to address trades that settle without accrued interest and the allocation of that interest in the event a loan ceases to be current pay. The Standard Terms and Conditions previously required the Buyer (when a loan settles without payment of accrued interest) to pay to the Seller, *upon receipt*, any interest received from the Obligor and attributable to the period prior to the Settlement Date, rather than a lump sum payment on the Settlement Date. This perpetual obligation to pay interest *whenever received* creates several administrative problems once a loan becomes non-performing. As a result, the LSTA determined to revise the Par/Near Par Trade Confirmation to provide a time limit on the Buyer's obligation to turn over to Seller such interest.

The amended "Settled Without Accrued Interest" language of the Standard Terms and Conditions now provides for the payment to the Seller by the Buyer of any interest received from the Obligor and attributable to the period prior to the Settlement Date *provided that*: (i) the Obligor made the interest payment on or before the due date; or (ii) the Obligor made the interest payment prior to the expiration of any applicable grace period *and* before a default by the Obligor in connection with any other payment obligations of the Obligor under the Credit Agreement. In the event no grace period is provided in the Credit Agreement, the payment by the Obligor to Buyer must have been made within 30 days of the due date. *However, if the interest is not paid by the Obligor to the Buyer on or before the due date or before the expiration of the grace period, or within 30 days of the due date if there is no grace period, the accrued amounts and any other accrued amounts due thereafter shall revert to the Buyer.*

Paid on Settlement Date

Also in 1997, several members noted that the provision governing treatment of interest "Paid on Settlement Date" as set forth in the Standard Terms and Conditions did not specify what happens if the interest payment advanced by the Buyer and paid to the Seller on Settlement Date is never paid by the borrower. Accordingly, the language has been revised and now specifies that:

> if the obligor(s) fail(s) to make payment thereof, unless otherwise specified in a Confirmation, Seller shall not be required to return such amount to the Buyer.

Delayed Settlement Compensation/Funding Costs

For purchases and sales that do not settle within the standard *T*+10 settlement period, the Seller agrees to pay the Buyer delayed settlement compensation. Members of the LSTA believed this was important because the Buyer assumes all credit and market risk for the transaction *from the trade date,* and because the Seller continues to receive interest as well as facility and commitment fees during the settlement period. Accordingly, if settlement occurs after *T*+10, the standard terms of trade require the Seller to pay to the Buyer the interest margin as well as all facility and commitment fees with respect to the purchase or sale amount from *T*+10 to the Settlement Date. The detailed calculation of this "delay compensation" is as follows:

- For funded loans:
  - ⇒ the applicable margin specified in the Credit Agreement multiplied by the amount outstanding for each day beyond *T*+10
- For unfunded commitments:
  - ⇒ the unfunded commitment amount for each day beyond *T*+10
- For the Facility Fee:
  - ⇒ if any specified in the Credit Agreement, calculated for each day, in each case calculated on the basis set forth in the Credit Agreement

Failed Trades/Close-Out Procedures

The Standard Terms and Conditions include procedures for "closing-out" failed trades. Members of the LSTA felt that establishing such procedures were necessary in order to avoid a loop hole in the standard confirmation which could otherwise inadvertently encourage "shorting" of loans. Different procedures apply depending on which party fails to perform.

No Fault

If a purchase or sale transaction cannot be closed because any of the required consents (such as Borrower/Issuer or Agent Bank) were withheld for any reason, and if the Seller and the Buyer cannot agree on an alternative means of settling the trade (for example, a participation instead of an assignment), the purchase or sale will be closed-out on a "no-fault" basis. The Seller will pay to the Buyer any delayed settlement compensation and the Buyer will pay to the Seller any funding costs incurred by the Seller on a non-performing loan, both as described above. The Seller will pay to the Buyer the price movement if the price has risen, or the Buyer will pay to the Seller the price movement if the price has fallen.

Buyer or Seller Fault

If a purchase or sale transaction cannot be closed because either the Seller or the Buyer fails to perform its obligations, the non-defaulting party can send to the defaulting party a notice informing the defaulting party of its intent to sell-out/buy-in the loan asset. After prescribed periods for the Seller and the Buyer to attempt to resolve their differences and to close the original trade, the loan in question may be sold-out/bought-in. If the loan is sold-out, the Buyer will pay to the Seller the amount (if any) by which the sell-out price is less than the original trade price plus, if the loan is not paying interest, the Seller's funding costs. If the loan is bought-in, the Seller will pay to the Buyer the amount (if any) by which the buy-in price is greater than the original trade price plus delayed settlement compensation.

In either a no-fault or a fault situation, the Standard Terms and Conditions have incorporated the concept of arbitration of price disputes if a party disputes the reasonableness of the price at which the purchase or sale will be closed-out. These arbitration procedures are described below in greater details.

The above description is intended only as a summary of the settlement procedures adopted by LSTA for par and near-par loan that fail to close. Set forth in Exhibits 3, 4, and 5 are details of the time table for failed trade procedures.

Arbitration

In either a no-fault or a fault situation, the Standard Terms and Conditions have incorporated the concept of arbitration of price disputes if a party disputes the reasonableness of the price at which the purchase or sale will be closed-out. Exhibit 6 summarizes the arbitration procedures adopted by the LSTA. The procedures promote efficiency and fairness by providing a confidential and expedited process whereby members submit disputes as to price to binding arbitration by a panel selected for its expertise in the loan trading industry. The panel has authority to decide *only* price disputes with respect to the purchase or sale of the loan asset on the date of execution of the cover transaction.

Exhibit 3: Buy-In Procedure

T+10	T+11 to T+15	T+21 to T+25	Arbitration	Compensation
Default:	Buy-In Notice:	Buy-In Date:		To Buyer:
Seller fails to deliver documentation. -or- Seller fails to deliver Loan Assets.	Buyer may send Buy-In Notice to Seller, and receipt of same shall be promptly acknowledged. Seller may cure default at any time prior to Buy-In Date (but must pay Delay Compensation to Buyer). During five business days following delivery of Notice, Seller shall use best efforts to identify a substitute party to perform its obligations.	Buyer may execute Buy-In Trade ten business days after sending Buy-In Notice to Seller. Buyer shall notify Seller of Buy-In Price no later than one business day following execution of Buy-In Confirmation.	Seller may dispute the reasonableness of the Buy-In Price by notice to Buyer no later than two business days following the receipt by Seller of notice of such Buy-In Price from Buyer.	On the Buyer Effective Date (T+31 to T+35), Seller shall pay the sum of: (i) Delay Compensation from and including T+11 to Buyer Effective Date; and (ii) the amount by which the Buy-In Price exceeds the Purchase Price.

Exhibit 4: Sell-Out Procedure

T+10	T+11 to T+15	T+21 to T+25	Arbitration	Compensation
Default:	Sell-Out Notice:	Sell-Out Date:		To Seller:
Buyer fails to execute documentation delivered by Seller. -or- Buyer fails to deliver Purchase Price.	Seller may send Sell-Out Notice to Buyer, and receipt of same shall be promptly acknowledged. Buyer may cure default at any time prior to Sell-Out Date (but must pay Seller's Cost of Carry if debt not fully performing). During five business days following delivery of Notice, Buyer shall use best efforts to identify a substitute party to perform its obligations. Seller has no obligation to pay Delay Compensation to Buyer.	Seller may execute Sell-Out Trade ten business days after sending Sell-Out Notice to Buyer. Seller shall notify Buyer of Sell-Out Price no later than one business day following execution of Sell-Out Confirmation.	Buyer may dispute the reasonableness of the Sell-Out Price by notice to Seller no later than two business days following Buyer's receipt of notice of such Sell-Out Price from Seller.	On the Seller Effective Date (T+31 to T+35), Buyer shall pay the sum of: (i) Cost of Carry for non-performing asset from and including T+11 to Seller Effective Date; and (ii) the amount by which the Sell-Out Price is less than the Purchase Price.

Exhibit 5: Failed Trade Procedure: "No Fault"

7+10	7+11 to 7+15	7+16	Compensation	Arbitration
Settlement Date fails to occur because necessary consents are not obtained.	Buyer and Seller will in good faith consider alternatives for resolving the trade.	Absent other agreement to terminate trade, Seller will use best efforts to sell the specified Debt. Notice of Sell-Out Price sent by Seller to Buyer one business day following execution of close-out confirmation.	*To Buyer:* If Sell-Out price is greater than purchase price, Seller will pay (i) such excess, *plus* (ii) Delay Compensation, if debt fully performing, *less* (iii) Cost of Carry, if debt not fully performing. *To Seller:* If Sell-Out price is less than purchase price, Buyer will pay (i) such loss, plus (ii) Cost of Carry, if debt is not fully performing, less (iii) Delay Compensation, if debt is fully performing.	Buyer may dispute reasonableness of Sell-Out price by sending the notice no later than two business days following receipt of notice of such Sell-out price from Seller.

Exhibit 6: Arbitration Procedures Timetable

Time	Time +2	Time +5	Time +10	Time +12	Time +14	Arbitration	Conclusion of Arbitration	Determination
Notice of Buy-In or Sell-Out price served (one day after Buy-In or Sell-Out date)'	Notice to Seller that Buyer disputes reasonableness of proposed Sell-Out price Notice to Buyer that Seller disputes reasonableness of proposed Buy-In price	Notice of Arbitration served Failure to serve timely Notice of Arbitration results in Determination that Buy-In or Sell-Out price was reasonable	Answer served Panel appointed by Administrator parties and Panel members notified of Panel members' identities, and Panel members receive copy of Notice of Arbitration	Any Panel member may recuse himself for conflict of interest Each party may strike one Panel member for any reason	Vacancies on Panel filled by Administrator New Panel members may recuse themselves, in which case vacancies will be filled within 2 days	Arbitration conducted at the discretion of the Panel	Arbitration concludes at close of hearing, if any, or at time of service of last written submission, whichever is later	Parties notified of Panel's Determination of price within 10 days of conclusion of Arbitration

Syndicate and Borrower Confidential Information

In 1997, the LSTA added provisions governing the use of Syndicate Confidential Information to the Standard Terms and Conditions for the Par/Near Par and Distressed forms of Confirmation. The Syndicate Confidential Information provision establishes the following procedures:

1. *Syndicate Confidential Information* is defined as material information provided by or on behalf of a borrower (or its affiliates) which is non-public except that it is deliberately made available by or on behalf of such borrower to all of the members and potential members of a particular lending syndicate. This is nonpublic information which the borrower intends to disclose only to syndicate members and potential syndicate members. This information is thus not confidential as among syndicate members and can be disclosed to prospective syndicate members upon compliance with any applicable confidentiality requirements. Syndicate confidential information includes (a) information provided in writing by or on behalf of the borrower in connection with origination of a loan and other information provided periodically in writing to the entire syndicate according to the terms of the applicable credit agreement and (b) information disseminated to the entire syndicate regarding developments or other special circumstances, whether provided in writing or orally, in each case, so long as it is material.

2. Representation by Buyer to Seller that:
   (i) Buyer is sophisticated and understands the nature and importance of Syndicate Confidential Information;
   (ii) Buyer understands the manner in which such information can be obtained; and
   (iii) If it desired such information, Buyer has requested such information from Seller or has otherwise obtained such information;

3. Representation by Seller that if Buyer has requested Syndicate Confidential Information, and Seller has agreed to provide such information, then Seller:
   (i) has used reasonable efforts to maintain Syndicate Confidential Information; and
   (ii) Seller has disclosed to Buyer all material Syndicate Confidential Information retained by it as of Trade Date; and

4. Buyer acknowledges to Seller that:
   (i) such Syndicate Confidential Information has been disclosed;
   (ii) the disclosed Syndicate Confidential Information may not be complete because Seller may not have retained all such information; and
   (iii) Buyer has taken all necessary steps to assure that it has the information it needs to make an informed decision regarding each transaction described in a Confirmation.

DISTRESSED DEBT

The Distressed Debt Committee, with representatives from both the buy and sell side, set as its initial goal the standardization of documents, including confirmations, assignment and participation agreements, and pricing letters. The Committee also decided to address trading conventions for non-performing loan assets.

The form of Distressed Trade Confirmation (shown in Appendix II) standardizes the allocation of pre- and post-settlement date interest, fees, and expenses between Buyer and Seller and permits the parties to agree in advance to default to a participation in the event the assignment of a loan asset cannot be effected. The Committee has also addressed the need to specify at the time of a trade the principal or agency status of the parties.

The standard LSTA Distressed Trade Confirmation, as stated earlier, is quite different from the LSTA Par/Near Par Confirmation. Listed below are the major differences between the standard Par/Near Par Trade Confirmation and the standard Distressed Trade Confirmation. These issues *must* be discussed *prior* to a trade of a distressed loan.

- Buyer and Seller must state whether they are acting as Principal or Agent
- Form of Purchase: Buyer and Seller must agree whether the trade will close on an Assignment basis, Participation basis, or a Subparticipation basis
- There is no standard settlement period for distressed loans. There, the Buyer and Seller must agree on one of the following Settlement Dates:
    1. As soon as practicable
    2. No later than _____, unless otherwise extended by mutual consent of Buyer and Seller, which consent shall not be unreasonably withheld
    3. No later than _____
- The payment of interest must be agreed upon prior to the confirmation of a trade. The choices are as follows:
    a. Paid on Settlement Date
    b. Settled Without Accrued Interest. As of 12/1/97, the LSTA's Distressed Trade Confirmation provides a limit on the Buyer's obligation to turn over to Seller interest. Under the new terms, for trades that settle without accrued interest, the Buyer is only required to turn over to Seller interest payments received from the Borrower and attributable to the period prior to the Settlement Date if:
        1. the Borrower makes the interest payment on or before the due date; or
        2. the Borrower makes the interest payment prior to the expiration of any applicable grace period and before a default by the Borrower in connection with any other payment obligation under the Credit Agreement; or

3. If no grace period is provided in the Credit Agreement, the payment by the Borrower to Buyer must have been made within 30 days of the due date.

c. Trades Flat (interest, commitment, facility and all other fees to Buyer)

• In the event that Buyer and Seller are unable to close the transaction as an Assignment, the Buyer and Seller may agree to use best efforts (subject to the term of the Credit Agreement) to settle the transaction as a Participation.

• The parties may agree that the trade shall be subject to the successful completion of either or both the prior purchase or sale of the loan asset to be sold to the Buyer or purchased from the Seller.

Assignment Agreement

The Distressed Debt Committee has been working on a standard form of "Assignment Agreement for Distressed Trades Commercial Credits," which it hopes to finalize and distribute to the distressed trading marketplace in 1998. The document format is a master agreement, with all variable terms to be reflected on annexed schedules. The Committee is optimistic that a model form of Assignment Agreement for distressed credits that has been endorsed by a broad segment of LSTA's membership will gain widespread market acceptance. It is hoped that a standard form of Assignment Agreement for distressed credits will reduce delay and expense in closing trades and thereby promote the LSTA's goals of efficiency and liquidity in the secondary trading market.

Trade Claims

Because the volume of new distressed bank loans has not kept pace with demand due to favorable economic conditions over the past few years, there is a rapidly growing interest in trade claims. Indeed, more and more secondary loan market participants have begun to buy and sell trade claims. The market for trade claims, however, is relatively new and there are few standards or conventions. Accordingly, the Distressed Debt Committee established a working group of institutions involved in trading of trade claims to attempt to develop standard forms and procedures for that market. The result of that work is a nearly completed form of *Distressed Confirmation for Trade Claims* and *Trade Claim Assignment Agreement*.

Unlike the Confirmations adopted by the LSTA for bank loans, the Trade Claim Confirmation is a much shorter document without standard terms and conditions. The detailed terms of trade are set forth in the Assignment, which is referenced in the Confirmation. Parties using the LSTA form of Confirmation will agree to close the trade using the Association's form of Assignment Agreement. It is expected that these documents, by bringing market standards and efficiencies to the trade claim market, will result in greater participation by institutions in the buying and selling of trade claims.

Binding Oral Trade Agreement Proposal

As a matter of custom and practice, unless otherwise agreed, parties to a trade generally intend to be legally bound by the terms of each transaction from the moment they reach agreement on such terms, whether orally or otherwise. The terms of trade generally are agreed upon over the telephone and are promptly memorialized by a written trade confirmation. It is industry practice — and the participants' expectation — that parities are bound to a trade as soon as they reach agreement, usually by telephone. However, absent "some writing," Section 1-206 of the New York Uniform Commercial Code ("Statute of Frauds") may prevent enforcement of oral trades of debt beyond $5,000.

Consequently, the Distressed Debt Committee determined in late 1996 to explore the measures which LSTA could take to ensure that trades of bank loans, trade claims or other commercial credits effected over the telephone are enforceable when the parties reach oral agreement on the terms of trade, rather than at the time written trade confirmations are exchanged. The *Agreement Regarding Binding Oral Trades* (the "Agreement") is intended to give legal effect to the industry custom and practice that the parties are bound to a trade from the time they reach agreement on the terms of the trade, whether by telephone or otherwise. Although developed by the Distressed Debt Committee, the Agreement will cover all secondary trading activity (including par and near par loans).

The Agreement contains (1) an undertaking not to assert as a defense to liability on an oral agreement to purchase or sell a commercial credit the lack of a writing that would otherwise be required to satisfy the Statute of Frauds; (2) an agreement to execute contemporaneously with each trade a writing (which may be in the form of a trade ticket to be provided by the LSTA) setting forth the basic terms of the trade, which will be adequate to satisfy the elements of the Statute of Frauds; and (3) an acknowledgment that the signatory intends only third parties with which it trades and who have signed a similar agreement to rely on its undertakings in the Agreement.

Procedurally, a party willing to be orally bound to a trade with a similarly bound counterparty would execute the LSTA Agreement, and the LSTA Administrator will publish monthly a list of all signatories. Any trading party — whether or not a member of the LSTA — could execute the proposed Agreement, and any party could withdraw from the Agreement by giving written notice directly to its trading counterparty or to the LSTA (as to all counterparites). However, this latter notice shall not be effective until 30 days following publication of such notice by LSTA.

The document is expected to be "rolled out" to the marketplace during the second quarter of 1998. As noted, it will be used in both the Par and Distressed Markets.

In addition to these activities, the Distressed Debt Committee also promulgated and adopted a standard form of *Bid Letter* for use in auctions and a standard form of *Trade Ticket* to record the necessary terms of trade.

OPTIONS ON LOANS

In November 1997, LSTA adopted a Standard Confirmation for options on loans. This Confirmation appears as Appendix III to this chapter. Listed below are the market practices that have been adopted in the Standard Confirmation for options:

1. options are *not* presumed to be cash settled
2. an option may be exercised in part or in full in denominations equal to minimum assignable amounts under the Credit Agreement
3. in the event of a complete paydown, the option is automatically exercised with the parties cash settling for the difference between the strike price and par (if economically beneficial to the Buyer);
4. in the event of a partial paydown, holder has until expiry to exercise the option (if exercised, the parties cash settle for the amount repaid based on the difference between the strike price and par and the remaining portion is settled in accordance with standard settlement provisions)
5. the holder of record maintains all voting rights
6. the option is transferable by the holder only with the writer's consent, which shall not be unreasonably withheld
7. the option may be exercised in parts or in full, provided it is exercised in the minimum assignable amounts provided for in the Credit Agreement; accordingly, the option writer is only obligated to pay one-half of one assignment fee
8. once an option is exercised it becomes subject to rules and procedures governing par trades as set forth in the Standard Term and Conditions for Par/Near Par Trade Confirmations

LSTA COMMITTEES

As I have stated earlier, most of the real work of the LSTA is achieved at the committee level. Members are able to identify the issues that are most important to them and can attend the Committees of their choice. As a result, the Committees are comprised of members of the business community that are most involved with the relevant issues. For example, the Distressed Debt Committee is made up of distressed loan traders, distressed buy-side institutions, individuals involved in the workout departments of several banks, and law firms involved in distressed loan activities. Consequently, the work that comes out of the various committees fairly reflects the many different interests represented in the market. Below is a brief description of the standing committees of the LSTA.

Settlement Committee

The Settlement Committee was formed to develop standardized documentation for trading par and near par loans and to address the issue of trades which do not settle on a timely basis. It was the Settlement Committee that developed and refined the Form of Confirmation for Par/Near Par Loans, which incorporates Standard Terms and Conditions for such trades. It was also the Settlement Committee that developed Close Out Procedures For Failed Trades and a Funding Memorandum (including Delay Compensation Calculation). The Committee has also adopted a standard Multilateral Letter Agreement and a Bilateral Netting Agreement. In addition to the above, the Committee also reached consensus on standardizing the allocation of assignment fees in multiparty trades when it voted to *have all parties involved in the trade split (per capita) the assignment fees.*

Distressed Debt Committee

The Distressed Debt Committee was formed in October 1996. Its goal was to deal with issues relating to trading of distressed loan assets — bank debt, private notes, and trade claims. This is one of the Association's most active committees. As noted above, it has developed a number of significant documents for use in the distressed loan market: Distressed Trade Confirmation together with Standard Terms and Conditions; Binding Oral Trade Agreement; Lost Note Affidavit and Indemnity; Confirmations and Assignment Agreement for Trade Claims; Bid Letter; and Trade Ticket. The Committee is also hard at work on developing a standard form of Assignment Agreement for Distressed Commercial Credits. Finally, the Committee regularly reports to its constituents on legal and regulatory developments that affect trading of distressed loan assets and credits.

Mark-To-Market Committee

The Mark-to-Market Committee was formed to facilitate the collection of loan valuation information and the preparation of aggregate average statistics for monthly dissemination to assist in the accurate valuation of loan assets for financial reporting purposes. The Mark-to-Market Committee has launched a project designed to facilitate this valuation, and LSTA has retained Loan Pricing Corporation to collect bid and offer price information from individual LSTA member-firms on a confidential basis, and to prepare aggregate average statistics for monthly dissemination to eligible LSTA members. The procedures that are followed are set forth in the "Revised Statement of Procedures for Collection and Dissemination of Loan Valuation Information," published by the LSTA.

Lawyers Group

The Lawyers Group was formed in mid-1996 in order to assist the other committees to identify, analyze and make recommendations with respect to the significant legal issues affecting existing and proposed market practices. The Committee's first project focused on the disclosure of confidential information in connection with the trading of loan assets. To date, the Committee has drafted proposed classifications and definitions of syndicate and borrower confidential information, as well as general policies regarding disclosure of such information in connection with trading activities. These definitions will be incorporated into the Association's Code of Conduct during 1998.

The Committee has also devoted considerable effort to refining the Binding Oral Trade Agreement. It has also provided invaluable assistance to the Distressed Debt, Syndications and Settlement Committees in their efforts to establish efficient market practices within the boundaries of the law.

Syndications Committee

The Syndications Committee has two primary goals: to standardize documentation and information flow surrounding the syndication process and to standardize primary syndication practices. The standardization of documents is proving to be an easier goal than the standardization of syndication practices. The Committee is close to recommending a standard Assignment Agreement and a standard Disclaimer and a Confidentiality/Nondisclosure Agreement. Listed below are the Committee's goals:

- *standardize documentation and information flow surrounding the syndication process*

    1. standard form of Assignment Agreement
    2. a Disclaimer and a Confidentiality/Nondisclosure Agreement
    3. transfer fees
    4. minimum assignments levels for partial assignments
    5. processing assignments during an amendment period
    6. standardization of certain portions of the Credit Agreement

- *standardize primary syndication practices*

    1. commitment deadlines
    2. closing syndications early
    3. lag of allocations following commitments
    4. disclosure of who has committed at various points in the syndication process
    5. a standard time-line with appropriate annotations addressing several circumstances which might affect the time period for commitment responses

In addition to the above, the Robert Morris Associates (RMA) has requested LSTA's assistance in updating certain of its published syndications guidelines. In 1977, RMA published a booklet on various topics relating to syndications. The booklet was last revised in 1983. As a result, the LSTA and the RMA are currently revising the booklet and intend to publish an updated version in the near future.

Establishment of Two New Committees

LSTA continues to honor its commitment to grow and to adjust to meet the needs of both the market and its members. Accordingly, the *Canadian Loan Syndications and Trading Committee* and the *Emerging Markets Committee* were established early in 1998. Each of these committees will address the particular needs and issues of members involved in trading Emerging Markets and Canadian loans and will, where appropriate, recommend trading standard and procedures that may differ from those established for loans originated in the United States. In addition, the Emerging Markets Committee has made its number one goal to attempt to deal with the "registration problem" within the different countries. In Mexico, for example, an investor must be registered with the Mexican government and be domiciled within a country that has a favorable tax treaty with the United States in order to receive a favorable tax basis on the loan. Currently, the Mexican government makes the registration process for a new investor in loans originated in the country very difficult to impossible. The LSTA has set up a task that will endeavor to recommend changes to the laws in Mexico and a number of other countries.

LSTA Forges Dialogue with
UK-Based Loan Market Association

In response to substantial growth in the European secondary loan market, several major financial institutions operating in Europe formed the Loan Market Association (the LMA) in mid-1996. Headquartered in London, the LMA was established "to create greater liquidity in the loan market ... through the development of a more active and efficient secondary market." The LMA believes that increased standardization in both documentation and procedures will encourage timely settlement, reduce costs, and enable participants to fully exploit the secondary loan market. The LMA's initial agenda addresses information, valuation, settlement and operational procedures and documentation *for par assets only*. However, the LMA fully expects to expand its focus in the future to include distressed loan assets.

Acknowledging the similar goals for their respective markets and the trend towards globalization of the United States, European, and Asian loan markets, the LMA and LSTA have agreed to keep each other informed of their progress towards a more efficient market.

What is important to recognize is that the LMA has devised standards that are different than the LSTA. For example, the standard LMA Confirmation for Par/Near Par Loans does *not* include delay compensation, close-out or arbitration procedures. The LMA Confirmation for Par/Near Par Loans *does*, however, allow the counterparties to compensate each other for breakfunding costs or benefits. Therefore, it is essential for a party to a trade to communicate with the counterparty as to which Confirmation one intends to use as it will affect the price of the loan.

CONCLUSION

As a result of the dramatic growth in trading volume in the secondary market, the LSTA was formed. Through the efforts of many in the market, a buyer and seller can now trade a loan in the secondary market and know they are "done" based on market standards. As a direct result of the work of the LSTA and its members, very few trade disputes arise in the marketplace today. We can now say that the secondary loan trading market is fair, efficient, and liquid.

APPENDIX I

[Seller Letterhead]

LSTA PAR/NEAR PAR TRADE CONFIRMATION

To: *Buyer Name*
         Contact Person
         Fax No.:
         Phone No.:

From: *Seller Name*
         Contact Person
         Fax No.:
         Phone No.:

We are pleased to confirm the following transaction, subject to the Standard Terms and Conditions for Par/Near Par Trade Confirmations as most recently published as of **October 1997** by the Loan Syndications and Trading Association, Inc. ("LSTA"), which Standard Terms and Conditions are incorporated herein by reference. The parties hereto agree to submit any dispute as to the reasonableness of a buy-in or sell-out price to binding arbitration in accordance with the LSTA "Rules Governing Arbitration Between Loan Traders With Regard to Failed Trades" in existence on the Trade Date.

Trade Date: _____, 199_
Seller: _____
Buyer: _____
Credit Agreement: _____
Purchase Amount/
Type of Debt: $_____   of   _____;
                            $_____   of   _____;
                            $_____ of _____.

Form of Purchase: Assignment/Participation
Settlement Date: _____   No later than _____, 199_.
                            _____   No later than the date 10 business days after signing of the Credit Agreement.
                            _____   No later than the date 10 business days after Trade Date.

Pricing:
                            Purchase Rate: _____%

Upfront Fee
(if any): _____   Payable: _____
(if other than the Settlement Date) by Seller/Buyer

Accrued Interest: Settled Without Accrued Interest/Paid on Settlement Date

Credit Documentation
to be provided: Yes/No

Other Terms of Trade: _____

Please provide the signature of a duly authorized officer or other signatory where indicated below and return this letter to the attention of *Closer's Name* no later than 5:00 p.m. (New York City time), _____, 199_, at the following fax number(s): _____.

If you have any questions, please contact *Closer's Name at Closer's telephone number.*

SELLER	*BUYER*
By:_____	By: _____
Name:_____	Name: _____
Title:_____	Title: _____
Date: _____	Date: _____

Standard Terms and Conditions for Par/Near Par Trade Confirmations

Published as of October 1997 by the Loan Syndications and Trading Association, Inc.

Settlement Date: The date of delivery and payment for the Debt specified in a Confirmation shall be the Settlement Date. Unless otherwise agreed, the date to be specified in a Confirmation under "Settlement Date" shall be the date ten business days after the Trade Date. Any Upfront Fee shall be paid on the Settlement Date in the amount and by the party specified in a Confirmation.

Purchase Amount: Unless otherwise specified in a Confirmation, Purchase Amount shall be allocated pro rata among the facilities under the Credit Agreement, including revolving credit, letter of credit and term loan facilities.

Permanent Reductions and Fees: The economic benefit of permanent commitment reductions and permanent repayments of principal (collectively, "Permanent Reductions") shall be allocated in accordance with the Purchase Price Calculation. Unless otherwise specified in a Confirmation, Buyer shall receive the benefit of payments of any amendment or other fees (other than commitment fees or facility fees, which shall be for the account of Seller) which are made in respect of the specified Debt from and after the Trade Date. Any and all unreimbursed fee or expense claims shall be for the account of Buyer.

Purchase Price Calculation: Buyer shall pay Seller a Purchase Price for the Purchase Amount of the specified Debt on the Settlement Date equal to the Purchase Rate multiplied by the funded principal amount of such Purchase Amount as of the Settlement Date <u>less</u> (100% minus the Purchase Rate) multiplied by any unfunded commitment obligation on the Settlement Date <u>less</u> (100% minus the Purchase Rate) multiplied by any Permanent Reductions after the Trade Date <u>plus</u> (unless otherwise specified in a Confirmation) one-half of the Recordation Fee or Transfer Fee.

Interest Payments and Fees: All interest and commitment, facility and letter of credit and other similar fees are based on contractual rates, as set forth in the Credit Agreement.

If "Settled Without Accrued Interest" is specified in a Confirmation, such accrued amounts to but excluding the Settlement Date shall be for the account of Seller and shall not be paid by Buyer to Seller on the Settlement Date, but shall be paid by Buyer to Seller promptly upon any payment thereof to Buyer by the obligor(s) under the Credit Agreement; <u>provided</u>, <u>however</u>, that unless such payment by the obligor(s) is made (a) on or before the due date thereof or the expiration of any applicable grace period, each as specified in the Credit Agreement as in effect on the Trade Date (or, if no such grace period exists, the expiration of thirty calendar days from such due date), and (b) before a default by the obligor(s) in connection with any other payment obligations of the obligor(s) under the Credit Agreement, such accrued amounts (if and when paid by the obligor(s)) and any other accrued amounts due thereafter shall be for the account of Buyer, and Seller shall not be entitled to any part thereof.

If "Paid on Settlement Date" is specified in a Confirmation, such accrued amounts to but excluding the Settlement Date shall be for the account of Seller and shall be paid by Buyer to Seller on the Settlement Date and, if thereafter paid to Seller, Seller shall promptly pay same to Buyer; provided, that if the obligor(s) fail(s) to make payment thereof, unless otherwise specified in a Confirmation, Seller shall not be required to return such amount to the Buyer.

Partial payments of interest shall be applied in the inverse order of payment dates unless otherwise specified in the Credit Agreement.

Breakfunding: No breakfunding compensation shall be paid for settlement of a transaction on a day other than an interest payment date in respect of the specified Debt unless otherwise specified in a Confirmation.

Recordation and Transfer Fees: Unless otherwise specified in a Confirmation, any recordation, processing or similar fee payable to the Agent under the Credit Agreement in connection with an assignment and any transfer fee payable to the seller of a participation in connection with the transfer of such participation shall be split equally between Buyer and Seller. As provided in the Purchase Price Calculation, Buyer shall pay its half (or, if otherwise specified in a Confirmation, its specified portion, if any) to Seller. Seller shall be responsible for paying the full amount of such fee directly to the Agent or such seller of such participation, as the case may be.

Costs and Expenses: Each of Buyer and Seller shall bear its respective costs and expenses in connection with the transaction described in a Confirmation. Seller shall be responsible for all costs, fees and expenses in respect of the Debt that are chargeable under the terms of the Credit Agreement to any period prior to but excluding the Settlement Date. Buyer shall be responsible for all costs, fees and expenses in respect of the Debt that are chargeable under the terms of the Credit Agreement to any period from and including the Settlement Date.

Transaction Documentation: Each transaction described in a Confirmation is subject to obtaining any necessary consents. In the case of an assignment, the parties shall execute an assignment agreement in the form stipulated in the Credit Agreement or, in the absence of same, a reasonably acceptable assignment agreement containing customary provisions. In the case of a participation, the parties shall execute a reasonably acceptable participation agreement containing customary provisions. Unless otherwise agreed, the Transaction Documentation shall be prepared by, and any required consents obtained by, Seller. Unless otherwise specified Seller shall send Buyer a Confirmation not later than one business day after the Trade Date, and Buyer shall respond prior to the date and time specified in the Confirmation. Unless otherwise specified, Seller shall endeavor to furnish Buyer an assignment or participation agreement, as appropriate, within four business days after the Trade Date, and (in the case of an assignment) the parties shall endeavor to execute and deliver to the Agent an assignment agreement within six business days after the Trade Date.

Credit Documentation; Confidentiality Agreement: If "Yes" is specified in a Confirmation, Seller shall furnish Buyer a true and complete copy of the Credit Agreement (including all schedules, and, if requested by Buyer, exhibits), together with all amendments thereto, as promptly as practicable following the Trade Date. If required by the Credit Agreement, Buyer shall execute and deliver to Seller a Confidentiality Agreement in the form stipulated in the Credit Agreement or, in the absence of same, a reasonably acceptable Confidentiality Agreement containing customary terms.

Syndicate Confidential Information: Unless otherwise specified, Buyer represents to Seller that Buyer is sophisticated, understands the nature and importance of syndicate confidential information (as defined in the LSTA Code of Conduct) and the manner in which such information can be obtained and has requested such information from Seller in connection with each transaction described in a Confirmation if it desired such information in such connection and that where it has not requested syndicate confidential information it has otherwise obtained such information as it has deemed appropriate under the circumstances to make an informed decision regarding each transaction specified in a Confirmation without reliance on Seller. If Buyer has requested Seller to provide syndicate confidential information, and Seller has agreed to provide such information to Buyer, unless otherwise specified, Seller represents to Buyer that it has used reasonable efforts to maintain syndicate confidential information and that it has disclosed to Buyer all material syndicate confidential information maintained by it as of the Trade Date, and, unless otherwise specified, Buyer acknowledges to Seller that such syndicate confidential information has been disclosed to it, that the syndicate confidential information so disclosed may not be complete because Seller may not have maintained all such information and that Buyer has taken all steps it deems necessary under the circumstances to assure that it has the information it deems appropriate to make an informed decision regarding each transaction described in a Confirmation.

Principal/Agency Status: Unless otherwise specified in a Confirmation, each of Buyer and Seller are presumed to be acting as principals in the transaction.

Nonreliance: Each party acknowledges to the other party that it is a sophisticated Buyer or Seller (as the case may be) with respect to the transaction described in a Confirmation, and has such information as it deems appropriate under the circumstances (however obtained), concerning for example the business and financial condition of the obligor(s) under the Credit Agreement, to make an informed decision regarding the purchase and sale of the Specified Debt. Each of Buyer and Seller hereby agrees that it has independently made its own analysis and decision to enter into the transaction described in such Confirmation, based on such information as it has deemed appropriate under the circumstances, which may include syndicate confidential information (however obtained) and without reliance on the other party (except for reliance on any express representation made by the other party in the Confirmation).

Delay Compensation/Cost of Carry: As used herein, "Delay Compensation" with respect to the Purchase Amount for specified Debt shall mean, for any day, a rate per annum equal to (i) for funded loans, the applicable margin specified in the Credit Agreement multiplied by the amount outstanding for each such day, and (ii) for unfunded commitments, the commitment fee (if any) specified in the Credit Agreement multiplied by the unfunded commitment amount for each such day, and (iii) the facility fee, if any, specified in the Credit Agreement, calculated for each such day, in each case calculated on the basis set forth in the Credit Agreement. As used herein, "Cost of Carry" with respect to the Purchase Amount for specified Debt shall mean, for any day, the interest that would accrue for each such day calculated at a rate per annum determined by Seller to be the applicable 3-month London Interbank Offered Rate for Dollar deposits as derived from the Reuter Monitor Money Rates Service (or, if such service is not available for any reason, from such other source as Seller shall reasonably determine).

Buy-in/Sell-out: If settlement does not occur on the Settlement Date specified in a Confirmation because of the failure of either Seller or Buyer to perform its obligations (excluding, however, failure to obtain necessary consents), the nondefaulting party may send to the defaulting party within five business days following such Settlement Date a written notice advising of the nondefaulting party's intent to terminate its obligations under the Confirmation and to effect a cover transaction for the specified Debt. Such cover transaction is a "buy in" if the Buyer purchases the specified Debt from a counterparty other than the original Seller, and is a "sell out" if the Seller sells the specified Debt to a counterparty other than the original Buyer. Such notice shall be substantially in the form most recently published by the LSTA, and the party receiving such notice shall promptly acknowledge receipt of same. The Trade Date for the buy-in/sell-out shall be the tenth business day following delivery of such notice (the "Close-Out Trade Date"). During the first five business days following delivery of such notice, the defaulting party shall use best efforts to identify a substitute party acceptable to the nondefaulting party to perform its obligations. If such an acceptable substitute party is identified, the buy-in/sell-out shall be made with such substitute party. If the defaulting party fails to identify such an acceptable substitute party, then both parties will in good faith consider other alternatives to settle or resolve the failed trade by mutual consent. The defaulting party may remedy its default at any time prior to the Close-Out Trade Date, with payment to be calculated in accordance with the Funding Memo as most recently published by the LSTA. Notice of the buy-in/sell-out price shall be sent within one business day following the date of execution of the Confirmation for the buy-in/sell-out (the "Close-Out Confirmation"). If the party receiving such notice disputes the reasonableness of the buy-in/sell-out price, it shall send notice of such dispute no later than the second business day thereafter. **Such price dispute shall be submitted to binding arbitration pursuant to, and shall be governed in all respects by, the "Rules Governing Arbitration Between Loan Traders With Regard to Failed Trades" ("Arbitration Rules") in existence on the Trade Date.** With respect to any arbitration conducted pursuant to the Arbitration Rules, the Seller and Buyer waive any right to a hearing and acknowledge that the arbitrators shall not be required to take an oath.

Buy-in Damages: Seller shall pay to Buyer on the Settlement Date of the buy-in (i) the amount (if any) by which the buy-in price exceeds the original Purchase Price for the specified Debt, plus (ii) if the specified Debt is fully performing, Delay Compensation with respect to the Purchase Amount for each day from (and including) the specified Settlement Date for the failed trade to (but excluding) the date that is earlier of (a) the actual settlement of buy-in or (b) ten business days following Close-Out Trade Date.

Sell-out Damages: Buyer shall pay to Seller on the Settlement Date of the sell-out (i) the amount (if any) by which the sell-out price is less than the original Purchase Price for the specified Debt, plus (ii) Seller's Cost of Carry if specified Debt is not fully performing for each day from (and including) the specified Settlement Date for the failed trade to (but excluding) the date that is earlier of (a) actual settlement of sell-out or (b) ten business days following Close-Out Trade Date.

Failure to Obtain Consents: If the Settlement Date fails to occur because necessary consents have not been obtained, the parties will in good faith consider alternatives for resolving the trade for five additional business days. Thereafter, unless the parties agree otherwise, Seller will use its best efforts to sell the specified Debt. If the sell-out price is greater than the original Purchase Price for the specified Debt, Seller will pay to Buyer on the Settlement Date specified in the Close-Out Confirmation (i) the amount by which the sell-out price exceeds the original Purchase Price plus (ii) if the specified Debt is fully performing, Delay Compensation for each day during the period (the "Fail Period") from (and including) the Settlement Date for the failed trade to (but excluding) the Settlement Date specified in the Close-Out Confirmation, less (iii) if the specified Debt is not fully performing, Seller's Cost of Carry for each day during the Fail Period. If the sell-out price is less than the original Purchase Price for the specified Debt, Buyer will pay to Seller on the Settlement Date specified in the Close-Out Confirmation (i) the amount by which the original Purchase Price exceeds the sell-out price plus (ii) if the specified Debt is not fully performing, Seller's Cost of Carry for each day during the Fail Period, less (iii) if the specified Debt is fully performing, Delay Compensation for each day during the Fail Period. Notice of the sell-out price shall be sent by Seller to Buyer within one business day following the date of execution of the Close-Out Confirmation. If Buyer disputes the reasonableness of the sell-out price, it shall send notice of such dispute no later than the second business day thereafter. **Such price dispute shall be submitted to binding arbitration pursuant to, and shall be governed in all respects by the Arbitration Rules in existence on the Trade Date.** With respect to any arbitration conducted pursuant to the Arbitration Rules, the Seller and Buyer waive any right to a hearing and acknowledge that the arbitrators shall not be required to take an oath.

When Issued Trades: For a transaction for which the Trade Date shall occur prior to signing of the Credit Agreement (a "when issued trade"), the relevant Confirmation shall specify under "Settlement Date" that the Settlement Date shall be not less than the date 10 business days after such signing. Except with respect to exchanging a Confirmation, all other times for when issued trades shall start on the later of the Trade Date or the signing of the Credit Agreement.

Confidentiality of Terms of Transaction: Both parties shall maintain the confidentiality of the terms of the transaction unless otherwise required by law or regulatory authority. Buyer shall be permitted to make any necessary disclosures to prospective purchasers from Buyer regarding the terms of the transaction described in a Confirmation (other than the Purchase Rate, Purchase Price or Upfront Fee), subject to same confidentiality constraints.

Binding Effect: The parties agree to be, and are, legally bound to the transaction on the Trade Date upon oral agreement to the terms thereof by Seller and Buyer (whether directly or through their respective agents). Seller and Buyer agree and acknowledge that events occurring subsequent to the Trade Date shall not relieve the parties of their obligations under the Confirmation.

Governing Law; Confirmation Controls: Each Confirmation and the Standard Terms and Conditions for Par/Near Par Trade Confirmations shall be governed by and construed in accordance with the law of the State of New York, without regard to the choice of law provisions thereof. In case of any variation between the terms of a Confirmation and the Standard Terms and Conditions for Par/Near Par Trade Confirmations, such Confirmation shall control.

Execution by Fax: Transmission by fax of an executed counterpart of a

Confirmation, Confidentiality Agreement or any other Transaction Document shall be deemed to constitute due and sufficient delivery of such counterpart. Buyer and Seller shall deliver to each other an original counterpart of the assignment or participation agreement (and, upon the request of either party, the Confirmation, Confidentiality Agreement or any other document) promptly after delivery of the fax, provided, however, that failure by either party to so deliver an original counterpart shall not affect the sufficiency of a fax of such counterpart (and the fact that such fax constitutes the due and sufficient delivery of such counterpart), as provided in the first sentence hereof.

APPENDIX II

[Seller Letterhead]

LSTA DISTRESSED TRADE CONFIRMATION

To: *Buyer Name*
Contact Person
Fax No.:
Phone No.:

From: *Seller Name*
Contact Person
Fax No.:
Phone No.:

We are pleased to confirm the following transaction, subject to the attached Standard Terms and Conditions for Distressed Trade Confirmations.

Trade Date: _____, 199_
Seller: _____ □ Principal □ Agent
Buyer: _____ □ Principal □ Agent
Credit Agreement: _____
Purchase Amount/
Type of Debt: □ Commitment Amount: $_____ of _____;
$_____ of _____; $_____ of
_____.

□ Claim Amount: $_____ of _____;
$_____ of _____; $_____ of
_____.

Form of Purchase: □ Assignment; □ Participation; □ Subparticipation
Settlement Date: □ As soon as practicable
□ No later than _____, 199_, unless otherwise
extended by mutual consent of Buyer and Seller, which
consent shall not be unreasonably withheld
□ No later than _____, 199_
Purchase Rate: _____%
Accrued Interest: □ Paid on Settlement Date
□ Settled Without Accrued Interest
□ Trades Flat
Credit Documentation
to be provided: □ Yes; □ No

Other Terms of Trade: ☐ In the event that Buyer and Seller are unable to close this transaction as an Assignment, each of Buyer and Seller agrees to use best efforts (subject to the terms of the Credit Agreement) to settle this transaction as a Participation.

☐ This transaction shall also be subject to the successful completion of the purchase by Seller of the Purchase Amount of the Debt to be sold to Buyer hereunder.

☐ This transaction shall also be subject to the successful completion of the sale by Buyer of the Purchase Amount of the Debt to be purchased from Seller hereunder.

☐ _____

Subject to: Negotiation, execution and delivery of reasonably acceptable contracts and instruments of transfer, to be prepared by ☐ Seller ☐ Buyer.

Please provide the signature of a duly authorized officer or other signatory where indicated below and return this letter to the attention of Closer's Name no later than _____ __.m. (New York time), _____, 199_, at the following fax number(s): _____.

If you have any questions, please contact *Closer's Name at Closer's telephone number.*

SELLER   *BUYER*

By:_____   By: _____

Name:_____   Name: _____

Title:_____   Title: _____

Date: _____   Date: _____

Standard Terms and Conditions for Distressed Trade Confirmations

Published as of December 1, 1997, by the Loan Syndications and Trading Association, Inc.

Settlement Date: The date of delivery and payment for the Debt specified in a Confirmation shall be the Settlement Date.

Purchase Amount: Unless otherwise specified in a Confirmation, the Purchase Amount shall be allocated pro rata among the facilities under the Credit Agreement, including revolving credit, letter of credit and term loan facilities. Seller shall indicate in the Confirmation whether the Purchase Amount is the Commitment Amount (principal only) of the Debt or the Claim Amount (principal as adjusted by other amounts) of the Debt. Unless otherwise agreed, Buyer is assuming all unfunded commitments relating to the Debt.

Permanent Reductions and Fees: The economic benefit of permanent commitment reductions and permanent repayments of principal (collectively, "Permanent Reductions") shall be allocated in accordance with the Purchase Price Calculation. Unless otherwise specified in a Confirmation, Buyer shall receive the benefit of payments of any amendment or other fees (other than commitment fees or facility fees, which shall be for the account of Seller unless "Trades Flat" is specified in a Confirmation) which are made in respect of the specified Debt from and after the Trade Date. Any and all unreimbursed fee or expense claims shall be for the account of Buyer.

Purchase Price Calculation: Buyer shall pay Seller a Purchase Price for the Purchase Amount of the specified Debt on the Settlement Date equal to the Purchase Rate multiplied by the Commitment Amount or the Claim Amount (as applicable) as of the Settlement Date less (100% minus the Purchase Rate) multiplied by the unfunded commitments assumed by Buyer as of the Settlement Date less (100% minus the Purchase Rate) multiplied by any Permanent Reductions after the Trade Date plus (unless otherwise specified in a Confirmation) one-half of the Recordation Fee or Transfer Fee.

Interest Payments and Fees: All interest and commitment, facility and letter of credit and other similar fees are based on contractual rates, as set forth in the Credit Agreement.

If "Trades Flat" is specified in a Confirmation, all unpaid interest and commitment, facility, letter of credit and other similar fees, whether accruing before, on or after the Trade Date, if and when paid, shall be for the account of Buyer and, if paid to Seller, Seller shall promptly pay same to Buyer.

If "Settled Without Accrued Interest" is specified in a Confirmation, such accrued amounts to but excluding the Settlement Date shall be for the account of Seller and shall not be paid by Buyer to Seller on the Settlement Date, but shall be paid by Buyer to Seller promptly upon any payment thereof to Buyer by the obligor(s) under the Credit Agreement; provided, however, that unless such payment by the obligor(s) is made (a) on or before the due date thereof or the expiration of any applicable grace period, each as specified in the Credit Agreement as in effect on the Trade Date (or, if no such grace period exists, the expiration of thirty days from such due date), and (b) before a default by the obligor(s) in connection with any other payment obligations of the obligor(s) under the Credit Agreement, such accrued amounts (if and when paid by the obligor(s)) and any other accrued amounts due thereafter shall be for the account of Buyer, and Seller shall not be entitled to any part thereof.

If "Paid on Settlement Date" is specified in a Confirmation, such accrued amounts to but excluding the Settlement Date shall be for the account of Seller and shall be paid by Buyer to Seller on the Settlement Date and, if thereafter paid to Seller, Seller shall promptly pay same to Buyer; provided, that if the obligor(s) fail(s) to make payment thereof, Seller shall not be required to return such amount to the Buyer. Partial payments of interest shall be applied in the inverse order of payment dates unless otherwise specified in the Credit Agreement.

Breakfunding: No breakfunding compensation shall be paid for settlement of a transaction on a day other than an interest payment date in respect of the specified Debt unless otherwise specified in a Confirmation.

Recordation and Transfer Fees: Unless otherwise specified in a Confirmation, any recordation, processing or similar fee payable to the Agent under the Credit Agreement in connection with an assignment and any transfer fee payable to the seller of a participation in connection with the transfer of such participation shall be split equally between Buyer and Seller. As provided in the Purchase Price Calculation, Buyer shall pay its half (or, if otherwise specified in a Confirmation, its specified portion, if any) to Seller. Seller shall be responsible for paying the full amount of such fee directly to the Agent or such seller of such participation, as the case may be.

Costs and Expenses: Each of Buyer and Seller shall bear its respective costs and expenses in connection with the transaction described in a Confirmation. Seller shall be responsible for all costs, fees and expenses in respect of the Debt that are chargeable under the terms of the Credit Agreement and that are attributable to any period prior to but excluding the Settlement Date. Buyer shall be responsible for all costs, fees and expenses in respect of the Debt that are chargeable under the terms of the Credit Agreement and that are attributable to any period from and after the Settlement Date.

Transaction Documentation: Each transaction described in a Confirmation is subject to obtaining any necessary consents (including, without limitation, any consents required by predecessors in interest to the Seller). In the case of an assignment, the parties shall execute an assignment agreement in the form stipulated in the Credit Agreement (if so stipulated) and a reasonably acceptable supplemental assignment agreement (taking into account related predecessor documents) containing customary provisions for the purchase and sale of distressed loan assets. In the case of a participation, the parties shall execute a reasonably acceptable participation agreement containing customary provisions for the purchase and sale of a participation in distressed loan assets. Unless otherwise specified, the Transaction Documentation shall be prepared by, and any required consents obtained by, Seller. Unless otherwise specified, Seller shall use best efforts to send Buyer a Confirmation not later than one business day after the Trade Date. Unless otherwise agreed, Seller shall use best efforts to furnish Buyer an assignment, supplemental assignment or participation agreement, as appropriate, together with any related predecessor documents (subject to applicable confidentiality provisions contained in such documents), within six business days after the Trade Date.

Credit Documentation; Confidentiality Agreement: If "Yes" is specified in a Confirmation, Seller shall furnish Buyer a true and complete copy of the Credit Agreement (including all schedules and exhibits, and any related documentation reasonably requested by Buyer), together with all amendments thereto, as promptly as practicable following the Trade Date. If required by the Credit Agreement, Buyer shall execute and deliver to Seller a Confidentiality Agreement in the form stipulated in the Credit Agreement or, in the absence of same, a reasonably acceptable Confidentiality Agreement containing customary terms.

Syndicate Confidential Information: Unless otherwise specified, Buyer represents to Seller that Buyer is sophisticated, understands the nature and importance of syndicate confidential information (as defined in the LSTA Code of Conduct) and the manner in which such information can be obtained and has requested such information from Seller in connection with each transaction described in a Confirmation if it desired such information in such connection and that where it has not requested syndicate confidential information it has otherwise obtained such information as it has deemed appropriate under the circumstances to make an informed decision regarding each transaction specified in a Confirmation without reliance on Seller. If the Buyer has requested Seller to provide syndicate confidential information, and Seller has agreed to provide such information to Buyer, unless otherwise agreed, Seller represents to Buyer that it has used reasonable efforts to maintain syndicate confidential information and that it has disclosed to Buyer all material syndicate confidential information retained by it as of the Trade Date, and, unless otherwise specified, Buyer acknowledges to Seller that such syndicate confidential information has been disclosed to it, that the syndicate confidential information so disclosed may not be complete because Seller may not have retained all such information and that Buyer has taken all steps it deems necessary under the circumstances to assure that it has the information it deems appropriate to make an informed decision regarding each transaction described in a Confirmation.

Bankruptcy Proceedings: In the case of a bankruptcy proceeding involving the obligor(s) under the Credit Agreement, (a) the Seller shall also use best efforts to provide to the Buyer within six business days after the Trade Date copies of any Proofs of Claim relating to the Debt specified in a Confirmation and (b) the Buyer shall be responsible for the preparation and filing of any necessary Bankruptcy Rule 3001(e) Notices of Transfer.

Standstill: With respect to the Purchase Amount of the Debt that is the subject of a Confirmation, until the Settlement Date Seller shall cease any discussions with other purchasers and shall decline all offers.

Principal/Agency Status: Each of Buyer and Seller shall indicate in the Confirmation whether it is acting as a principal or an agent in the transaction. A Buyer or Seller that holds itself out in a Confirmation as a "principal" is directly liable for the completion of the transaction. A principal may, however, specify in the Confirmation that its obligation to complete the transaction is subject to successful completion of the purchase or sale from a third party of the Debt specified in a Confirmation.

A Buyer or Seller that holds itself out to a counterparty in a Confirmation as an "agent" acts on behalf of one or more principals to the transaction contemplated by the Confirmation and is not itself a party to the transaction. Accordingly, a Buyer or Seller that holds itself out as an agent: (i) is not liable to such counterparty for the successful completion of the transaction (unless the parties otherwise agree); and (ii) for the avoidance of doubt, shall have no liability or obligation to such counterparty in connection with the transaction contemplated by the Confirmation. However, a Buyer or Seller that indicates in a Confirmation its status as an agent does represent to the counterparty its authority to bind its principal(s) to the terms of the transaction set forth in the Confirmation, and shall disclose the identity of such principal(s) no later than the Trade Date.

Nonreliance: Each party acknowledges to the other party that it is a sophisticated Buyer or Seller (as the case may be) with respect to the transaction described in a Confirmation, and has such information as it deems appropriate under the circumstances (however obtained), concerning for example the business and financial condition of the obligor(s) under the Credit Agreement, to make an informed decision regarding the purchase and sale of the Specified Debt. Each of Buyer and Seller hereby agrees that it has independently made its own analysis and decision to enter into the transaction described in such Confirmation, based on such information as it has deemed appropriate under the circumstances, which may include syndicate confidential information (however obtained) and without reliance on the other party (except for reliance on any express representation made by the other party in the Confirmation).

Confidentiality of Terms of Transaction: Both parties shall maintain the confidentiality of the terms of the transaction unless otherwise required by law or regulatory authority, except that the parties may disclose the terms of the transaction to their respective attorneys, accountants, and other professionals. Buyer shall be permitted to make any necessary disclosures to prospective purchasers from Buyer regarding the terms of the transaction described in a Confirmation (other than the Purchase Rate or Purchase Price), subject to same confidentiality constraints.

Binding Effect: The parties agree to be, and are, legally bound to the transaction on the Trade Date upon oral agreement to the terms thereof by Seller and Buyer (whether directly or through their respective agents), subject to all the other terms and conditions set forth in the Confirmation. Seller and Buyer agree and acknowledge that events occurring subsequent to the Trade Date shall not relieve the parties of their obligations under the Confirmation.

Governing Law; Confirmation Controls: Each Confirmation and the Standard Terms and Conditions for Distressed Trade Confirmations shall be governed by and construed in accordance with the law of the State of New York without regard to the choice of law provisions thereof. In case of any variation between the terms of a Confirmation and the Standard Terms and Conditions for Distressed Trade Confirmations, such Confirmation shall control.

Execution by Fax: Transmission by fax of an executed counterpart of a Confirmation, Confidentiality Agreement or any other Transaction Document shall be deemed to constitute due and sufficient delivery of such counterpart. Buyer and Seller shall deliver to each other an original counterpart of the assignment or participation agreement (and, upon the request of either party, the Confirmation, Confidentiality Agreement or any other document) promptly after delivery of the fax, provided, however, that the failure by either party to so deliver an original counterpart shall not affect the sufficiency of a fax of such counterpart (and the fact that such fax constitutes the due and sufficient delivery of such counterpart), as provided in the first sentence hereof.

APPENDIX III

[Seller Letterhead]

LSTA OPTION TRADE CONFIRMATION

To: *Buyer Name*
Contact Person
Fax No.:
Phone No.:

From: *Seller Name*
Contact Person
Fax No.:
Phone No.:

Seller has agreed to sell, and Buyer has agreed to buy, an option in respect of the debt described below (the "**Option**") on the terms set forth below and in the Standard Terms and Conditions for Option Trade Confirmations as published by the Loan Syndications and Trading Association, Inc. as of **October 1997** (which are incorporated herein by reference) (collectively, the "**Option Trade Confirmation**"):

Trade Date: _____, 199_
Seller: _____
Buyer: _____
Option Style: [American][European]
Option Type: [Call][Put]
Exercisability: Permitted in full or in part so long as the amount so exercised will constitute an amount permitted to be assigned under the Credit Agreement

Debt Subject
to the Option: $_____ of the _____ [Commitment][Loans] (the "**Purchase Amount**") under the Credit Agreement dated as of _____ among _____ as borrower (the "**Borrower**") and the lenders party thereto and _____, as [Administrative] Agent (the "**Credit Agreement**").

Exercise Time: Up to 5:00 p.m. New York time
Expiration Date: _____, 199_
Expiration Time: 5:00 p.m. New York time
Pricing:
Purchase Rate: ____%

Premium:	$_____ (____ basis points on the aggregate principal amount of the Debt subject to the Option as specified above).
Relevant Currency:	US Dollars
Accrued Interest:	Settlement Without Accrued Interest/Paid on Settlement Date
Credit Documentation to be provided:	Yes/No
Cash Settlement:	No
Amendments and Restructurings:	Transferor of the Debt subject to the Option retains full voting rights with respect to any Debt it may hold through and until settlement of any transfer or transfers of all or a portion thereof
Settlement by Participation:	Yes/No/Acceptable if assignment is unavailable
Transferability:	Transferable by Buyer only with Seller's prior consent, which consent shall not be unreasonably withheld
Other Terms of Trade:	_____

If you agree with the terms and conditions described herein, please provide the signature of a duly authorized officer or other signatory where indicated below and return this letter to the attention of *Closer's Name* no later than 5:00 p.m. (New York City time), _____, 199_, at the following fax number(s): _____.

If you have any questions, please contact *Closer's Name at Closer's telephone number*.

ACCEPTED AND AGREED:

SELLER	*BUYER*
By:_____	By: _____
Name:_____	Name: _____
Title:_____	Title: _____
Address:	Address:
Fax No.:	Fax No.:

Standard Terms and Conditions for Option Trade Confirmations

Published by the Loan Syndications and Trading Association as of October 1997

Exercise of the Option: Unless otherwise specified in the Option Trade Confirmation, the Option may be exercised in full or in part with respect to amounts of Debt which constitute assignable amounts under the Credit Agreement, (i) in the case of an American Option, on any business day up to and including the Exercise Time on the Expiration Date or (ii) in the case of a European Option, only on the Expiration Date before the Exercise Time. Exercise of the Option shall be made by oral notification followed by written notice by Buyer to Seller (together an "**Exercise Notice**") substantially in the form of Exhibit A hereto, provided that such Exercise Notice must be received by Seller prior to the Exercise Time on the Expiration Date. An Exercise Notice may be transmitted by Buyer to Seller by any means, including, without limitation, by facsimile, hand delivery or courier. (In the case of either an American Option or a European Option, if the Expiration Date specified in the Option Trade Confirmation is not a business day, the Expiration Date shall be deemed to be the next succeeding business day). In the case of an American Option, if the Exercise Notice is received by Seller after the Expiration Time on any day prior to the Expiration Date, such Exercise Notice shall be deemed to be given on the opening of business on the next business day. In the case of an American Option exercise shall be effective on the date such notice is given. In the case of a European Option, an Exercise Notice may be given to Seller prior to the Expiration Date, but such Exercise Notice shall be irrevocable once given with respect to the amount of the Debt specified therein and such exercise shall be effective only as of the Expiration Date. As used herein, "**business day**" shall mean any day on which commercial banks are not authorized or required to close in New York City. Unless expressly otherwise provided herein, "Trade Date" shall mean the Trade Date specified in the Option Trade Confirmation.

Upon giving of an Exercise Notice in respect of a Call Option, Seller shall be obligated to sell to Buyer that portion of the Debt specified in such Exercise Notice at the specified Purchase Price (as defined below). Upon giving of an Exercise Notice in respect of a Put Option, Seller shall be obligated to purchase from Buyer that portion of the Debt specified in such Exercise Notice at the specified Purchase Price. Notwithstanding anything in this paragraph to the contrary, in the event that a complete or partial permanent paydown has occurred with respect to the Debt to be transferred upon exercise, the trade shall be settled in accordance with the terms and conditions set out under the headings "Complete Paydowns" or "Partial Paydowns" below (as applicable).

Settlement: Except as otherwise provided in the Option Trade Confirmation, Seller and Buyer agree to consummate the assignment of (or, if applicable, sale of participation in) the Debt that is the subject hereof in accordance with the procedures applicable to the settlement of par trades as set forth in the LSTA's Standard Terms and Conditions for Par Trade Confirmations (the "**LSTA Standard Par Trade Terms**"); provided that, for purposes thereof, the "Trade Date" with respect to any assignment or participation shall refer (i) in the case of an American Option to the date the relevant Exercise Notice from Buyer is given and effective and (ii) in the case of a European Option to the Expiration Date; and provided further that provisions with respect to fees and documentation expense in case of multiple exercise set forth below shall be applicable. The transfer of the Debt subject to each exercise shall be effected by assignment or, if agreed to in the Option Trade Confirmation, by participation, subject in each case to compliance with applicable restrictions in the Credit Agreement. If the parties do not specify in the Option Trade Confirmation whether the transfer is to be effected by assignment or participation, the transfer shall be effected by assignment. If the parties specify in the Option Trade Confirmation that participation is acceptable if assignment is unavailable, then settlement shall be by assignment, unless Credit Agreement requirements for an assignment, such as borrower or agent consent or minimum assignable amount, can not be met, in which case settlement shall be by participation. The party who transfers the Debt (or who would transfer the Debt if the Option were to be exercised) (by way of assignment or participation) shall be referred to herein as the "**Transferor**" and the party to whom the Debt is so transferred (or to whom the Debt would be so transferred if the Option were to be exercised) shall be referred to herein as the "**Transferee**". Each partial exercise shall be effected by a separate settlement.

Unless otherwise agreed to by the parties in the Option Trade Confirmation, all payments made by either party in respect of the Option (including, without limitation, the Purchase Price and the Premium) shall be made in US Dollars, which shall mean the lawful money of the United States of America.

Purchase Price: The Purchase Price for the portion of the specified Debt subject to each exercise of the Option shall be calculated in accordance with the Purchase Price Calculation under the LSTA Standard Par Trade Terms and shall relate to the exercised portion of the Debt and/or Commitment covered by the relevant Exercise Notice and shall be determined as if the Trade Date referred to therein were the Trade Date determined as set forth under the caption "Settlement" above.

Premium: The Premium (if any) specified above shall be payable by Buyer to Seller on the date which is two business days after the Trade Date. If Buyer fails to pay the premium when due, the Seller shall have the option to cancel the trade by prompt written notice to the Buyer, in which case neither party shall have any further obligation to the other.

Purchase Amount: Unless otherwise specified in the Option Trade Confirmation, Purchase Amount shall be allocated pro rata among the facilities under the Credit Agreement, including revolving credit, letter of credit and term loan facilities.

Recordation and Transfer Fees: Unless otherwise specified above, any recordation, processing or similar fee payable to the Agent under the Credit Agreement in connection with an assignment and any transfer fee payable to the seller of a participation in connection with the transfer of such participation shall be split equally between Seller and Buyer. Where an Option is exercised in part multiple times, however, Seller shall only be obligated to pay half of one recordation, processing or similar fee in connection with the initial transfer and Buyer shall be obligated to pay in full all remaining such fees for all subsequent transfers (the Purchase Price Calculation under the LSTA Standard Par Trade Terms to be adjusted accordingly).

Documentation: Unless otherwise specified in the Option Trade Confirmation, the Transferor shall prepare the settlement documentation in accordance with the LSTA Standard Par Trade Terms. However, in the case of multiple exercises of a Call Option, Buyer/Transferee shall prepare all trade documentation except for those prepared in connection with the initial exercise and transfer.

Transferability: Buyer shall have the right to sell, assign or transfer this Option [(in whole only)], to the extent not exercised, to an eligible assignee under the Credit Agreement only with Seller's prior consent, which consent shall not be unreasonably withheld.

Complete Paydowns: If the Option is an American Option or a European Option as to which paydown occurs on the Expiration Date, then in the case of a complete permanent paydown the Option will automatically expire upon such paydown, and, to the extent economically beneficial to the Buyer on the basis of the following cash settlement computation, the Option will be deemed to have been automatically exercised immediately prior to such expiration and a cash settlement shall be made in respect of such exercise as set forth below. In the case of a Put Option, (a) the Paydown Price (as defined below) shall be subtracted from the Purchase Rate and (b) the difference if positive shall be multiplied by the amount of the Debt subject to the Option. In the case of a Call Option, (a) the Purchase Rate shall be subtracted from the Paydown Price and (b) the difference if positive shall be multiplied by the amount of the Debt subject to the Option. In each case where the difference is positive, the Seller shall owe the Buyer the resulting amount, which amount shall be payable within three business days of notice of the complete paydown given by Transferor to Transferee (which shall be given as soon as practicable after the Transferor learns of the paydown).

If the Option is a European Option and the paydown occurs prior to the Expiration Date for such Option, then in the case of a complete permanent paydown the Option will expire and not be exercisable.

Partial Paydowns: In the case of a partial permanent paydown of Debt subject to an Option the settlement of each exercise of such Option shall be made as follows: The Paydown Percentage (determined as set forth below) shall be multiplied by the amount of Debt subject to such exercise (herein the "**Exercise Amount**") and settlement shall be made in respect of such exercise in accordance with the paragraph captioned "Settlement" above in an amount of Debt equal to such product. The balance of the Exercise Amount shall be settled in cash as follows: In the case of a Put Option, (a) the Paydown Price (as defined below) shall be subtracted from the Purchase Rate and (b) the difference, if positive, shall be multiplied by such balance. In the case of a Call Option, (a) the Purchase Rate shall be subtracted from the Paydown Price and (b) the difference, if positive, shall be multiplied by such balance. In each case where the difference is positive Seller shall owe the Buyer the resulting amount which shall be payable on the date when the settlement occurs in respect of the portion of the Option settled in accordance with the paragraph captioned "Settlement" above. The "**Paydown Percentage**" in respect of an Option shall equal (a) the total aggregate outstanding principal amount of the issue of the Debt which is subject to such Option (including any undrawn commitment) minus the amount of such Debt permanently paid down (including undrawn commitment permanently terminated) divided by (b) such aggregate outstanding principal amount of the issue of Debt. "**Paydown Price**" in respect of any Option shall be expressed as a percentage equal to the amount paid to extinguish a portion of the issue of Debt the subject of such Option (excluding accrued interest) divided by the amount of such Debt so extinguished. Where the paydown constitutes only reduction of a commitment the Paydown Price shall be 100%.

Representations and Warranties: Seller hereby represents and warrants to Buyer, and Buyer hereby represents and warrants to Seller at and as of the date of the Option Trade Confirmation and upon each exercise of the Option:

(i) it is duly organized and validly existing under the laws of the jurisdiction of its organization;

(ii) neither the execution and delivery of the Option Trade Confirmation nor the consummation of the transactions contemplated by the Option Trade Confirmation, nor the performance of its obligations under the Option Trade Confirmation violates (i) any law, regulation, decree or other legal restriction applicable to it, (ii) its charter, by-laws or other constitutional documents, or (iii) any material instrument or agreement to which it or any of its assets is subject or by which it is bound;

(iii) there is no legal requirement of any governmental authority (including any requirement to make any declaration, filing or registration or to obtain any consent, approval, license or order) which is necessary to be met in connection with its execution, delivery or performance of the Option Trade Confirmation;

(iv) the Option Trade Confirmation has been duly authorized, executed and delivered on its behalf and constitutes its legal, valid and binding obligation, enforceable against it in accordance with its terms except as such enforceability may be limited by bankruptcy, insolvency or other laws of general applicability relating to or affecting the rights of creditors and by general equitable principles;

(v) in the normal course of its business, Seller or Buyer (as the case may be) engages in transactions similar to the Option;

(vi) it is a sophisticated institutional investor and is buying or selling the Option for its own account and not with a view to any distribution and is able to bear the economic risk of doing so in violation of any law; and

(vii) it is a sophisticated market participant with respect to the transaction described in the Option Trade Confirmation, and has such information as it deems appropriate under the circumstances (however obtained), concerning for example the business and financial condition of the obligor(s) under the Credit Agreement, to make an informed decision regarding the purchase and sale of the Option and the Debt subject to the Option, and it has independently made its own analysis and decision to enter into the transaction described in such Option Trade Confirmation, based on such information as it has deemed appropriate under the circumstances, which may include syndicate confidential information (however obtained) and without reliance on the other party (except for reliance on any express representation made by the other party in the Option Trade Confirmation).

Additionally, unless otherwise specified, Transferee represents to Transferor that Transferee is sophisticated, understands the nature and importance of syndicate confidential information (as defined in the LSTA Code of Conduct) and the manner in which such information can be obtained and has, prior to the Trade Date specified in the Option Trade Confirmation, requested such information from Transferor in connection with the transaction described in the Option Trade Confirmation if it desired such information in such connection and that where it has not so requested syndicate confidential information it has otherwise obtained such information as it has deemed appropriate under the circumstances to make an informed decision regarding the transaction specified in the Option Trade Confirmation without reliance on Transferor. Unless otherwise specified, if Transferor discloses to Transferee syndicate confidential information, Transferor represents to Transferee that it has used reasonable efforts to retain syndicate confidential information and that it has disclosed to Transferee, prior to the Trade Date specified in the Option Trade Confirmation, all material syndicate confidential information retained by it as of such Trade Date, and, unless otherwise specified, Transferee acknowledges to Transferor that such syndicate confidential information has been disclosed to it, that the syndicate confidential information so disclosed may not be complete because Transferor may not have retained all such information and that Transferee has taken all steps it deems necessary under the circumstances to assure that it has the information it deems appropriate to make an informed decision regarding the transaction described in the Option Trade Confirmation.

Changes in Terms of Underlying Debt: In the case of a Call Option, if Buyer of the Call Option desires to know whether the terms of the principal amount, interest rate, maturity, commitment, fees or collateral for the Underlying Debt have changed prior to exercise, but subsequent to the Trade Date, Buyer shall ask Seller (prior to exercise) for such information, and Seller shall promptly provide such information to Buyer. In the case of a Put Option, Buyer of the Put Option shall, in its Exercise Notice, indicate whether the terms of the principal amount, interest rate, maturity, commitment, fees or collateral for the underlying Debt have changed subsequent to the Trade Date.

Credit Documentation; Confidentiality Agreement: If "Yes" is specified above, Transferor shall furnish Transferee a copy of the Credit Agreement (including all schedules and exhibits), together with all amendments thereto, as promptly as practicable following the Trade Date with respect to the Option. If required by the Credit Agreement, Transferee shall execute and deliver to Transferor a confidentiality agreement in the form stipulated in the Credit Agreement or, in the absence of same, a mutually acceptable confidentiality agreement containing customary terms.

Events of Default: The occurrence at any time with respect to either party of any of the following events constitutes an event of default (an "**Event of Default**") with respect to such party:

(i) Failure by such party to make, when due, any payment or delivery under the Option;

(ii) A representation by such party in or pursuant to the Option Trade Confirmation proves to have been incorrect or misleading in any material respect when made;

(iii) Failure by either party to perform any other term or provision of or incorporated in the Option Trade Confirmation and such failure is not cured within 30 days of the occurrence thereof;

(iv) Such party: (1) is dissolved (other than pursuant to a consolidation, amalgamation or merger); (2) becomes insolvent or is unable to pay its debts or fails or admits in writing its inability generally to pay its debts as they become due; (3) makes a general assignment, arrangement or composition with or for the benefit of its creditors; (4) institutes or has instituted against it a proceeding seeking a judgment of insolvency or bankruptcy or any other relief under any bankruptcy or insolvency law or other similar law affecting creditors' rights, or a petition is presented for its winding-up or liquidation, and, in the case of any such proceeding or petition instituted or presented against it, such proceeding or petition (A) results in a judgment of insolvency or bankruptcy or the entry of an order for relief or the making of an order for its winding-up or liquidation or (B) is not dismissed, discharged, stayed or restrained in each case within 30 days of the institution or presentation thereof; (5) has a resolution passed for its winding-up, official management or liquidation (other than pursuant to a consolidation, amalgamation or merger); (6) seeks or becomes subject to the appointment of an administrator, provisional liquidator, conservator, receiver, trustee, custodian or other similar official for it or for all or substantially all of its assets; (7) has a secured party take possession of all or substantially all its assets or has a distress, execution, attachment, sequestration or other legal process levied, enforced or sued on or against all or substantially all its assets and such secured party maintains possession, or any such process is not dismissed, discharged, stayed or restrained, in each case within 30 days thereafter; (8) causes or is subject to any event with respect to it which, under the applicable laws of any jurisdiction, has an analogous effect to any of the events specified in clauses (1) to (7) (inclusive); or (9) takes any action in furtherance of, or indicating its consent to, approval of, or acquiescence in, any of the foregoing acts.

(v) An "Event of Default" shall occur with respect to such party with respect to any other option regarding a loan between the parties hereto which is documented pursuant to an LSTA Option Trade Confirmation (an "**Other Option**").

Right to Terminate Following Event of Default: If at any time an Event of Default with respect to either party (the "**defaulting party**") has occurred and is then continuing, the other party (the "**nondefaulting party**") may, by not more than five days notice to the defaulting party specifying the relevant Event of Default, designate a day not earlier than the day such notice is given as a Termination Date in respect of this Option (or this Option and all (but not fewer than all) Other Options), provided, however, that any date on which an Event of Default specified in paragraph (iv) above has occurred, shall be and be deemed to be a Termination Date without any notice or other act in respect of this Option (or this Option and all Other Options).

Termination and Close-Out: Upon the occurrence of a Termination Date, this Option, or, as applicable, this Option and all (but not fewer than all) Other Options shall be terminated and all obligations thereunder shall be accelerated and become immediately due and payable on such Termination Date. If the applicable Event of Default with respect to the Option occurs after the exercise thereof, then the settlement otherwise due thereunder shall result in a "failed trade" under the LSTA Failed Trade Rules, and such LSTA Failed Trade Rules shall govern. For all other Options, the nondefaulting party shall in a commercially reasonable manner replace the economic benefit of the positions represented by such Options ("**Gain**"), or determine the lost economic benefit resulting from the termination of such Options ("**Loss**"). If the Option and Other Options are being simultaneously terminated, then the Loss payable hereunder and under such Other Options shall be determined on a net basis taking into account any Gain to the nondefaulting party resulting from the termination of the Option and Other Options which shall be set off and netted against any Loss from the Option and Other Options. In the event that a Loss to the nondefaulting party results after such set off and netting, the defaulting party shall pay to the nondefaulting party an amount sufficient to compensate the nondefaulting party for such Loss. In the event that a Gain to the nondefaulting party results after such set off and netting, the nondefaulting party shall pay to the defaulting party an amount equal to such Gain.

Setoff: In addition to any rights of setoff a party may have as a matter of law or otherwise, upon the occurrence of an Event of Default with respect to either party, each party will have the right (but will not be obliged) without prior notice to the other party or any other person to setoff any obligation of the other party owing to such party (whether or not arising under any Option, whether or not matured, whether or not contingent and regardless of the currency, place of payment or booking office of the obligation) against any obligation of such party owing to the other party (whether or not arising under this Agreement, whether or not matured, whether or not contingent and regardless of the currency, place of payment or booking office of the obligation).

Amendments and Restructurings: If an amendment or waiver occurs with respect to a Debt on which an Option has been written, (a) the Transferor (although it may, as a courtesy only, consult with the other party to the Option) retains the right to exercise any voting rights it may have (including any right to elect whether and for what other assets the Debt will be exchanged as part of a restructuring) with respect to the Debt, regardless of whether or not the Option has been exercised, and (b) upon settlement of an exercised Option on a Debt that has been exchanged for other assets, the Transferee of the exchanged Debt pursuant to the Option will receive such other assets (as well as any related obligations) or, if the Debt was a part of a larger amount of an asset held by the Transferor, a ratable portion of all assets (as well as any related obligations) for which such larger amount has been exchanged. In exercising any such voting rights, Transferor shall have no duty to Transferee with respect to the legal consequences which may result from the manner in which Transferor exercises any such voting rights on the exercisability of the Option by Transferee.

Confidentiality: Both parties shall maintain the confidentiality of the terms of the Option and this Option Trade Confirmation unless otherwise required by law. Buyer shall be permitted to make any necessary disclosures to prospective purchasers from Buyer of its rights under the Option (other than Purchase Rate and Premium), subject to same confidentiality constraints.

Costs and Expenses: Except as specifically provided herein, each of Seller and Buyer shall bear its respective costs and expenses in connection with this Option Trade Confirmation and the transactions contemplated hereby.

LSTA Standard Par Trade Terms: Unless otherwise agreed, once exercised an Option (and any trade occurring thereunder) shall be governed by the LSTA Standard Par Trade Terms; provided, however, that the language in this Option Trade Confirmation regarding syndicate confidential information shall govern instead of that in the Standard Par Trade Terms.

Binding Effect: The parties agree to be, and are, legally bound to the Option on the Trade Date upon oral agreement to the terms thereof by Seller and Buyer (whether directly or though their respective agents).

Severability: If any term or provision of this Option Trade Confirmation or the application thereof to any person or circumstance shall to any extent be invalid or unenforceable, the remainder of this Option Trade Confirmation, or the application of such term or provision to persons or circumstances other than those as to which it is invalid or unenforceable, shall not be effected thereby, and each term and provision of this Option Trade Confirmation shall be valid and enforceable to the maximum extent permitted by law.

Governing Law: This Option Trade Confirmation shall be governed by and construed in accordance with the law of the State of New York.

Notice of Exercise

From: Seller Name
      Address

      Contact Person
      Fax No.:
      Phone No.:

      Reference is made to the Option Trade Confirmation (the "**Option Trade Confirmation**") dated as of _____, 199_ by and between _____ ("**Seller**") and _____ ("**Buyer**"). Terms used but not defined herein have the meanings stated in the Option Trade Confirmation.

      Notice is hereby given pursuant to the Option Trade Confirmation of the exercise of the Option for the following amount of _____ [Commitment][Loans]:

      _____ [Commitment Amount][Loans] $_____

      Previously Exercised [Commitment]
      [Loans] (Total) $_____

      Amount of Debt remaining subject
      to the Option $_____

The calculation of the Purchase Price is set forth on Schedule I hereto.

                            [BUYER]

                            By:_____
                            Name:

Chapter 7

Latin American Loan Syndications in the 1990s

Meredith W. Coffey
Director — Public Data Analysis
Loan Pricing Corporation

INTRODUCTION

The loan syndication market and the economic history of Latin American bear a striking similarity in their cyclical nature. Both the loan market and Latin American borrowers have gone through numerous boom and bust cycles in the last century. The Lost Decade of the 1980s, in which a cycle of loan defaults swept through Latin America profoundly shaking the international banking system, is generally considered the most recent cycle in Latin America.

In fact, syndicated lending to Latin America has gone through several distinct mini-cycles in the 1990s. While bilateral trade lines with relationship borrowers existed throughout the 1980s, broadly syndicated lending, often with trade or export credit agency support, began to inch its way forward in the early 1990s — generally following on the heels of the Brady agreements and the stirrings of a Eurobond market.

By early 1994, a true syndications market had developed out of the cocoon of trade finance. It was a year of battling adversity, with syndicators wading through interest rate increases, uprisings, kidnappings, and assassinations. In the end of the year, adversity — in the form of the bungled Mexican peso devaluation — triumphed over sometimes foolhardy courage. It was, however, a temporary triumph.

The so-called "Tequila effect" washed over the rest of Latin America as investors fled from the region. Argentina was hard hit, nearly following Mexico to the brink of insolvency. The capital markets closed for six months (far less than generally anticipated in early 1995) for the strongest Latin American issuers (weaker issuers and countries were left on the sidelines for the entire year), leaving bankers wondering what to do with their bridge loans. In fact, the 6-month window allowed bankers to forge closer ties with Latin American borrowers, and loan issuance increased substantially in several countries.

By the end of 1995, Latin America, with new battlescars over the old, was back on the track it had followed before Mexican peso crisis. For 1996 and most of 1997, the region enjoyed boom years; competition for loan mandates increased substantially and lenders poured money in, driving down pricing. However, the crisis in Asia in 1997 crossed over into Latin America, with some countries, notably Brazil, hard hit. The question, at the time of this writing, is whether syndicated lending to the continent is moving back to a mini-bust cycle, or whether the markets will rebound quickly in 1998.

EMERGENCE FROM THE LOST DECADE: 1990-1992

Like most new or reviving markets, the Latin American syndicated loan market returned with a whimper, not a roar, in the early 1990s. While regional banks fled the market following the 1982 Debt Crisis, a number of large money center banks maintained bilateral trade lines with major Latin American and multi-national clients throughout the 1980s. These facilities, however, were seldom syndicated or sold down.

Several events needed to take place before most retail lenders were willing to consider voluntary lending to Latin American borrowers. The most crucial event was the development of the Brady agreements (or other resolutions to the debt crisis — such as Chile and Colombia structured). Until the Brady agreement took place, few lenders evidenced interest in voluntary lending to borrowers with defaulted debt still outstanding. The next major step was the active trading in Bradies, which created substantial liquidity for Latin American debt. While this did not affect syndicators directly, most felt reassured by the presence of more institutional investors in the market.

The nascent voluntary syndicated loan market, however, was vastly eclipsed by the Eurobond market. Because most Latin American issuers had serviced their bond debt throughout the 1980s, it was generally considered to be effectively senior to the loans. Because institutional investors had not been particularly burned in the 1980s, they were more willing to enter the market once it showed some signs of liquidity. Further, this was a way for some flight capital to find its way back into Latin America. Bond issuance was mostly comprised of sovereign debt (see Exhibit 1). Unlike the late 1970s and early 1980s, when most syndicated lending went to state entities, bankers began targeting corporate borrowers in the 1990s.

Because banks were cautiously wading back into syndicated lending in Latin America in the early 1990s, they were taking many steps to ensure a safer market. One route was to choose a relatively highly-rated country. While Chile was a small country, it was the first to get its house in order following the crisis. For this reason, several banks chose to focus on the country (which received an investment-grade rating in 1992).

Borrowers in Chile were regularly tapping markets for smallish ($10-$30 million) trade finance and export-credit agency deals. Tenors in the early years began at less than one year, but rapidly increased to 18 months, two years, and

then three years. While early credits were closely linked to actual trade receivables, deals soon became linked to general trade flows, and then to the company
stating the deal would be used for trade purposes. Many bankers speculate that
these were pure working capital deals.

These deals were widely priced, according to a number of sources, with
spreads sometimes hitting LIB+300. Because banks had such low limits for Latin
American paper, arrangers generally needed to sell the paper down. While the
early Chilean loans were not syndicated in the classical sense, they often were
structured as a series of promissory notes — either sold straight or in strips by
maturity. For instance, a $20 million amortizing 3-year trade note might be split
into 10 promissory notes, with maturities ranging from 12 months to three years.

With the wide spread, arrangers often were able to skim substantial fees
off the deal, before selling the promissory note.

While bankers looked geographically for comfort — hence their interest in
Chile — they also looked to structural enhancements and pre-export finance to
increase their security. Credits structured with export credit agency (Exim, EDC,
Jexim, etc.) guarantees took on a risk profile similar to the guarantor, easing the minds
of the lenders. Meanwhile, advances linked to specific export receivables were also
considered much safer than straight lending, and were also a way for lenders to get
exposure to certain Latin American companies while minimizing country exposure.

Exhibit 1: Latin American Bond Volume (Bank and Corporate, Sovereign)

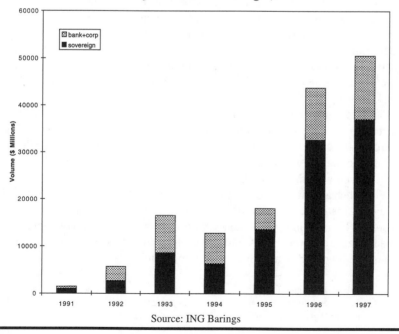

Source: ING Barings

These deals were structured around contracts between a Latin American exporter and an OECD-country importer (and often a relationship borrower). The bank would advance the funds, and would set up an offshore trust that collected the cash flows governed by the export contract. The banks would be paid first through the contracted exports, the remainder would flow to the Latin American company.

Trade finance deals were considered structurally senior to straight bank lending. Throughout the 1980s, companies (with government support) honored their trade facilities, realizing that they needed this financing avenue. Because these lines were serviced, they — like bonds — were considered senior to the syndicated loans.

Trade related financing was relatively advanced in Mexico by 1991. The majority of credits were either guaranteed by an export credit agency (primarily U.S. Eximbank) or were advanced by the same entity. The numbers were surprising: Eximbank alone had $4.3 billion of accumulated business and $2.3 billion in the pipeline in mid-1991. In fact, Mexico was that agency's largest market.[1] Much of that paper, however, was sold in private placement form.

While a number banks were uncomfortable with extending trade finance uncovered by an ECA to more than a year, some institutions were willing to go far further. For instance, J.P. Morgan and NMB in mid-1991 arranged a 5-year pre-export facility for copper concern Mexcobre. The deal was backed by contracts with Belgium's Sogem.[2] This facility, which was priced on a swap basis at roughly LIB+325, was extremely long for its type.

Argentina and Brazil also looked to tap trade finance in this period, though tenor generally remained short for borrowers from these countries.

Competition for Latin American bond mandates increased in 1991, and some banks used underpriced bridge loans to compete for those mandates. For instance, Bankers Trust in late 1991 arranged a bridge loan to its bond take out for Venezuelan oil concern PDVSA. The spread on the bridge loan was 37.5 bps over LIBOR[3] — at a time when there was little market appetite for uncovered Venezuelan risk at any price.

The securitized deals and ECA-backed credits continued into 1992. As comfort with Latin American countries increased, competition began eating into the margins and structures on these deals. Tenors began to lengthen, while pricing started to decline. However, because it was considered extremely safe, a number of banks stayed with that structure.

At the same time, project finance began to take on a larger profile. Latin American infrastructure was in dismal shape, and needed billions in investment on an annual basis. While many banks were wary from the white elephant projects they had financed in the 1970s and the early 1980s, this time the multinational agencies got involved. Chilean copper mine Quebrada Blanca received a $250

[1] "Mexico: Eximbank Bundling More for Mexico," *Project and Trade Finance* (June 1991), p. 18.

[2] "Mexico: Mexcobre and Copper-Bottomed Finance," *Project and Trade Finance* (April 1991), p. 52.

[3] "Venezuela: Bankers Trust Lands New PDVSA Mandate," *Euroweek* (June 28, 1991), p. 10.

million credit from Union Bank of Switzerland. That deal, which was priced at 87.5 to 168 bps over LIBOR, ran nine years.[4]

Latin American borrowers also began to look abroad for acquisitions following a decade of focussing inward. Mexican cement company Cemex was, by mid-1992, implementing its plan to become a global company. A major step in that direction was the roughly $1.8 billion acquisition of Spanish cement companies Valenciana and Sanson. Citibank backed the acquisition with a $1.2 billion bridge loan.[5] The 364-day credit, which was expected to carry blended US-Mexican-Spanish risk, was priced at 275-325 bps over LIBOR.

EMERGENCE OF BROAD SYNDICATIONS: 1993-1994

As competition for mandates became increasingly intense in Latin America, tenors lengthened and pricing fell on trade finance deals. Further, the size of the non-ECA backed receivables deals increased substantially. By 1993, lending in several countries was beginning to shift from receivables-backed and ECA-backed credits to uncovered syndicated loans.

By 1993, Chilean borrowers were able to tap bankers for medium-term, syndicated working capital facilities. Mexico, while considered less desirable than Chile, began receiving medium-term syndicated trade finance and short-term corporate deals. Brazil, on the other hand, generally was still limited to 364-day to two-year trade finance deals completely linked to contracts.

Beginning in late 1993, liquidity began returning to the developed syndicated loan markets, with lenders anticipating a surge in pricing pressures. With competition likely to increase in the United States and Europe, those lenders comfortable with emerging markets assets began to look to the region to bolster sagging returns elsewhere. However, spreads had fallen significantly since 1991 on trade finance credits, meaning lenders would need to look to riskier countries, longer tenors on trade deals, or look to move away from trade-backed or ECA-backed credits. Bankers took all approaches.

In August 1992, Chile became the first Latin American country to receive an investment-grade rating, and by 1993, Chilean corporates were beginning to tap the international banking community for medium-term working capital deals. Moreover, pricing was substantially lower than it had been on trade finance from several years earlier. For instance, in mid-1993, Chilean energy holding company Enersis was able to contract a 5-year corporate credit from a syndicate of banks led by CSFB. The credit was priced at 100-137.5 bps. Banco del Estado de Chile received a $100 million credit from a J.P. Morgan-led syndicate. That deal, which

---

[4] "Chile: Loans Signed — Compania Minera Quebrada Blanca SA — $250M — Construction Loan," *Euroweek* (December 18, 1992).

[5] Kelley Holland, "Citicorp Leads $1.2 Billion Bridge Loan for Cemex," *American Banker* (August, 14, 1982), p.1.

was a trade facility, was priced at 137.5 bps over LIBOR, again, well below what the borrower had paid several years previously on shorter facilities.

Bankers were also becoming more comfortable with Mexico in 1993. With NAFTA approved in November and the country preparing for OECD membership, Mexico appeared to be leaving its troubled past behind.

As comfort levels increased through the course of 1993, bankers moved from medium-term trade finance to shorter-term corporate finance deals. Dutch bank International Nederland (ING) provided a number of the Mexican credits that emerged that year. In the summer, ING arranged a $400 million, 6-year credit for metals concern Grupo Industrial Minera Mexico. The deal was broadly syndicated, with roughly 18 banks joining, and reintroduced a number of banks to Latin America. Part of the appeal came from the fact that the credit was secured by export proceeds of subsidiaries' metal exports and a hedging program to reduce commodity price risk. Further, the credit was priced at 300 bps over LIBOR at a time when spreads were beginning to slide in the United States.

Later in the year, ING arranged a $140 million, 364-day bridge facility for Mexican Coke bottler Panamerican Beverages (remember that name). The 1-year credit was priced at 325 bps over LIBOR, stepping up by 50 bps per quarter after the first two quarters. The deal created a stir in the market because the financials of the company were strong (and probably would have qualified the company for investment-grade status were it not located in Mexico): an interest coverage ratio of 8.6:1 and a debt to cash flow ratio of 1.2:1.[6] With the strong financials and wide pricing, the deal served as an eye opener for a number of New York syndications shops, making them realize that wide margins on good credits were available as liquidity prepared to increase in the United States.

While both Chile and Mexico had ventured into the realm of short- to medium-term syndicated corporate finance, much of the rest of Latin America remained in trade finance, albeit with longer tenors, in 1993.

By 1994, syndicated lending to the region began in earnest. While it was a year of political uncertainty and turmoil, it was also a year in which banks — for better or worse — appeared to make full-fledged commitments to the region. It was also a year in which pricing fell to what many, in retrospect, consider foolish levels, especially for relatively untested markets.

While trade deals remained the financing *du jour* in a number of countries (Venezuela, Brazil), medium-term, syndicated activity picked up. The majority of these credits were for very specific purposes — acquisitions, project finance, etc. Working capital deals generally were the province of Chilean borrowers.

The year began, for Mexico, with an uprising in Chiapas. However, lenders did not let that dissuade them. Because Mexico was close to home, because it had Nafta under its belt, because it became an OECD member in the summer, it

---

[6] Steve Miller and Meredith Coffey, "Hungry for Assets, Banks Return to Latin America," *Gold Sheets* (October 13, 1993), p. 24.

was considered relatively secure. Further, the county was rated BB+ by Standard & Poor's, and lenders were waiting for Mexico to become investment-grade. So, despite repeated political upheavals, assassinations, and kidnappings, lenders remained optimistic.

In 1993, the bond market, which absorbed $16.4 billion of Latin American paper, was far more favorable to Latin American issuers than the still-cautious loan markets. There appeared to be no competitive advantage to borrowing in loan format.

Then, in early 1994, the Federal Reserve began raising U.S. interest rates. The pricing advantage of bonds began to deteriorate as Treasury rates began to climb, while, at the same time, commercial bankers began to look very seriously at Mexico. The result was a substantial increase in syndicated loan activity despite very serious political uncertainty.

The above-mentioned Panamerican Beverages returned to the syndicated loan market in March for a $400 million credit backing the purchase of shares of subsidiary Inversiones Azteca. Despite intense market turmoil (presidential candidate Luis Donaldo Colosio was assassinated during syndication), pricing still fell from LIB+325 to LIB+250. The borrower was able to return to market at the end of the year (before the peso devaluation) and receive another credit, led by Citibank. Pricing fell to LIB+125. The company managed to lower its borrowing cost by 200 bps over the course of 16 months (see Exhibit 2).

Petroleos Mexicanos also returned to galvanize the market. Since 1979, Pemex had a bankers acceptance facility outstanding from Bank of America. The credit had been rolled over, with varying levels of enthusiasm from participant banks, every two years since its inception.

In the summer of 1994, however, Pemex restructured its credit, splitting it between Bank of America, J.P. Morgan, and Industrial Bank of Japan. Banks poured into the credit (split between bankers acceptances and letters of credit) despite its thin pricing (all facilities were priced at less than 100 bps), realizing that Pemex would be handing out substantial business in the years to come.

The new credit was well received, oversubscribed, and increased from $1.1 billion to $1.4 billion. Further, the terms on the credit reflected the euphoria of the times: one tranche offered pricing step-downs assuming a ratings upgrade, but no pricing step-ups in case of a downgrade. Another tranche contained a clause stipulating that pricing would be renegotiated were Mexico upgraded.

Exhibit 2: Panamerican Beverages Pricing: 1993-1995

	Pricing (bps over LIBOR)
August 1993	325 bp
April 1994	250 bp
December 1994	125 bp
May 1995	500 bp

Source: Loan Pricing Corp/Gold Sheets

This enthusiasm passed on to Argentina, a country that had been relatively ignored in the syndications market up to now. Argentina, in order to subdue hyperinflation, had in 1991 imposed a currency board, pegging the peso to the dollar at parity. While the markets had met this originally with skepticism, the peg appeared to be holding, and inflation was dropping at a tremendous rate. From a high of nearly 5,000% in 1989, inflation had fallen to 7.4% in 1993.

Bankers, who had previously only offered trade finance and some project finance, began to sit up and take notice. The Argentine Eurobond market was becoming increasingly competitive in 1994 and arranging banks began competing for bond mandates by offering below-market pricing on bridge loans (a strategy they would come to regret).

Gas distribution company Metrogas received at $100 million bridge loan priced at 87.5 bps over LIBOR. At the time, the company's rating was limited by a BB− sovereign ceiling. Further, in the United States, BB non-leveraged companies were paying a drawn spread of, on average, LIB+104, according to Loan Pricing Corporation's BSL Grid.[7] In its haste to win the mandate, the arranging bank priced the loan below US levels.

CIESA, holding company of Transportadora de Gas del Sur, also tapped the market for a bridge loan leading to a capital markets issue. Again, pricing began at LIB+87.5 (again, sub-U.S. pricing), with step-ups through its 2-year maturity.

Telefonica de Argentina awarded Bankers Trust, J.P. Morgan, Salomon Brothers, and Goldman Sachs the mandate to lead a $300 million Eurobond. Attached to the mandate was a $250 million, 2-year bridge loan. Pricing began at LIB+70.

A final bridge loan, a $500 million, 18-month facility for the Republic of Argentina, was large enough to overwhelm this nascent market. While priced at LIB+125–150 — still considered thin for Argentina, despite being priced well-above CIESA and Metrogas — the credit struggled in syndication, as lenders ran into their still-tiny country limits. With banks full, syndications activity slowed for the remainder of the year.

Colombia was something of a banker's paradise for those lenders that could overcome the drug taint. The country did not formally default upon its debt in the 1980s, and consequently never needed to restructure.[8] Further, it was one of two major investment-grade countries in Latin America in 1994. Yet the drug taint did repel a number of lenders. For this reason, those banks that did business with Colombia reaped substantial rewards.

In 1994, Colombia was in the midst of a privatization push that included primarily banks and cellular communications systems. A number of banks stepped up for widely-priced credits backing the sell-offs. Dutch bank ING was prominent among these, arranging a $115 million credit backing Bancol's purchase of Banco de Colombia; pricing was 300 bps over the U.S. prime rate. Special purpose vehicle Ganadero Share Trust paid P+200 for a credit backing its

---

[7] "Broadly Syndicated Loan Grid," *Gold Sheets* (May 23, 1994), p. 1.

[8] William R. Cline, *International Debt Reexamined* (Washington, DC: Institute for International Economics, 1995).

acquisition of Banco Ganadero. Chemical Bank arranged a $50 million credit for Fedecafe's acquisition of Banco Cafetero; pricing was LIB+250.

Not as richly-priced, but still attractive were a series of short-term credits backing the auctions of cellular concessions. Chemical Bank arranged a $150 million, 2-year bridge loan for consortium Comcel's bid for a region; pricing was LIB+300 initially. Santander arranged a $300 million credit for Bavaria, which bought concessions in another region; pricing rumors were in the 300s over LIBOR. Bank of America arranged a $150 million credit backing consortium Cocelco's acquisition of another region at a relatively thin spread of LIB+150 initially.

Brazil and Venezuela, in this period, tended to remain in the field of trade finance and occasionally project finance. Resource-rich Venezuela, which had been a favorite of bankers in the early 1990s, was mired in its banking crisis. A number of controls had been placed on foreign exchange and prices; few lenders expressed interest in straight lending to the country.

On the other hand, things were looking up for Brazil. The country had pegged its currency, the real, to the dollar, and appeared to be gaining the upper hand over its hyperinflation (it had fallen from 50% per month in July to 3% per month in November). Also, Cardoso, the architect of the real plan (to link the currency to the dollar, like Mexico and Argentina) in October beat populist candidate "Lula" in the presidential election. The reforms and optimism, however, were too new for lenders to venture far beyond the tried-and-true trade finance and letter of credit-backed commercial paper programs (see Exhibit 3).[9]

THE CRASH: 1994-1995

The nascent Latin American syndications market of 1994 came crashing down following the bungled Mexican peso devaluation in mid-December. Mexico had been running an unsustainable current account deficit, financed by very large capital inflows;[10] the currency had been tied to the dollar to tame inflation, and was substantially overvalued. While the syndications market was blasé about any tur-

---

[9] Another way lenders found to tap the rich spreads coming from Latin American debt while minimizing risk was through the use of syndicated letters of credit that backed commercial paper issuance. Bank of America was the largest proponent of the market, and did the bulk of the arranging. Latin American issuers could not tap the U.S. commercial paper market because their ratings were too low. However, if they received backing in the form of a letter of credit, the CP issue would then receive the rating of the letter of credit issuer. Consequently, Bank of America or Barclays Bank (the two biggest arrangers of this structure) would enlist a highly rated (often European) bank to act as the fronting bank for the letters of credit. A syndicate would then take risk participations on the credit. The structure took off in the mid-1990s, as lenders saw these structures as being particularly safe. The risk participation fee varied based on how volatile the market was at the time. Initially, the credits ran only 364 days, however, as risk appeared to decline, the tenor extended to two and three years.

[10] Sebastian Edwards, *Crisis and Reform in Latin America, From Despair to Hope* (New York, NY: Oxford University Press, 1995).

bulence in the Mexican market, local investors were more concerned. Mexico that year had witnessed an uprising in Chiapas, seen its presidential front-runner, Colosio, and PRI secretary general Francisco Ruiz Massieu assassinated; Alfredo Harp Helu, the chairman of financial group Banamex-Accival was kidnapped; businessman Carlos Cabal's empire began to sour, and he subsequently fled the country (just before signing a $450 million syndicated credit backing his company's acquisition of Del Monte). Further, Mexico has always seen substantial economic turmoil during election years; the currency is routinely devalued following the election.

Thus, while Mexico was enjoying a near-investment grade rating (with expectations of going investment grade in the near future), local investors were beginning to funnel their money out of the country, putting pressure on reserves and jeopardizing the fixed exchange rate. The Finance Ministry was defending the peso (at roughly 3.5 pesos to the dollar), but reserves fell so low that the currency could no longer be defended. On December 20, the peso was devalued to roughly 4:1; the next day, following heavy selling, the currency band was abandoned. The peso immediately fell to 5:1. Over the next several weeks, the peso fell to 6:1, and flirted with 7.5:1.

While the currency was no longer overvalued, for many companies (without easy access to dollars), their foreign currency debt had effectively doubled.

Exhibit 3: Latin American Letter of Credit-Backed Commercial Paper Programs

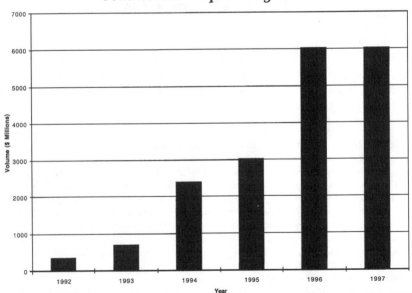

Bond markets panicked: spreads on Mexican (and other Latin American) bonds soared to thousands of bps over Treasuries as liquidity dried up. Several new bond deals — such as $300 million Tepic-Guadalajara toll road note and a $75 million note for Embotteladores Mexicanos de Pepsi-Cola — were pulled.[11]

For several weeks, Mexico appeared to be teetering on the brink of default. Further, troubles were not confined to Mexico, the so-called Tequila effect swept through Latin America, though much of its fury was targeted at Argentina, which also had an overvalued currency and a current account deficit.

The United States, the IMF, and the BIS in February put into place a $51 billion bailout plan for Mexico. In addition, J.P. Morgan and Citibank attempted to arrange a $3 billion credit for the United Mexican States, priced at 125 bps over LIBOR. The credit fell apart, however, over questions about subordination. (It was replaced later in the year with a $1 billion floating-rate note.)

Other banks stepped up on their own to support lenders: Santander was rumored to have arranged a $500 million credit for the United Mexican States, Citibank put together a $150 million credit for cement concern Cemex.

Mexico, after making strides toward medium-term, unsecured syndicated loans, appeared to be reduced to trade finance and securitizations (if lucky). A humbling moment came in March when proud Pemex returned to market to do its annual roll-over of its 364-day trade finance deal. In 1994, the $150 million credit was priced at 75 bps over LIBOR. Recognizing the market was skittish, Pemex increased pricing to 100 bps over LIBOR. This, however, underestimated market nervousness. In the end, only $65 million of the commitments were rolled-over, far below the anticipated $150 million.

Argentina found itself tarred with the same brush. With its overvalued currency and current account deficit, many lenders expected the country might not be able to meet its payments. That country, too, received funds for stabilization: $2.4 billion from the IMF, $1.3 billion from the World Bank, $1 billion from the Inter-American Development Bank, $1 billion from a local "patriotic" bond issuance, and $1 billion in the form of a Citibank and Deutsche Bank-led floating-rate note that was targeted toward commercial banks.[12] The commercial bank tranche ran three years, and was priced at LIB+300.

Syndications activity returned briefly for one special borrower: oil giant YPF. While the sovereign was struggling to receive funds to avoid insolvency, the well-regarded oil colossus tapped the market for $800 million backing the acquisition of Maxus energy. The credit, however, was primarily syndicated offshore — with Maxus and several Indonesian companies taking on debt. Still, even the Argentine portion, which was priced around 150 bps over LIBOR, survived syndication relatively unscathed.

The rest of the country did not do so well. For the remainder of the year, syndications volume remained muted, and the country more or less stayed on the sidelines while other countries slowly regained favor in the international markets.

---

[11] Meredith Coffey, "Latin Debt Market Remains Volatile," *Gold Sheets* (January 9, 1995), p. 24.
[12] Meredith Coffey, "International Banks Consider Argentina," *Gold Sheets* (March 20, 1995), p. 24.

SIGNS OF RECOVERY: 1995

While most market commentators expected Mexican syndications to be closed for the year, in fact, syndicated corporate lending revived (expensively) after six months. Preparing the market for corporates was a $500 million (increased to $1 billion) floating-rate note for the United Mexican States. The deal was put in place both to increase liquidity and to tempt bankers back into the market. At LIB+537.5, the deal was priced to tempt banks into rethinking Mexican deals. The strategy worked; the credit received $1.8 billion in commitments and paved the way for the return of corporate syndicated loans far earlier than expected. Corporate borrowers took two approaches to tap the loan market: trade finance/ securitizations or immensely widely priced unstructured loans.

Syndications market veteran Panamerican Beverages chose the latter, returning to market in June for a $150 million credit. The 3-year facility was priced at 500 bps over LIBOR (substantially above the LIB+150 the company had paid six months previously, but not unreasonable considering what had happened to the market, according to the general consensus).

Cola holding company Grupo VISA also chose that route, paying LIB+500-600 for its $240 million credit. Conglomerate Empresas La Moderna also accepted a wide spread for an uncovered deal: its $130 million credit had initial pricing of 500 bps over LIBOR.

With the peso devaluation making exports very competitive, a number of exporting companies returned to market for trade finance or securitizations. J.P. Morgan brought dollar-based financings to several companies in this manner by mid-1995: Steel concern Hylsamex received a $175 million credit priced at LIB+300. Another steel concern, Ahmsa, received a $115 million credit securitizing offshore receivables; pricing was LIB+250.

The Mexican peso crisis had little negative impact on Chile and Colombia; if anything it improved the climate for syndicated lending to entities in these countries because lenders committed to Latin America fled to the relative safety of these investment-grade countries.

Chile saw a boom of lending in 1995. Not only did bankers fleeing from other Latin American countries arrive in Chile, but European lenders — who were fleeing extremely low pricing in Central and Eastern Europe following intense competition there — also began settling on Chile as a destination. Further, the Japanese banks were allowed to do unstructured deals in Chile and Colombia, further increasing the number of buyers.

In 1995, the Japanese and European banks seldom led Chilean deals. However, the fact that they were eager to buy increased liquidity for those deals, and consequently allowed the (often U.S.) arrangers to bid spreads down aggressively.

Further, demand for credit by Chilean companies was not that strong. The top Chilean companies simply could not absorb all the paper that was thrust in their direction. Further, government, working to reduce short-term capital inflows, required a substantial percentage of foreign loans to be placed, interest-free, in an account at the Central Bank, substantially increasing the cost of borrowing.

Because of the supply/demand imbalance, spreads fell drastically. For instance, Chilean energy company Endesa (which was then rated BBB+), returned to market to refinance a credit from 1992. The deal was priced at LIB+125 when the issuer returned to market. Pricing on the new facility fell to LIB+62.5. Telecommunications company CTC returned to market to refinance existing debt and lower pricing. The new, 5-year $275 million credit was priced at LIB+85. Energy company Enersis was also able to reduce pricing to 75 bps over LIBOR in 1995.

While most lenders did complain about spreads falling precipitously, most were unwilling or unable to participate in deals for other countries. Consequently, the majority of Chilean deals from 1995 were substantially oversubscribed. For instance, the $150 million credit for Enersis received commitments totaling more than $300 million.

While Colombia also benefited from the flight to quality, its benefits were somewhat more qualified by two factors. First, because of the drug taint, fewer banks were eager to commit to Colombian deals despite the investment-grade rating. Second, Colombia had substantial needs for infrastructure finance in 1995. Thus, liquidity for loans was lower, while Colombian demands for credit were higher. There was not the supply and demand imbalance that existed in Chile; for this reason, while pricing fell substantially, it did not hit the levels seen in Chile.

Chemical Bank arranged a nearly $700 million credit backing an oil pipeline from the Cusiana oil fields to the Caribbean coast. While this was a very substantial amount of paper out of this previously reticent country and thus hit country limits hard, two factors reduced the hit. First, co-arranger Industrial Bank of Japan syndicated some $130 million in Japan. Second, a substantial portion of the credit was slated to be taken out by an Eximbank facility, thus reducing provisioning substantially.

Even with the substantial volume of paper hitting the market, Colombia was able to receive some substantial pricing concessions. For instance, the Republic of Colombia came to market to set a benchmark for pricing: LIB+125 — substantially lower than it would have received in the Eurobond market. Again, like most of the 1995 Chilean deals, European and Asian banks bought most of the paper.

RESURGENCE OF THE BROADLY SYNDICATED LOAN MARKET: 1996

While in January 1995 bankers were pondering whether Mexico and Argentina were teetering on the brink of default, by January 1996, lenders were preparing to ramp up their lending to those countries. Chile, which had come off a record-breaking year in 1995, was also revving up to shatter new budgets. On the other hand, Colombia, with more than $2 billion of debt issued in December, was revving down in the new year. Across the continent, all was forgiven — and appeared to be forgotten — and bankers were preparing to break records as the developed loan markets appeared less and less lucrative. As a result, syndicated lending to the region soared past $29 billion in 1996 (see Exhibit 4).

While Mexico began to recover in 1995, with extremely widely priced short-term loans, competition for mandates surged in 1996. Early Mexican deals offered solid risk/return profiles: spreads were high (average pricing was LIB+400 in the first quarter), tenors were low (average tenor was a mere 15 months), and deals were well-secured. However, lenders rapidly began competing on the basis of tenor. By the end of the first quarter, some deals were coming out with three year terms. While loan life had increased, spreads remained wide: a 3-year credit for conglomerate Grupo Alfa was priced at 480 bps over LIBOR, while a 3-year credit for retailer CCM offered a spread of 500 bps over LIBOR.

By mid-year, lenders were considering 5-year credits, and several had made their way through the syndications market by year-end. Spreads were also being trampled: average Mexican pricing had declined to LIB+200 bps, while average tenor increased to 48 months (see Exhibit 5).

Exhibit 4: Latin American Loan Volume, 1996-1997

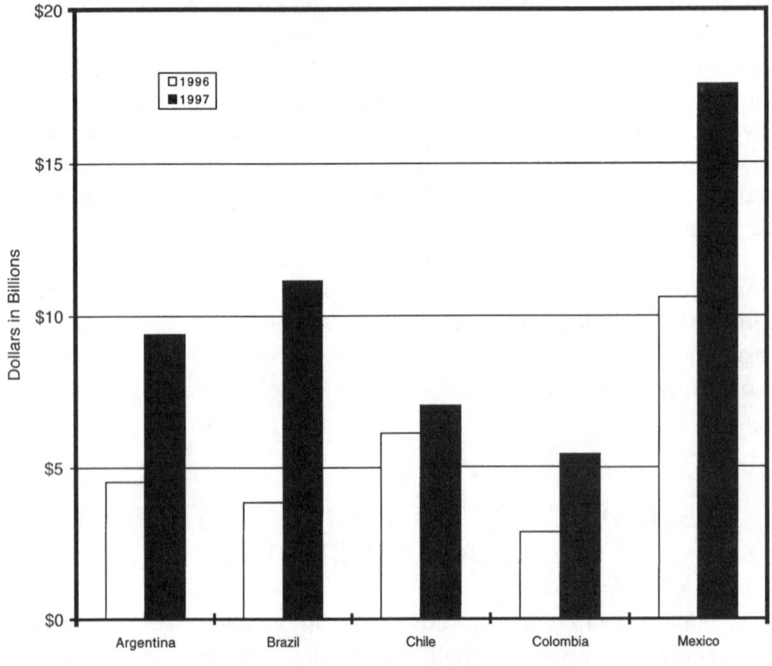

Source: Loan Pricing Corp/Gold Sheets

Exhibit 5: Argentine and Mexican Top Corporate Spreads

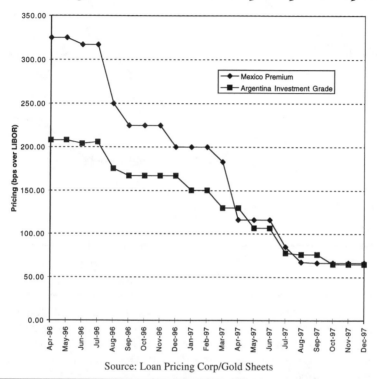

Source: Loan Pricing Corp/Gold Sheets

In 1996, lenders also came back to market to refinance (and reduce spreads by an average of 47%) on their widely priced deals of the previous year.[13] For instance, state electricity concern CFE reduced pricing from LIB+375 to LIB+175 (with a 5-year tenor). Mexican bank Banorte rolled over its 364-day letter of credit backed commercial paper program; the risk participation fee fell from 400 bps to 150 bps. Cemex also renewed its letter of credit commercial paper program, with the fee falling from 375 bps to 175 bps. Grupo Alfa, which inaugurated the 3-year corporate market for Mexico in the summer, received an amendment reducing pricing by 200 bps by winter.

While Argentina was all-but ignored by the syndication market in 1995, its story was similar to Mexico in 1996: average LIBOR spreads fell by more than 50%, while tenors increased by more than 80%.[14] Argentine pricing for the first quarter averaged 300 bps over LIBOR, while the average tenor was 24 months (see Exhibit 6).

---

[13] Meredith Coffey, "Increasing Competition Takes a Bite Out of Excess Latin Returns," *Gold Sheets Emerging Markets Fax* (February 10, 1997), pp. 1-4.

[14] Meredith Coffey, "As Spreads Thin and Structure Weakens, Lenders to Latin America Eye New Frontiers," *Gold Sheets* (February 10, 1997), p.22.

Exhibit 6: Mexican and Argentine Tenors

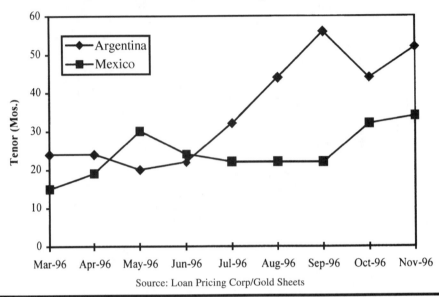

Source: Loan Pricing Corp/Gold Sheets

In the first quarter of 1996, borrowers Metrogas and Telefonica de Argentina received $100 million credits. The 18-month Metrogas deal was priced at LIB+325, stepping up to LIB+475; the 3-year Telefonica de Argentina credit was priced at LIB+250, stepping up to LIB+350. The stronger credit characteristics quickly deteriorated.

Competitive pressures elsewhere in Latin America, especially in Chile, played a major role in credit statistics in Argentina. In early 1996, lenders to Chile were becoming increasingly dismayed by low spreads in the region. A number of retail buyers (especially the German banks) began considering lending to Argentine borrowers to improve returns. As more lenders became comfortable with Argentina, liquidity surged, allowing arranging banks to bid pricing down in competition.

Lenders also began hawking bridge loans to bond issues, structures that proved risky in 1994. For instance, gas company TGS and holding company CIESA both received 18-month bridge loans to bond takeouts. The TGS deal was initially priced at LIB+200, while the CIESA credit was priced at LIB+220. Both companies had received bridge loans in 1994, with initial pricing of LIB+87.5, to bond market takeouts. When the bond market disappeared following the Peso crisis, the arrangers were left holding thinly-priced Argentine loans. Both of the new deals refinanced the still-outstanding 1994 bridge loans.

While some arrangers were nervous to see deals that relied on a skittish bond market for refinancing, others felt that the deals (which offered substantial pricing step-ups over time) were sufficiently widely priced to be held for a substantial period.

As competition increased, structure and pricing deteriorated. By the end of the year, 4- and 5-year bullet deals were beginning to emerge from Argentina and pricing fell to an average of LIB+146. Further, loan structure deteriorated. In the middle of the year, three deals (for YPF, Perez Companc, and Telecom Argentina) came to market without financial covenants. Despite the level of competition, the deals fared poorly in syndication, and the covenant-free deals were abandoned as a bridge too far.

With spreads for top-tier corporates falling so rapidly, some arranging banks began considering leveraged deals and M&A transactions to boost return. Spreads in that category averaged 428 bps over LIBOR as compared to 146 bps over LIBOR for top corporate deals at year end.

While volume surged in Argentine in 1996 to $4.5 billion, at the end of 1996 the Argentine government threw a wrench into the works in the form of an increased withholding tax on syndicated loans. The tax increase was sufficiently punitive to devastate the syndicated loan market. However, syndicators found a loophole by structuring their credits as floating-rate notes, with commercial banks being the targeted investors.

While Argentina and Mexico became increasingly acceptable to retail buyers in 1996, lenders remained the most comfortable with Chile. For most of the year, investors continued to pour money into the country, contributing to $6 billion in syndicated loan volume for the year. Further, the massive liquidity allowed arrangers to continue bidding down pricing in competition for mandates. LIBOR spreads for A– corporates, which were constrained by the Chilean sovereign ceiling, fell by 58%, from 56.1 bps in the beginning of the year to 23.3 bps at the end (see Exhibit 7).

The intense competition at the underwriting level proved too tempting to the top corporates, and a number of them returned to market to cut spreads. Energy company Enersis cut its pricing from LIB+75 to LIB+35, telecommunications concern CTC sliced pricing from LIB+85 to LIB+50 and Banco de Chile reduced pricing from LIB+75 to LIB+50.

In fact, in mid-year, a $500 million credit for state copper company Codelco came to market priced (at LIB+22.5) at spreads more attractive than an A- borrower would receive in the U.S. market. As spreads deteriorated, lenders began to look to alternatives to increasing spreads. One approach was to leave the market altogether. In fact, a number of lenders began to lend to Argentina to receive a yield pick-up (and subsequently driving down pricing in that country).

Lenders also looked for a yield pick-up by moving down market, both to the BBB sector and to the non-investment grade sector in Chile. The effect of that move was to reduce pricing in those arenas: spreads on BBB Chilean credits fell to 54 bps over LIBOR at the end of 1996.

By the end of 1996, Chilean spreads had stabilized at only a few bps over U.S. levels. However, most lenders were beginning to cast their eyes elsewhere, figuring that there simply was not enough juice left in the Chilean market.

Exhibit 7: Chilean A- Corporate Pricing

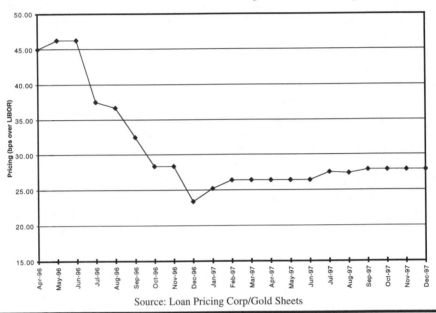

Source: Loan Pricing Corp/Gold Sheets

After posting volume of more than $2 billion for the fourth quarter of 1995 alone, Colombian syndications began to fall off in 1996. There was some residual business early in the year as several institutions came to market for pricing concessions in the wake of the new pricing benchmark (LIB+125) set by the Republic of Colombia in late 1995. Government energy financing concern FEN garnered pricing of LIB+137.5, as did telecommunications concern Nortel Colombia, while Banco de Bogota received a credit priced at LIB+162.5.

Substantial appetite emanated from Japanese banks as Colombia (having never formally defaulted on its debt in the 1980s) was one of the few countries that Japanese banks could lend to while avoiding punitive reserve requirements. For instance, Japanese banks comprised eight of the 16 lenders in the FEN credit, while only one U.S. bank joined.

The Colombian government also eased restrictions on foreign loans to the country. Previously, borrowers needed to hold a substantial portion of foreign loans in an interest-free account at the Central Bank if the credit had a tenor of less than five years. In early 1996, the government eased the restriction initially to four years, and then reduced it further to three.

However, 1996 lending to Colombia was hit by a number of factors, primarily political. First, the country was decertified by the Clinton administration as an ally in the war on drugs. Because of this, the U.S. Eximbank and OPIC could no longer participate in credits to the country, thus drying up needed guaranty facilities for Colombian projects. In fact, the OCENSA pipeline project was immediately hit because Exim was forced to pull out at the last minute, thus effectively doubling banks' Colombian exposure and eating into relatively small country limits.

Moreover, questions emerged about new President Samper's link to drug money, causing some to call for his resignation, and further worrying an already nervous investor base. The result was that lenders began to withdraw from Colombia: loan syndication volume fell to $2.85 billion in 1996, as compared to more than $2 billion for fourth quarter 1995 alone.

LENDING MANIA: 1997

The first three quarters of 1997 were incredibly strong for Latin America. Syndicated loan volume surged to $54 billion, nearly double the volume ($29 billion) of the previous year. At the same time, average pricing fell by 67% in Mexico and 56% in Argentina, as lenders flung themselves wholeheartedly into those markets. At the same time, pricing fell too far in Chile, disillusioning bankers and volume deteriorated as lenders fled that market in search of more fertile ground. Brazil, after years of talk, began privatizing in earnest, with subsequent widely priced syndicated credits.

However, a pall was cast over the fourth quarter in the form of the Asian flu. A liquidity crisis in Korea (at the time of writing) is bringing that country to the brink of default. The crisis rapidly traveled to Eastern and Central Europe, decimating bond and loan markets in that region. After several weeks of calm, panic descended into Latin America. Unlike in the previous emerging markets crisis in 1995, Mexico, rather than being the epicenter of the crisis, was in fact considered a safe haven. Meanwhile, Brazil, which shook off the 1995 crisis, was hit hard by the new backlash. Argentina, a victim of the Tequila effect in 1995, appeared likely to be hit from uncertainties in Brazil.

Mexico threw off the last stigma of the 1995 emerging markets crisis in 1997. Having gotten their feet under them in 1996, lenders flung themselves into Mexico in 1997, driving volume to $17.5 billion, some 70% above the numbers posted in 1996. Meanwhile, average pricing for top corporates collapsed, falling 67% from 200 bps over LIBOR in January to 66.5 bps in December.

Early in the year, top corporates tested the market by demanding extremely tight spreads, but accepting short tenors in return. Having determined that banks were willing to offer thin pricing, top corporates then moved to demand longer tenors. In fact, spreads on top corporate credits (which would likely be considered investment-grade were they not confined by the Mexican BB sovereign ceiling) fell below pricing on BB U.S. credits.

While syndication became difficult for a number of these loans, most survived unchanged. For instance, average U.S. BB credits were receiving pricing of LIB+74 in October; at the same time, Mexican top corporates were receiving spreads of LIB+66.5 on average. For instance, conglomerate Grupo Carso attempted a $500 million, 5-year credit priced at LIB+70 (the deal was downsized to $350 million) while bread maker Grupo Bimbo paid LIB+67.5 on a $100 million, 5-year credit.

Pemex was able to self-syndicate a $1 billion credit, which offered a trade facility priced at LIB+37.5 and term loan priced at LIB+50-87.5. A group of bankers received a 20 bps undrawn spread on a $2.5 billion self-syndicated back-up facility for the United Mexican States.

Attempting to pick up some yield, bankers moved somewhat downmarket, driving down spreads for those borrowers as well. Retailer CCM received a $150 million refinancing which offered starting pricing of LIB+150; the company paid LIB+500 in 1996.

Then, in October, the Asian flu crossed over into Latin America. While Mexico had been the epicenter of the last two emerging markets crises, this time the country, with its strong exports and competitive currency had become a safe haven. While lenders hunkered down, trying to wait out the storm in Brazil and Argentina, Mexican syndications continued unabated in the fourth quarter.

The syndicated loan market all-but changed to the syndicated floating-rate note (FRN) market in 1997 as new Argentine financial regulations increased the withholding tax on foreign loans from roughly 3% to more than 13% in late 1996. Commercial bankers were nimble enough to structure FRNs to suit their needs, and lending continued relatively unabated. In fact, volume for Argentine lending soared to $9.3 billion, some 120% above where it stood in 1996.

The most momentous occasion for the Argentine loan market came in May: Standard and Poor's cut the string that bound corporate foreign currency ratings to the sovereign level. The Republic of Argentina was upgraded from BB– to BB; several weeks later, a series of top corporates and financial institutions were upgraded to BBB–. The rationale was that the Argentine economy was sufficiently dollarized that the government would not be able to control foreign exchange. For this reason, many top-rated corporates could be considered better credits than the country in which they resided.

The upgrade encouraged Argentine corporate officials to renegotiate pricing on their deals. Average pricing on the newly investment-grade corporates fell from LIB+150.3 in the beginning of the year to LIB+65 by the end of the year. For instance, oil company YPF received at credit priced at LIB+75, oil company Astra received LIB+70 on its deal. Banco Rio received a $500 million, 2-tranche FRN; pricing was LIB+55 on the 1-year facility, LIB+87.5 on the 2-year facility.

In the fourth quarter, however, Argentina again began suffering from another country's problems. With Brazil hit by the Asian crisis, investors began to worry about Argentina's overvalued currency and its ability to export to Brazil. Several deals ran into trouble: a $1 billion credit for Cablevision struggled visibly in the syndication market, while a deal for supermarket Tia was cut from $90 million to $60 million, and initial pricing increased from 140 to 200 bps over LIBOR.[15]

---

[15] Bill Craighead, "Latam Volume, Pricing Shatter Records in '97; Lenders, Eyeing Asia Woes, Treading Lightly in '98," *Gold Sheets* (January 12, 1998), pp. 21-22.

Throughout much of the 1990s, lenders talked about when Brazil was going to return to the loan syndications market. Brazil, the Goliath of South America, promised vast volumes of activity at wide spreads. However, until 1997, the overwhelming majority of lending to Brazil took the form of structured trade finance and letters of credit backing commercial paper programs. That all changed in 1997 when Brazil began to privatize in earnest. A case in point: syndicated loan activity was less than $4 billion in 1996, but soared to more than $11 billion in 1997. As U.S. corporations began to look to investment in Brazil, they brought their relationship banks along.

In mid-year, a syndicate led by NationsBank structured a $1.2 billion credit backing the winning bidders in the privatization of mining giant CVRD. The B Band cellular concessions were auctioned off in 1997, with subsequent multi-billion dollar credits backing the winners. BankAmerica arranged a $1 billion recourse syndicated loan/floating-rate note backing the winners. J.P. Morgan and Merrill Lynch structured a $1.2 billion credit backing a BellSouth-led consortium's cellular acquisition.

Further, a number of power companies were auctioned off. The privatization of state power company CEEE engendered two credits: a $600 million deal from BankBoston and ANZ, and a $400 million credit from ABN AMRO and Santander.

Few of these credits were syndicated, however, before Brazil was felled by the Asian crisis. Because of the country's overvalued currency (pegged to the dollar to subdue chronic inflation), investors began scrambling for the exits. Lenders began worrying about whether they would be able to syndicate their underwritten credits. By year end, most bankers were hunkering down, trying to determine how best to cope with the latest shift in Brazil's popularity.

LOOKING FORWARD

As lenders enter 1998, Latin America is facing its second emerging markets crisis in three years. Unlike 1995, when Mexico was the epicenter and bore the brunt of the market's fury, lenders are currently eyeing that region as a storm-tested safe haven. Brazil, which emerged from the 1995 crisis relatively unscathed, is currently the Latin American focal point of investor unrest. Meanwhile, poor Argentina, which was hard hit in the 1995 crisis due to is similarities to Mexico, appears shaken by its links to Brazil.

The near-term horizon for Latin American lending is cloudy; it is not yet clear whether investors are preparing to flee back to the safe havens of the developed world (thus precipitating another mini-bust cycle in Latin America's famously cyclical history) or whether the current downturn will be seen as an opportunity to invest still more money in what has been a rocky, but often rewarding, emerging continent.

Chapter 8
Securitization of Commercial and Industrial Loans

Anthony V. Thompson
Director of ABS Research
Goldman, Sachs & Co.

INTRODUCTION

Long before anyone had ever heard of a home equity loan or even a credit card, there were commercial and industrial loans. Surprisingly, this asset class — the bread and butter of many large commercial banks — has been slow to find its way into the multi-billion-dollar securitization market. But this is changing. A number of large financial institutions (some highly rated, others not) are rethinking how capital and funding should be allocated to their commercial and industrial (C&I) loan business. An estimated $34 billion of securities were issued in 1997 and the market is expected to grow significantly in 1998. While some structures look like traditional asset-backed securities, others have more in common with secured borrowings, credit derivatives, or CLO hybrids. None of them, however, are quite like anything the market has seen before.

Most of what we consider to be the traditional ABS market has been built on the securitization of consumer receivables (credit cards, autos, and home equities). These assets are relatively homogenous and easily repackaged. Rating agencies are generally comfortable assigning credit enhancement levels to deals because the large number of obligors is suited to a statistical analysis. Securitization of commercial loans has been slow to catch on, but this is changing and the market could be substantial. According to recent FDIC data, these assets represent over 25% of loans in the U.S. banking system (see Exhibit 1).

We see three factors behind the recent increase in activity in the sector. First, a number of financial institutions are looking to alleviate capital pressures through asset securitization; well-diversified pools of C&I loans (especially those to U.S. borrowers) are a logical starting point. Second, recent advances in securitization technology have enabled institutions to sell loan participations without borrower notification in a manner similar to traditional ABS deals. And third, with investor demand at a record high, the ability to execute C&I transactions at levels competitive to other, more traditional asset classes, is providing a further incentive to issuers.

Copyright 1997 by Goldman Sachs

Exhibit 1: U.S. Banking Industry: Loan Portfolio Summary

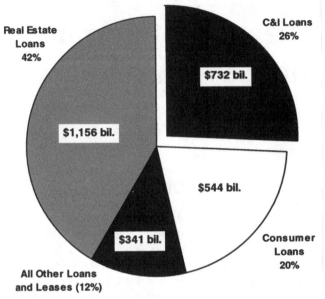

Loans and leases of insured commercial banks as of first quarter, 1997.
Source: FDIC

DISTINGUISHING COMMERCIAL LOAN SECURITIZATIONS FROM CLOs

The current generation of C&I loan securitization is quite different from its CLO/CBO predecessors, which may be more familiar to asset-backed investors. To understand C&I loan securitization, a brief review of their CBO/CLO cousins is in order. Broadly speaking, CBOs (collateralized bond obligations) and CLOs (collateralized loan obligations) are essentially secondary market arbitrage-driven securitizations. In a CLO or a CBO, a collateral manager establishes a bankruptcy-remote investment vehicle to purchase bank loans, corporate bonds, sovereign debt, or other high yielding securities. The vehicle issues asset-backed debt, and the collateral manager retains a layer of equity. The incentive for the collateral manager to do the transaction is driven by the return that can be earned on the equity layer; this will be based on the credit spread between the investment vehicle's assets (high yield loans and bonds) and its liabilities (higher quality asset-backed securities). The economics of the CLO are also influenced by the size and cost to fund the retained equity layer, as well as the market limitations associated with stringent rating agency guidelines.

There are two types of CBO/CLO transactions: cash flow and market value. In a cash flow transaction, the rating on the securities is derived from the ability to service bondholder interest and principal through cash generated by interest payments and redemptions on the underlying loans and bonds. In a market value transaction, securities issued by the investment vehicle are expected to be repaid through the sale of underlying collateral. Rating agencies require a regular marking to market of the securities in a market value transaction.

The first CBO was rated in 1988 (a transaction backed by high yield bonds); the first CLO was rated in 1990 (U.S. bank loans). Moody's estimates that about $70 billion of CBOs and CLOs have been issued to date, mostly in the private market. Volume has accelerated in recent years, fueled by low default experience in the high yield and emerging markets. And with other spread product at record tight levels, investors have been drawn to the attractive incremental yield and stable cash flows associated with CBOs and CLOs.

While CBOs and CLOs have been a part of the ABS market for quite some time, commercial loan securitizations are relatively new. Prior to 1996, securitizations of commercial loans in a traditional ABS format had been mostly limited to issuance by finance companies where the collateral is either small-business loans or secured by small and medium-size ticket equipment loans and leases. But these deals are quite different from the commercial bank loans that are now coming to market, where balances tend to be much larger, multilateral (or syndicated) facilities more common, and loan terms less standardized.

The first large-scale, non-arbitrage securitization of commercial bank loans took place at the end of 1996. The $5 billion deal was sponsored by NatWest and issued under the name R.O.S.E. Funding. A number of transactions have since followed. In our opinion, three points distinguish a commercial loan securitization from a traditional CLO transaction.

First, commercial loan securitizations are not driven by secondary market arbitrages; instead, the issuer is more likely to be motivated by capital efficiency created by funding the assets off balance sheet. These are the same reasons that would motivate a traditional ABS issuer to securitize.

Second, in a commercial loan securitization, the transaction sponsor is the underwriter/originator of the assets; in a CLO, loans are typically purchased in the secondary market. The sponsor of a commercial loan securitization therefore has a preexisting underwriting and servicing relationship with the borrower, similar to a typical consumer ABS deal. This is distinct from arbitrage CLO transactions, where the relationship between the collateral manager and the obligors is incidental and somewhat artificial based on availability of assets in the secondary market subject to rating agency diversity and credit criteria.

Third, in commercial loan securitizations, as in traditional ABS deals, loans are originated and serviced by a lender whose primary business is the granting and monitoring of credit. In a CLO, since the pool often has yet to be generated, there is more reliance on the credit quality criteria imposed by rating agencies (e.g., industry/obligor concentration limits) and the ability of the collateral manager to earn sufficient returns based on such criteria.

Exhibit 2: C&I Loan Securitization: Generic Structural Outline

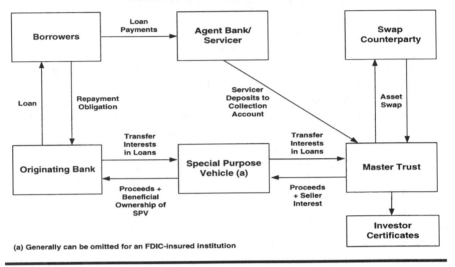

(a) Generally can be omitted for an FDIC-insured institution

A SUMMARY OF STRUCTURAL AND CREDIT ISSUES TO LOOK FOR IN A COMMERCIAL LOAN SECURITIZATION

Much of the portfolio and structural analysis behind a commercial loan securitization is not unlike the analysis used to evaluate any other asset-backed deal. Here are a few key criteria.

Insolvency Risk

Not all commercial loan securitizations are alike when it comes to seller insolvency. For ABS investors seeking to reduce third-party risks, it is essential to understand to what degree the assets are insulated from the seller's insolvency. Several highly rated European banks have executed transactions with ratings tied to those of the underlying bank. Recent trends, however, have been toward more traditional ABS structures, where investors are "de-linked" from the seller (i.e., assets are isolated from the seller in the event of insolvency). For example, a bank not regulated by the FDIC (such as a branch of a foreign bank) would generally have to use a true-sale of assets to a special purpose, bankruptcy-remote vehicle in order to achieve Aaa/AAA ratings (see Exhibit 2).

Concentration Risk

Commercial loans typically have historical loss levels that are a fraction of consumer assets. However, the larger loan balances could expose investors to less-predictable risks if not properly managed. Many deals include limitations on borrower and industry concentrations. The limits would generally apply on an ongoing basis to current assets in the pool and to any new additions.

Servicing Risk

An inexperienced seller or servicer can adversely affect the performance of any asset-backed transaction. Generally, the servicing of C&I loans is less systems-intensive than consumer assets because of higher average loan balances. Furthermore, an active secondary market for commercial loans increases the ability to liquidate non-performing assets before a default occurs.

Multilateral Versus Bilateral

There are two basic types of C&I loans: loans where the lender is acting alone (bilateral) and loans where the lender is extending credit as part of a larger syndication with other banks (multilateral). Generally, multilateral facilities diversify underwriting risk among a larger pool of lenders.

Set-Off Risk

When a borrower has a loan from a bank where it also has a deposit, if the bank becomes insolvent and the deposit is lost, the borrower may be able to reduce ("set-off") the amount of its loan repayment by the size of the forfeited deposit. Lenders can obtain waivers from borrowers with respect to set-off. Any amounts subject to set-off can be addressed similar to dilution in a credit card deal, the risks of which can be reduced by appropriately increasing the seller's interest.

Interest Rate Mismatch Risk

There are two potential sources of mismatch in a C&I structure: basis risk and spread risk. *Basis risk* arises to the extent that there is a mismatch between interest rates on the underlying loans and the floating-rate asset-backed securities. Even in C&I portfolios that are predominately floating rate, a mismatch could still occur to the extent that loans are pegged to different floating-rate indexes with different reset dates. Also, many C&I loans carry spread risk because loan terms often provide for an increase or decrease in the loan rate if a borrower's financial condition changes. Both of these risks can be eliminated or substantially reduced through the use of a swap issued by a highly rated counterparty. To protect investors from deterioration in the counterparty, swap replacement clauses and amortization events can be incorporated that are similar to swap provisions in credit card structures.

Moral Hazard

Without sufficient incentive, a lender might be expected to let a loan portfolio deteriorate once it has been sold. In C&I securitizations, like other asset-backed transactions, this risk is offset by the lender's investment in the first loss tranche of the securitization, and its ongoing right to receive regular and excess servicing income. The desire to re-access the market also provides the lender with an incentive not to "abandon" a securitized pool.

A FEW POINTS ON RELATIVE VALUE

Liquidity Premium Relative to Generic ABS Product

The market for securitized C&I loans is still in its very early stages, and, until a standard template emerges, investors will command a premium for the deal-by-deal analysis. This will eventually change, as we believe issuers (especially those rated lower than double-A) will favor a standard ABS structure that provides investors with insolvency protection. Because most transactions are executed in the 144A market and are not uniformly eligible for ERISA, investors can command a several-basis-point premium relative to generic ABS product.

Cash Flow Stability

Many C&I loan portfolios have payment rates similar to those of credit cards. Using a master trust structure (revolving period followed by accumulation/amortization), investors can expect extremely predictable cash flows. In addition, as with credit card deals, C&I revolving structures contain early amortization events to protect investors from unforeseen credit deterioration in the pool or the servicer. The triggering of early amortization would reduce a security's average life; however, the investment impact should be less of a concern since most securities are likely to be issued as floating rate.

Asset Diversification

We see the growing market for commercial loans as an excellent diversification for floating-rate ABS buyers. In the past, third-party event risk has been a drawback for many investors, but we believe this is changing in light of structural innovations. Pools backing recent deals have exhibited solid fundamentals, and we think they are approaching the effective level of borrower diversification common to more generic ABS product.

Chapter 9

Collateralized Loan Obligations: Markets and Analysis

Ronald E. Thompson Jr.
Vice President
Citicorp Securities, Inc.

Eva F.J. Yun
Associate
Citicorp Securities, Inc.

INTRODUCTION

The collateralized loan obligations (CLOs) and their forerunners, collateralized bond obligations (CBOs), clearly demonstrate the rapid innovation of the asset-backed securities market over the past few years. Structural nuances have developed, driven by issuers' purpose in creating these securities and ensuring that the securities perform as expected.

Investors may find solid yield advantages in this relatively underdeveloped and evolving asset class, along with relatively stable average lives. These securities offer an opportunity to increase incremental yield without assuming undue risk.

In the search for improved returns on investment, CLOs offer a structured solution for both investors and issuers. For investors, CLOs offer a method in which to participate in loan markets without the commensurate investment in staff and analytics to track individual loans. Investors are able to access diversified portfolios that offer non-correlated returns versus more traditional asset classes. For bank issuers of these structures, CLOs offer a method to de-lever the balance sheet by selling loans yet still participate through residual holdings and sharing of the servicing income.

The authors wish to thank David S. Blackwelder of Citicorp Securities, Inc., Darron Weinstein and Jennifer Wright of Citibank International, PLC for their helpful comments and suggestions. We also wish to thank Peg Pisani for her editorial guidance.

Exhibit 1: CLO, CBO, MV, and SLT Issuance, 1996 versus 1997* (Dollars in Billions)

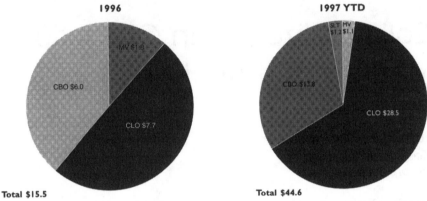

1996

1997 YTD

Total $15.5   Total $44.6

* Through October 14, 1997. CBO Collateralized bond obligation. CLO Collateralized loan obligation. MV Market value. SLT Secured loan trust.

Source: Citicorp Securities, Inc.

CASH FLOW-BACKED INVESTMENTS: GROWTH OF THE MARKET

The CLO and CBO markets have experienced tremendous growth and garnered significant notice from the investment community. While CBOs have existed for some time as leveraged equity transactions, a unified market for debt issued by these entities has grown markedly. Although CLO issuance has increased dramatically, securitized loans have encompassed only either homogeneous consumer loans or large corporate loans. Much of the growth of CLOs has been dominated by so-called *cash flow structures*. These structures utilize cash flow from, in general, buy-and-hold instruments to service the cash flow requirements of the CLO. Recently, a number of structures have included transactions that rely on the skill and timing of the portfolio manager to achieve market value gains. These "market value" transaction represent a smaller portion of the market (see Exhibit 1). Over time, CLOs are expected to incorporate a broad range of loans, including small commercial and industrial (C&I) loans.

Bolstering the development of the CLO and CBO markets has been a strong investor appetite across the globe for investment products offering better yields without incremental risk. Investors have sought alternatives to traditional markets, but often lack the resources to assess and monitor the risks embedded in these alternatives. The CLO/CBO markets frequently offer simpler methods through which investors may access higher returns, while hedging some of the exposures by using an experienced manager with economic incentives to temper risk.

Exhibit 2: CLO Transactions — Arbitrage- versus Balance Sheet-Driven Structures

Arbitrage (Investor Driven)	Balance Sheet (Issuer Driven)
Assets typically bought out of the secondary market	Originator sells assets for off-balance sheet treatment
	Regulatory rules act as catalyst; seller originates assets
More active trading	Less active trading
Manager acts as investment advisor	Originator acts as investment advisor
Manager may take only a nominal economic stake in the transaction	Originator generally retains a sizable economic stake in the transaction

Source: Citicorp Securities, Inc.

The current capital weakness of the Japanese banks will foster future CLO market development through these issuer-driven transactions as the banks seek regulatory and GAAP capital relief by reducing assets. In our view, many of the European and U.S. banks will experience intensified earnings and shareholder pressures, forcing them to sell lower-yielding assets. Thus, although the CLO market will likely mature and stabilize over time, we foresee considerable growth ahead.

INVESTOR-DRIVEN AND BALANCE SHEET-DRIVEN CLOS

Within the CLO submarket, two distinct lines have emerged based on transaction orientation: (1) the *investor-driven arbitrage transaction*; and (2) the *balance sheet-driven transaction*. Investor-driven arbitrage transactions have long dominated the market (see Exhibit 2). These transactions have been prompted by investors' desire to increase yield through investments in other, riskier markets using skilled managers who purchase distressed or par loans in the secondary market. Recently, issuers have learned to apply securitization technology to large, high-quality loans, bringing the rise of issuer/balance sheet-driven transactions. These issues tend to have loans that exhibit solid credit quality but pay below-hurdle yields for banks on-balance sheet. Banks have sought capital relief from carrying these loans by securitizing them and financing them off-balance sheet.

The CLO asset class has evolved into several subclasses, although these lines are blurring. From a cash flow and a credit standpoint, the differences are sometimes more subtle than apparent between investor-driven and balance sheet-driven transactions, but nonetheless, they remain important. For the most part, balance sheet-driven CLOs represent buy-and-hold investments in high-quality C&I loans that typically have lower default and loss severity rates than their leveraged loan and high-yield bond counterparts. However, investor-driven CLOs generally represent more actively managed asset pools.

Structurally, arbitrage and balance sheet transactions tend to have similar characteristics. Most start with a special purpose vehicle that purchases loans or bonds directly from the issuers or from the secondary market (see Exhibit 3). This vehicle may take the form of a special purpose corporation, a limited liability corporation, or a limited partnership and is typically bankruptcy-remote from other entities that may arrange or support it. The vehicle usually has strict limitations on its activities, including borrowing funds and distributing dividends. Aside from investors in the trust structure, other parties to a transaction may include a portfolio manager and/or a servicer, a trustee for asset-backed bond holders, credit enhancer(s), and, as necessary, a swap provider.

To support its capital structure, the vehicle may issue a number of classes of debt and an equity interest. Certain transactions have been structured with additional credit enhancements to bolster the rating value or to increase their marketability. Such credit enhancements may include additional equity, a mezzanine-type structure with junior lenders to the vehicle, or a surety wrap. In addition to credit enhancements, many transactions may have other protections, including excess spread or cash reserves, that bolster the credit quality of the vehicle.

The typical structure calls for a revolving period when the portfolio is actively managed, followed by an amortization period during which principal is paid to investors. To offer a more stable cash flow to investors, the structure may include a lock-out on principal payments, which builds cash reserves through excess spread generated by the cash flows in the vehicle. These structures generally restrict trading.[1] Many of the structures may offer partial or early-amortization triggers, which enhance principal protection but may increase reinvestment risk for investors.

Exhibit 3: Simplified CLO Structure

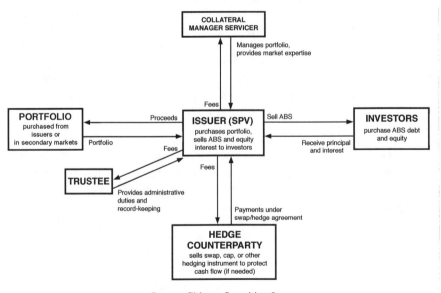

Source: Citicorp Securities, Inc.

[1] Trading in these types of CLOs generally is limited to loan credit improvement, price improvement, or credit impairment.

Another type of structure, a so-called "market-value" transaction, derives its income not only from investment interest on invested assets, but also from trading strategies that may draw heavily on market timing and valuation. Because this asset class uses an actively managed, leveraged equity strategy, it deserves extensive analysis of the portfolio manager to perform in all types of markets and conditions within the manager's abilities and constraints. Under the market-value structure, the underlying assets supporting the transaction will likely change dramatically from those present at the initial offering. These structures may purchase distressed loan assets in the secondary market and aggressively trade the loans based on potential price improvements. Many of these structures carry provisions to invest in various types of assets.

Another recent innovation is in the alternative collateral CLO or secured loan trust. This structure is similar to a cash flow CLO, but instead of buying loans for cash, it uses total return swaps with counterparties that are long a desired portfolio. This structure allows the counterparties to reduce exposures to particular markets without selling the portfolio. Conversely, the trust cuts execution costs by entering into swaps rather than purchasing the underlying assets.

BALANCE SHEET-DRIVEN CLO MARKET — OFFERING A CAPITAL AND MARKET ARBITRAGE FOR BANKS

The balance sheet-driven CLO market has undergone tremendous growth as banks have sought to arbitrage their risk-based capital requirements for markets where investors require less equity. While banks have other constraints such as tax, legal, confidentiality, and accounting practices, the primary driver for issuers lies in the capital required to support loans. Many of the structures target 2%-3% "capital" through the sale of a junior tranche or retention of the seller's equity piece.

In bank balance-sheet securitizations, issuers structure the CLO to obtain regulatory and/or GAAP capital relief, targeting 2%-3% "equity" versus 8% for on balance sheet. Under Bank of International Settlements (BIS) risk-based capital requirements, banks must hold capital against assets based on risk weighting. Currently, banks must hold 8% Tier 1 capital (a combination of tangible common equity and certain types of preferred securities) against loans, which are counted with a 100% risk weighting.

In the United States, the Federal Financial Institutions Examination Council recently proposed changing the capital allocation rules for banks holding investment-grade and other rated securities. This change may accelerate the development of these securitizations because of banks' ability to arbitrage the capital rules for loans. To generate a 15% return for shareholders, a bank using an 8% equity-to-assets ratio must produce a 1.2% return on assets. If banks are able to hold a 20%-risk asset for a AAA-rated CLO versus a 100%-risk asset for a loan, the required return drops from 1.2% to 0.3% on regulatory accounting principles (RAP) assets. This lower funding cost enables banks to rechannel resources to seek out higher-risk assets for origination and portfolio.

Exhibit 4: Credit-Linked Note Sale to Issuers — Advantages and Disadvantages

Advantages	Disadvantages
BIS capital relief	Rating linked to originator/issuer
Administratively simple/flexible	Unsecured debt capacity diminished
Funding costs comparable to a participation-interest CLO	Structure only for highly rated banks
	More expensive than "true sale" CLO
No borrower notification requirement	No GAAP benefit

Source: Citicorp Securities, Inc.

Exhibit 5: SBC Glacier Finance Ltd. — Credit-Linked Note Program Structure

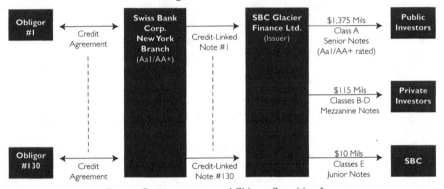

Source: Company reports and Citicorp Securities, Inc.

Credit-Linked Notes: Regulatory Relief But No GAAP Benefit

Recently, the traditional CLO market began to include new asset types such as derivatives and fee receivables. Many of these exposures are linked to the trust through credit-linked notes rather than a true sale of assets. This sale of notes provides RAP capital relief, but offers no GAAP benefit. However, other benefits (see Exhibit 4), such as no borrower approval requirements, create for issuers a simpler and cleaner structure than that of traditional CLOs. These structures are similar to issuer-offered credit derivatives, but allow for a blended "sale" of exposure in an investor-blind pool.

SBC Warburg launched the first of these synthetic CLOs in 1997 with a $1.7 billion offering of a vehicle known as SBC Glacier Finance Ltd. (see Exhibit 5). Through the offering, SBC Warburg sold credit exposure to a portfolio referenced to more than 100 of its investment-grade borrowers in a five-tranche structure. This structure references credit exposures through the trust, rather than sell participations in bank loans in the traditional structure. In both structures, investors bear risk to the pooled risk, but, for the credit-linked notes structure, they do not own the bank loans, merely the references to them. No "true-sale" opinion, which is critical to obtaining off-balance sheet treatment for GAAP purposes, may be obtained because the credit-linked notes reference the loans as opposed to owning an interest in them. Therefore, the strength and ratings of credit-linked notes structure depend heavily on the strength and ratings of the issuer.

AN ANALYTICAL FRAMEWORK

To examine the CLO market, investors should use an analytical framework to identify relative value between issues (see Exhibit 6). In an analytical framework, investors may utilize a top-down analytical approach that focuses first on macro issues, then considers the peculiarities and nuances of each structure. We believe that this approach ferrets out the quality of the issue and enables the analyst to assign weights for pricing decisions. When analyzing balance sheet and investor-driven CLOs, most investors consider similar variables, but the reliance and weighting given to each factor differentiates the two asset types. While disclosure details vary from transaction to transaction, investors should try to evaluate as many of these as practicable. In any case, the analysis of the issuer/servicer and portfolio manager ranks as the primary fundamental factor or parties, followed by an analysis of the portfolio investment parameters and constraints.

As with any asset-backed investment using a top-down strategy, investors generally focus the first analysis on the economic conditions that may drive or hinder the market for the underlying collateral. Next, investors evaluate several key areas pertinent to each transaction. We have outlined a number of these areas and an approach to evaluating each one.

Exhibit 6: Collateralized Loan Obligation (CLO) Investments —
Analytical Framework

Balance Sheet CLO	Arbitrage CLO
Originator/Servicer/Manager	Portfolio Manager
Structure Analysis/Credit Enhancement Review	Structure Analysis/Credit Enhancement Review
Collateral Credit Analysis	Collateral Credit Analysis
· Underwriting Criteria	Weighted-Average Credit Rating
· Portfolio Heterogeneity	Weighted-Average Maturity
· Event of Default Actions	Default Analysis
Weighted-Average Credit Rating	· Default Probability
Weighted-Average Maturity	· Default Severity
Default Analysis	Cash Flow Analysis
· Default Probability	Amortization Trigger Events
· Default Severity	Prefunding Amounts and Periods
Cash Flow Analysis	Redemption Rights (Optional/Mandatory)
Legal Considerations	Legal Considerations

Source: Citicorp Securities, Inc., Duff and Phelps Credit Rating Co., Fitch Investors Service, LP,
Moody's Investor Service, Inc., and Standard & Poor's.

Originator/Servicer/Portfolio Manager

Most investors focus first on the abilities of the asset manager or servicer. In arbitrage (investor-driven) CLO transactions, this analysis is crucial to establish potential manager risk from poor market timing and valuation decisions. In most balance sheet (issuer-driven) CLOs, much of the credit hinges on the issuing bank's ratings and its reputation risk if actions in the portfolio were to prove sour; thus, the question may arise whether the issuer is likely to intervene. Therefore, investors should feel comfortable with the quality and credit judgment of the issuing bank.

Structure Analysis/Credit Enhancement Review

After the investor is satisfied with the abilities of the portfolio manager or originator/servicer, the structure and attendant credit enhancement should receive solid scrutiny to ascertain cash flow waterfalls[2] for interest and principal, prepayment conditions and triggers, the rights and roles of senior tranches and credit enhancement, reserve account requirements, and allocation methods for defaults and recoveries. Credit enhancement generally takes several forms including excess spread, surety wraps, reserve accounts, and subordinate pieces.

Collateral Credit Analysis

The extent and type of collateral analysis depends on the type of structure analyzed. In balance sheet CLO transactions, portfolio collateral tends to be less heterogeneous and of higher quality than in investor-driven transactions and underlying assets trade less frequently, if at all. Therefore, investors need to focus on three areas: underwriting criteria and skills, portfolio heterogeneity, and actions undertaken on behalf of asset-backed holders in the event of default. Underwriting quality and parameters are fundamental to this analysis, but investors need to feel comfortable with the originating bank's approach, its markets, and its skill in curing faults. Many of these CLO transactions have "lumpy" collateral. In many cases, the investors purchase increments smaller than the average loan size, and therefore, depend on the issuer's skill in selecting a diverse pool of loans. Conversely, in arbitrage-type CLOs, the collateral is generally traded and is unlikely to remain the same from period to period. Therefore, investors should examine the investment parameters and restrictions on the portfolio manager and his track record with similar constraints.

Weighted-Average Credit Rating and Maturity

As part of CLO reviews, investors focus next on loss rates that could stress the portfolio. This analysis determines the proper size of the credit enhancement, but also points out stress scenarios that may trigger early-amortization events. Under early amortization, investors may face reinvestment risk as the portfolio pays out. Therefore, several default scenarios should be run, examining the effect of the credit enhancement and on the prepayment triggers.

---

[2] "Cash flow waterfall" is a descriptive term in asset-backed securities used to refer to the allocation of interest and principal to each tranche in a series. If excess cash flows are allowed to be shared with other series, then the cash flows are reallocated through the "waterfall," cascading back through the tranches.

Prepayment events would not be as highly correlated with interest rates as negatively convex products such as mortgage pass-throughs, but a recessionary environment may cause credit deterioration while prompting declining interest rates. Compounding the issue may be imbedded calls by issuers. Therefore, investors should review these events in light of several interest rate scenarios in their cash flow analysis.

Default Analysis

We recommend that investors use a combination of rating agency approaches to develop default scenarios. For example, the approaches by Moody's and Standard & Poor's segregate the two underlying factors fundamental to default analysis: (1) probably of default, and (2) severity. While the first factor is easy to conceptualize, the latter incorporates recovery rates by asset type (senior bank loans rank higher in priority after defaults and therefore have higher recovery rates than unsecured debt, for example). This second variable may be expanded or contracted based on economic outlook. However, the combination of probability and severity determine cash flows within the trust and may accelerate or extend the expected maturity.

Another component of the Moody's approach incorporates a diversity score, in an attempt to evaluate the underlying collinearity of the credits in the pool. Each credit in the portfolio is classified by industry groupings — a total of 32 groups under the Moody's model — credit in each industry group, a certain value is assigned. Each subsequent credit in the same industry is assigned a diminishing value. For example, five different credits in five different industries may be each assigned a value of one point for a total diversity score of 5.00 points. Each second credit added to each industry may be assigned a value of 0.50 points, and each third credit added to an industry group may be assigned a value of 0.25 points, and so on.

A higher value in this diversity index indicates greater diversity within the underlying collateral pool. Balance sheet transactions generally exhibit greater diversity than arbitrage deals, because they are less actively managed. Typically, balance sheet deals have indexes of 70-80, while arbitrage deals typically start with indexes of 35-40. Investors should be cautious about relying only on diversity scores because diversity scores are not dollar-weighted and may lead to credit concentrations despite the appearance of a balanced portfolio; therefore, investors should ascertain and evaluate portfolio exposure limits to any one industry or credit. While most transactions do not let investors monitor individual credits in the managed pool, investors can and should monitor diversity scores and adherence to portfolio guidelines.

Cash Flow Analysis

Incorporating many of the default parameters and remedies, investors generally next focus on cash-flow scenario analysis, ensuring that the effects of cash-flow waterfalls in normal and distressed scenarios are tested and compared against total returns in varying interest rate scenarios. While this process is generally less vigorous for floating-rate transactions than for fixed-rate ones, investors look at forward rates to determine reinvestment risk expectations.

Other Considerations

For many transactions, investors consider the implications of other features, such as prepayment triggers for ratings or default changes, bankruptcy remoteness of the vehicles, dependence on issuer ratings, prefunding amounts, whether CLO securities are callable and by whom, and rights for investors under stressful scenarios to change portfolio managers or to collapse the structure.

THE ECONOMICS OF CLOS — AN EXAMPLE

A CLO transaction is, at its essence, an arbitrage: either a market, capital or regulatory arbitrage. For example, bank-issued balance sheet-driven CLOs are basically regulatory arbitrages. Banks are driven by regulatory discipline to maintain certain levels of capital to support their loan books, whereas CLOs are driven by market discipline to develop and maintain sufficient capital or its market costs will rise. If market demands are lower than regulatory ones, a bank's return on capital is enhanced by securitizing assets for sale to investors.

The economics of a investor-driven, cash flow CLO are fairly simple. To examine a market arbitrage transaction, an example may help explain the dynamics. (See Exhibit 7.) We start with an investor that may wish to obtain return exposure to the funded, high-yield loan market. While returns may be high, the investor may multiply the return by leveraging the investment and betting on default performance. The spread difference between the investment-grade market and the high-yield loan market may be such that this leverage magnifies the return.

In our example, we start with an investor who wants to place $40 million into the high-yield market. The investor works with an arranger to create a trust (usually in a tax-friendly country). Nominally capitalizing the trust, this investor seeds the newly created trust with the $40 million as a junior tranche (Class B) noteholder. The arranger seeks out investment-grade investors looking for above-average yields, but highly-rated risk.

We assume that our exemplary trust has a reinvestment period of five years, with an expected seven-year average life. Principal is reinvested for five years, then paid out on straight-line basis, first to the Class A noteholders, then to the Class B noteholders. Using a debt-to-equity gearing of seven to one, the trust issues $280 million of senior notes which are wrapped by a surety. The notes receive a Aaa/AAA rating because of the wrap and $40-million junior tranche. If the combined $320-million portfolio is assumed to earn 9.5% with defaults of 50 basis points and the Class A noteholders demand some premium to Treasuries, the transaction in our example yields the Class B investor $9.2 million annually during the portfolio's reinvestment period. After the reinvestment period, the returns drop and the effect of any portfolio deterioration is heightened as the transaction's leverage and resulting income fall.

Exhibit 7: Economics of a Typical CLO Transaction

Transaction During Reinvestment Period (Dollars in Millions)

	Amount	Rate	Annual Income/(Expense)
Portfolio	$320	9.50%	$30.4
Assumed Defaults*		0.50%	(1.6)
Class A Notes	$280	6.75%	(18.9)
			$9.9
Expenses**			2.2
Residual Available to Class B Notes			$7.7
Annual Rate of Return			19.4%

Transaction During Reinvestment and Amortizatlon Periods (Dollars in Millions)

	Reinvest Period	Amortization Period			
	Years 1-5	Year 6	Year 7	Year 8	Year 9
Portfolio Balance	$320	$240	$160	$80	$0
Class A Notes	280	200	120	40	0
Portfolio Income	$30.4	$26.6	$19.0	$11.4	$3.8
Defaults*	(1.6)	(1.4)	(1.0)	(0.6)	(0.2)
Class A Note Interest	(18.9)	(16.2)	(10.8)	(5.4)	(1.4)
	9.9	9.0	7.2	5.4	2.3
Expenses**	(2.2)	(1.9)	(1.5)	(1.1)	(0.6)
Residual Available	$7.7	$7.1	$5.7	$4.3	1.6$
Annual Rate of Return	19.4%	17.7%	14.3%	10.9%	5.4%

* Defaults are assumed to be 50 bps of the average balance outstanding through the life of the transaction.

** Expenses are assumed to be 55bps of the outstanding portfolio plus $400,000.

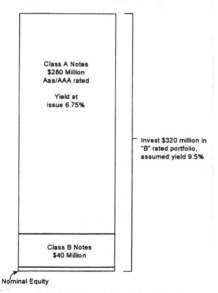

Class A Notes
$280 Million
Aaa/AAA rated

Yield at
issue 6.75%

Invest $320 million in
"B" rated portfolio,
assumed yield 9.5%

Class B Notes
$40 Million

Nominal Equity

Source: Citicorp Securities, Inc.

If the Class B noteholder has the right to call the senior class, it often will call the senior notes to limit its exposure to losses. Also, as the transaction de-levers, the returns fall relative to the Class B principal outstanding. Therefore, investors in the senior securities generally look for a make-whole premium to offset a call.

CONCLUSION

Investors looking to gain exposure to alternative market sectors or asset classes can use CLOs to create cost-effective returns from these markets. Using a portfolio manager to focus on a particular sector where the investor lacks expertise can improve yields, without incurring incremental costs to establish and maintain large infrastructures to manage alternative investment risk. Accordingly, high-grade investors can access incremental yields through this market without incurring substantial incremental risk.

Chapter 10

Corporate Loan Portfolio Management

Elliot Asarnow
Managing Director
ING Capital Advisors

Michael McAdams
Managing Director
ING Capital Advisors

INTRODUCTION

The management of portfolios of corporate loans (by which we mean floating-rate senior secured loans primarily to non-investment grade corporations) is a relatively new and growing area of portfolio management. Traditionally, loans to corporations were originated by banks acting either individually, in a series of bilateral arrangements with the borrower or as part of a "club" which shared the loan. In each of these cases, corporate loans were the exclusive domain of banks participating in a private quasi-market with essentially no secondary liquidity. The lending banks were hand-picked by the borrower on the basis of long-term lending relationships.

Given the number, size and non-investment grade nature of transactions, the wave of corporate restructurings, strategic acquisitions, and leveraged buy-outs of the late 1980s inevitably contributed to the development of a professionalized syndication market for corporate loans. The syndicate members were still overwhelmingly banks, but at this time a small number of retail mutual funds emerged which specialized in managing portfolios of corporate loans. Indeed, one of the authors of this chapter was the founding manager of the first such fund. This configuration of market participants continued through the early 1990s. In the past few years, non-bank investors including retail mutual funds as well as insurance companies, hedge funds, and other institutionally oriented asset management firms such as our own have experienced rapid growth in loan assets under management.

While the syndicated corporate loan market remains predominantly an inter-bank market, the influence of non-bank investors is apparent. Most obvious is the emergence of longer-dated delayed amortization tranches as a standard feature in senior secured loan transactions. These tranches were designed specifically for non-bank investors who are concerned that their funds will remain fully

171

invested as opposed to banks who typically prefer more rapid amortization. Stimulated by the growth in number of non-bank investors as well as the accelerating development and acceptance of portfolio management practices by banks, the secondary market for syndicated loans has rapidly expanded.

In light of the dramatic growth and evolution of the bank loan market and increased institutional investor participation, this chapter describes a corporate loan portfolio management process which can be applied by non-bank investors. We also draw comparisons with the high yield bond market, as well as the manner in which commercial banks generally approach the corporate loan market.

CORPORATE LOAN MARKET VERSUS HIGH YIELD BOND MARKET

Some observers believe that a convergence of markets is occurring as investors freely move between the high yield bond market, the corporate loan market, and even the private placement market seeking to maximize relative value. And indeed there are additional signs of increasing market convergence apart from the increased liquidity of corporate loans and overlapping investor bases. These additional signs include the determined efforts of the major rating agencies to gain market acceptance for corporate loan ratings, the emergence of the Loan Syndication and Traders Association with a primary goal of standardizing key market practices such as settlement procedures and valuation, and the growth of loan-based derivatives such as total return swaps.

There are, however, structural features which can be expected to continue to distinguish, for example, the high yield bond and corporate loan markets. Not the least of these is differences in the instruments themselves, including for loans and bonds respectively floating versus fixed rate, senior versus subordinated, secured versus unsecured, unrestricted prepayment versus call protection, and revolving credits and term loans versus only fully funded instruments. As would be expected, these differences in senior secured loans versus subordinated bonds have fundamental portfolio management implications.

For both loans and high yield bonds the dominant form of risk is default loss. Therefore, in both cases the emphasis is on fundamental credit analysis focused on the issuer's prospects of generating sufficient cash flow to service debt. However, since loans are senior and secured and have various covenant protections, much additional analysis focuses on the nature, value, and liquidity of collateral, which is viewed as the "second way out" in the event of the borrower's inability to repay debt from cash flow, as well as on the completeness of the covenant package and the structure and trigger levels of individual covenants. Covenants serve, among other things, to restrict undesirable actions by the issuer (e.g., incurring additional debt) and to establish performance standards (e.g., minimum interest coverage ratios) which if not met give investors the standing to take early corrective action.

Whereas high yield bonds are exposed to two fundamental forms of risk, default loss risk and interest rate risk, loans are only exposed to default loss risk. Therefore duration in the traditional sense is not an important consideration in analyzing corporate loans. Even the prepayment risk in loans is not primarily a function of the absolute level of interest rates but rather of changes in issuer credit quality and general required spread levels in the market. In fact, to the extent that most loans are sold in the primary market at a discount (that is, at "par" minus a share of the agent bank's origination fees which is paid to the investor), prepayment accelerates taking the discount into income and thereby improves the total return received by the investor.

LOAN PORTFOLIO MANAGEMENT AT BANKS

Prior to outlining a model loan portfolio management process, one further issue needs to be addressed, namely the contrast between loan portfolio management as practiced by commercial banks and by non-banks. In almost all commercial banks the approach to portfolio management, even of syndicated loans, is dramatically different than that practiced by non-banks.

Most commercial banks define their strategic approach to corporate banking as that of relationship management. The premise is that by developing long-term lending relationships with its clients a bank can successfully market multiple products to them and thus maximize its overall profitability. A corollary to this strategy is that banks tend to be buy-and-hold investors. They are inhibited in selling their loans due to the appearance that they may be reducing their commitment to a client, which could lead to a decline in non-lending business from the client. A further corollary is that banks tend not to be as sensitive about loan pricing as non-bank investors since they view loan pricing in the context of the overall profitability of a client relationship, and performance measurement and compensation related to loan portfolio management per se tend to be vague or even dysfunctional (e.g., by rewarding volume and not controlling sufficiently for risk-adjusted return and by using accrual accounting, a lagging indicator, rather than mark-to-market measurement procedures).

Another defining strategy of bank lenders is the tendency to focus on a limited number of industries or geographic areas in order to establish a competitive advantage in their marketing and loan origination efforts. This specialization, which may constitute a strength from an origination perspective, almost ensures that the bank will originate loans in those industries or geographies since that is what the specialized lenders are being paid to do. When combined with a relationship management strategy, the overwhelming tendency is to hold disproportionately large exposures to these self-originated loans, resulting in highly concentrated exposures to selected industries and geographies on the bank's balance sheet, which is clearly not desirable from a pure loan portfolio management perspective.

The bank may derive comfort in the face of these concentrations from the depth of its credit expertise in its specialized industries. However, one need only look at the experience of many southwestern institutions in the late 1970s which failed or are no longer independent entities despite their previously renowned lending expertise in energy and real estate. In short, concentrations of exposure no matter what the reason are still concentrations and should be minimized.

NON-BANK PORTFOLIO MANAGEMENT PROCESS

The loan portfolio management process we will describe below is that which we employ. This process is most applicable for non-banks given the way commercial banks are structurally organized and strategically focused. While a number of banks have made significant improvements to their loan portfolio management processes in the past few years, some of the structural barriers described in the previous section cannot be avoided and fundamentally shape the types of controls and analytic tools that are needed to support the process in ways that are not always applicable to non-banks.

Loan Acquisition

The portfolio management process we employ can be described as a market-tempered credit process. While each loan purchase is viewed as a potential long-term portfolio position and is subjected to the full evaluation process, the immediate and short-term view of the loan by the market is a valuable input into each investment decision. Additionally, each loan in the portfolio, even if it was expected to be a long-term hold when purchased, is always available for sale based on market conditions as well as on an ongoing assessment of credit quality.

Maximize Deal Flow

The foundation of the process is to always have available a wide selection of viable investment opportunities for each investment that must be made. Maintaining a strong flow of investment opportunities from a wide range of sources helps to increase diversification and reduces the likelihood that a less-than-desirable loan will be purchased merely because it is the best of a bad lot. In the corporate loan market, stimulating the flow of investment opportunities can involve developing relationships with U.S. branches of foreign banks, regional banks, and finance companies in addition to the money center banks who dominate the loan syndication market. The process can be facilitated by employing a buy-side trader.

Preliminary Screening

As with any other portfolio managed on behalf of third parties, the available opportunities are then screened for compliance with the prospectus/investment management agreement, both at an individual transaction level in terms of permissibility and return potential, and at a portfolio level with regard to concentration limits such as those for individual issuers and industries. Apart from considering contractual concentration limits, the senior portfolio manager will typically have a view of the macro-economy and various industries which translates into portfolio-level criteria such as the desired degree of issuer-level diversification and the desired portfolio weights of specific industries or groups of industries. More issuer-level diversification can reduce the risk of extraordinary losses due to a recession. If the senior portfolio manager is especially concerned about a particular factor such as oil prices or interest rates, he will seek to reduce aggregate exposure to industries that share a high sensitivity to that factor.

An important function of the preliminary screening is to reduce the number of loans that are then subjected to the in-depth credit analysis that follows. This credit analysis focuses on default risk, i.e., the possibility that a company will be unable to service its debt, and is essentially the same as that conducted by well-disciplined commercial banks and high yield bond and private placement analysts. Again, the absence of structural barriers relative to banks is an important advantage. In non-banks, an enormous amount of experience and information can accumulate within a small group whose composition tends to remain intact, that sees essentially all the major transactions in the market, that has short lines of communication, clear authority, unambiguous and appropriate performance measures and a relative absence of structural frictions such as those caused by having narrowly defined origination groups. Critically, rewards for staff are based on portfolio total return and volatility minimization over time, not merely on volume.

Credit Analysis

The credit analysis is conducted on both a top-down as well as a bottom-up basis. The top-down analysis includes the articulation of a view of the macro-economy and an analysis of the prospects of a given industry in light of the macro-economic view and broader competitive considerations. The bottom-up analysis considers numerous factors, such as the issuer's longevity, size, product diversification, competitive position in its target markets, competitive exposure to changes in technology, fashion and regulation, susceptibility to specific macro-economic factors, quality of management, and its business and financial strategy.

Apart from the fundamental analysis of the issuer's business, detailed analysis is conducted on the issuer's financial statements. This includes adjusting the financial statements to reflect economic reality, for example with respect to actual or contingent off-balance sheet assets or liabilities or with respect to extraordinary earnings, as well as ratio analysis (e.g., capital structure, interest coverage) and trend analysis (e.g., historical earnings growth). Since there is limited potential for appreciation with non-distressed loans, the search is for issuers with good prospects for stable or slowly growing earnings rather than for issuers with expected rapid earnings growth as might appeal to an equity investor.

Accordingly, stress test analysis at the individual issuer level plays an important role since it is explicitly focused on the risk of a cash flow shortfall. Forecasted base case financial statements are developed, possibly taking into account projections from company management, and various downside scenarios are tested, often based on the performance of the company or industry peers in prior difficult periods. An assessment of management, its strategy, and the implications for the company of competitive and macro-economic issues are normally made through personal due diligence visits and meetings with management (typically, but not exclusively, as part of the agent bank-arranged syndication process). Evaluating specific industry issues, facility modernity or product developments may require plant tours which may be supplemented or supplanted by the analysts' prior firsthand knowledge of the issues.

Analysis of Collateral, Structure, and Covenants

At this point, the loan's collateral is analyzed from a valuation, liquidity, and legal perspective. The significance of collateral should not be underestimated. It is the key to the superior recovery rates of senior secured bank loans in the event of payment default. In a recent Moody's study, the recovery rate for defaulted senior secured bank loans averaged 71% by one method and 79% using a different method.[1] This contrasts with average recovery rates of 34% for subordinated bonds and 46% for senior debentures.

Collateral for senior secured loans can run the gamut from claims on customer receivables to finished goods inventory, plant and equipment, intangibles such as trademarks, copyrights and patents, and the stock of operating subsidiaries. Legal issues may include assuring that the investor has perfected liens on key assets and that those assets would not transfer undue legal (e.g., product liability) or regulatory (e.g., environmental) risk to the investor. Ongoing business value is determined in the usual manner, i.e., by discounted cash flow analysis and examination of comparables. For key assets the investors individually or as a group may obtain appraisals. In all cases, the collateral analysis needs to be incorporated into a contingency plan for disposing of the business and/or its assets in the event of a distressed situation.

Ongoing Monitoring and Rebalancing

Together with the collateral analysis, the structure of the loan is analyzed to determine if the investor is at risk of being structurally subordinated while having the appearance of being in a senior secured position. This can occur, for example, when a loan that is extended to a holding company is secured by the stock of the operating companies but where other investors have prior claims on the assets of the operating companies.

---

[1]   Lea V. Carty and Dana Lieberman, "Defaulted Bank Loan Recoveries," *Moody's Investors Service Special Report* (November 1996).

It is then appropriate also to consider the experience and reputation of the agent and co-agents for the loan and, at times, even the composition of the bank group. An inexperienced group of lenders voting in majority to take actions against the wishes of a few more experienced lenders can be a material problem that is relatively unique to loan syndicates.

As stated earlier, additional analysis is conducted on the loan's covenants to determine the completeness of the covenant package and the structure and trigger levels of individual covenants. Again, the objective is to ensure that the intended loan structure is maintained and that in the event of unanticipated developments the lenders can take action promptly to maximize the likelihood of full repayment.

Incorporating Market Feedback

If a loan passes the preceding tests, it is still subject to further scrutiny from a market-based perspective. The trader provides market feedback as to credit risk issues and investor demand for the loan and thus probable liquidity. Negative sentiment in the market is taken very seriously, at a minimum leading to a re-evaluation of the credit and often a reversal of the previous favorable conclusion. Weak investor demand, even if not based on credit risk concerns, can also lead to a rejection or reduced purchase size of a loan due to concerns about subsequent liquidity. Conversely, if strong demand is observed, a larger purchase may be desirable, both because of concern about receiving a smaller-than-requested allocation in the syndication and because of the opportunity to generate a capital gain by selling a portion of the loan into the secondary market at a later date. At this point relative value considerations also come to the fore as the expected return of the loan is compared to other available opportunities of similar risk. Other considerations include the likelihood and timing of closing the purchase as a result of deal-specific documentation complexities; a loan whose risk/return is acceptable may need to be re-evaluated if the purchase cannot be completed in a reasonable time.

Quantitative Tools

Quantitative tools also can be helpful at this point in the process. An objective, statistically-validated debt rating model can help in assigning debt ratings while a loan pricing model can be useful in calculating the fair value of a loan in light of the many features that can distinguish two loans that may be similar in terms of general factors such as debt rating, industry, and tenor.

Fluid Process, Formal Documentation

Throughout the purchase analysis, there are frequent discussions among the various team members as a consensus is developed about a particular loan, with the senior portfolio manager making the ultimate decision in the event a consensus does not emerge. These fluid discussions provide most of the advantages of a formal credit committee, in terms of reality testing and probing by a group of peers, while avoiding most of the disadvantages, such as long lines of communication, potential rigidity, political interference, and diffusion of responsibility. The key considerations leading to the purchase of a loan are formally documented in a credit memo together with the extensive supporting financial analysis.

The ongoing monitoring of the loan portfolio and individual loans benefits from a rich flow of information from many sources, particularly for those issuers who also have public securities outstanding. In the latter case, the portfolio managers are likely to have access to research reports of high yield bond and equity analysts as well as to more widely available public information. Clearly there is great value to be derived from observing the trading prices and patterns of the issuers' public securities. However, the unique aspects of managing a corporate loan portfolio pertain to the access to non-public information. This information may include the issuer's own forecasted financial statements, more frequent actual financial statements than are reported publicly, periodic collateral valuations, and detailed covenant calculations with supporting data. This information is disseminated to the bank group by the agent bank, which is one of the banks that played a lead role in the original syndication and which serves the equivalent of a trustee function thereafter. In addition, an important tool of investors is that generally they have direct access to the issuer's senior management for questions about financial performance and strategy and are consulted on corporate actions or performance that may cause covenant violations.

Reassessing Hold Positions

The desired position size of each loan is continually reassessed in light of the loan's perceived relative value in the market and the portfolio managers' dynamic, fundamental view of the credit. In the great majority of cases, execution simply means to buy, hold or sell. In the case of problem credits including defaults, the portfolio manager must also consider various possible workout scenarios, including restructuring the loan to avoid a bankruptcy filing or the potential outcomes of a bankruptcy proceeding as well as the implications of these scenarios for the fair value of the loan. The portfolio manager may sell and accept a limited loss if he believes the market has not yet fully discounted the loan. In other cases, the portfolio manager may judge that he can realize greater value by riding the loan through the workout. This conclusion may result from the manager's belief that the benefit of senior secured status may provide for repayment of the senior bank debt in full despite default or bankruptcy.

Workouts

Workouts are lead by the administrative agent bank, which generally would be expected to maintain a position in the loan in its own portfolio to encourage the alignment of its economic interests with those of other holders. The agent's intimate involvement and direct economic stake in the credit from its inception stand in sharp contrast to the traditional role of a bond trustee. Apart from the lead role played by the agent bank, it is common for the other loan investors to take a more active role in workouts than is usual for corporate bond investors.

Feedback from Operations Staff

Operations support does not normally enter discussions of portfolio management. However, given the complex, dynamic and non-public nature of loans, feedback from the operations staff to the portfolio managers is vital. Since interest payment periods are reset repeatedly and may frequently change in length over the life of a single loan, the portfolio manager must rely on the operations staff to call attention to late interest or principal payments. Even a subtlety such as a change in interest rate basis can be significant. If the issuer switches from LIBOR to prime-based pricing, it may well be that the issuer plans to refinance the loan soon and wishes to avoid paying possible LIBOR breakage costs. Unusually heavy usage of a revolving credit facility may be an early warning of liquidity problems associated with declining credit quality.

Also crucial is the role of the operations staff in initial trade compliance, monitoring portfolio concentrations and ensuring that all required information, much of which is non-public, is provided as scheduled by the issuer and the administrative agent bank. Repeated delays by an issuer in providing information may be another indication of a developing problem, whether in the area of systems or credit.

Completing the Circle

With the description of the ongoing monitoring and management of the portfolio, we have come to the conclusion of the portfolio management process. However, the conclusion of the process is linked to the beginning of the process in a type of feedback loop. From a zero-based budget perspective, on any given day loans in the portfolio that are not sold have implicitly been repurchased. Thus, the portfolio manager's views on the macro-economy and industries, among other considerations, are applied to the existing portfolio as well as to prospective new loans. In effect, the opportunity set is a combination of existing portfolio loans as well as available loans in the market, with as little bias as possible placed on retaining existing portfolio loans. This perspective helps provide the basis for a selling discipline, which is well known to be one of the most difficult aspects of managing any portfolio. Finally, to fully close the loop, the emphasis on maintaining a strong flow of investment opportunities that was noted earlier encourages adherence to a buying and selling discipline, both psychologically as well as economically, by reducing the likelihood that a less-than-desirable loan will be held only because of a lack of attractive alternatives.

Chapter 11
Credit Derivatives in Bank Loan Management

Mark J. P. Anson, Ph.D., CFA, CPA
Portfolio Manager
OppenheimerFunds, Inc.

INTRODUCTION

Credit derivatives are financial instruments which are designed to transfer the credit exposure of an underlying asset or issuer between two or more parties. They are individually negotiated financial contracts which may take the form of options, swaps, forwards, or credit-linked notes where the payoffs are linked to, or derived from, the credit characteristics of a referenced asset or borrower. With credit derivatives, a portfolio manager can either acquire or hedge credit risk.

Most large commercial banks consider syndicated loans as part of a broader client relationship and these relationships may influence a bank to accept excess credit exposure with respect to a particular client. Credit derivatives offer an efficient way to hedge this exposure. Conversely, institutional investors may use credit derivatives to target specific exposures as a way to enhance portfolio returns. In each case, the ability to transfer credit risk and return provides a new tool for bank managers and portfolio mangers to improve performance.

We begin this chapter with a short discussion on the role of credit risk in the commercial loan market. We then review the four main types of credit derivatives: credit options, credit forwards, credit swaps, and credit-linked notes. We describe their structure and consider their practical applications. Lastly, we discuss some important risks associated with the use of these new derivatives.

CREDIT RISK AND THE BANK LOAN MARKET

A commercial loan investment represents a basket of risks. There is the risk from changes in interest rates (duration and convexity risk), the risk that the borrower will refinance the debt issue (call risk) and lastly, the risk of defaults, downgrades, and widening credit spreads (credit risk). The total return from a commercial loan is the compensation for assuming all of these risks. Depending upon the rating on the borrower, the return from credit risk can be a significant part of the total return.

The corporate bank loan market typically consists of syndicated loans to large and mid-sized corporations. They are floating-rate instruments, often priced in relation to LIBOR. Corporate loans may be either revolving credits (known as revolvers) that are legally committed lines of credit, or term loans that are fully funded commitments with fixed amortization schedules. Term loans tend to be concentrated in the lower credit rated corporations because revolvers usually serve as backstops for commercial paper programs of fiscally sound companies. Therefore, this chapter will primarily focus on the application of credit derivatives to term bank loans.

Term bank loans are repriced periodically. Because of their floating interest rate nature, they have reduced market risk resulting from fluctuating interest rates. Consequently, credit risk takes on greater importance in determining a commercial loan's total return.

Over the past several years, the bank loan market and the high yield bond market have begun to converge. This is due partly to the relaxing of commercial banking regulations which has allowed many banks to increase their product offerings, including high yield bonds. Contemporaneously, investment banks and brokerage firms have established loan trading and syndication desks. The credit implications from this "one-stop" shopping is twofold.

First, the debt capital markets have become less segmented as commercial banks and investment firms compete in the bank loan, junk bond, and private placement debt markets. This has led to more flexible, less stringent bank loan constraints. For instance, the average cash flow sweep for bank loans has declined from 68% in 1994 to 64% in 1996. Additionally, over the same time period, the average prepayment requirement from equity issuance has declined from 82% to 74%.[1] Lastly, in 1996, the average debt to cash flow multiple climbed to 5.5, its highest level in the 1990s.[2] Bottom line, the increased competition for business in the commercial loan market has resulted in more favorable terms for debtors and less credit protection for investors.

Second, hybrid debt instruments with both bank loan and junk bond characteristics are now available in the capital markets. These hybrid commercial loans typically have a higher prepayment penalty than standard commercial loans, but only a second lien (or no lien) on assets instead of the traditional first claim. Additionally, several commercial loan tranches may now be offered as part of a financing package where the first tranche of the bank loan is fully collateralized and has a regular amortization schedule, but the last tranche has no security interest and only a final bullet payment at maturity. These new commercial loans have the structure of high yield bonds, but have the floating rate requirement of a bank loan. Consequently, the very structure of these hybrid bank loans makes them more susceptible to credit risk.

---

[1] See Keith Barnish, Steve Miller, and Michael Rushmore, "The New Leveraged Loan Syndication Market," *Journal of Applied Corporate Finance* (Spring 1997), pp. 79-88.
[2] See Loan Pricing Corporation, "Gold Sheets 1997 Annual," Vol. III, No. 1 (1997), p. 38.

In addition to default risk for bank loans, there is the risk of credit downgrades and the risk of increased credit spreads. Downgrade risk occurs when a nationally recognized statistical rating organization such as Standard & Poor's, Moody's Investment Services, Duff & Phelps, or Fitch's reduces its outstanding credit rating for a borrower based on an evaluation of that debtor's current earning power versus its capacity to pay its fixed income obligations as they become due. Credit spread risk is the risk that the interest rate spread for a risky commercial loan will increase after the loan has been purchased, resulting in a diminution of loan value. Credit spreads can change based on changes in credit rating — a microeconomic analysis — but they can also increase or decrease based on macroeconomic events such as recession or expansion.

For instance, during the U.S. economic recession of 1990-1991, the credit spread for B rated bank loans increased on average from 250 basis points over LIBOR to 325 basis points, as default rates climbed to 10%.[3] Not surprisingly, over this time period the total return to B rated bank loans underperformed the total return to BBB and BB rated bank loans by 6.41% and 8.64%, respectively. Conversely, during the economic expansion years of 1993-1994, the total return to B rated bank loans outperformed the total return to BBB and BB rated bank loans by 3.43% and 1.15% as the default rate for B rated loans declined in 1993 and 1994 to 1.1% and 1.45%, respectively.[4]

In the event of a default, commercial bank loans generally have a higher recovery rate than that for defaulted high yield bonds due to a combination of collateral protection and senior capital structure. Nonetheless, estimates of lost value given a commercial bank loan default are about 35% of the loan value.[5] Even for asset-backed loans, which are highly collateralized and tightly monitored commercial loans where the bank controls the cash receipts against the collateralized assets, the average loss of value in the event of default is about 13%.[6]

The loss in value due to a default can have a significant impact on the total return of a bank loan. For a commercial bank loan the total return comes from two sources: the spread over the referenced rate (LIBOR+) and the return from price appreciation/depreciation. As might be expected, B rated bank loans are priced on average at higher rates than BBB rated bank loans — an average 250-300 basis points over LIBOR compared to 50 basis points over LIBOR for BBB rated loans. Yet, over the time period 1988-1994, the cumulative return to B rated bank loans was 10 percentage points less than that for BBB rated loans.[7]

---

[3] See Elliot Asarnow, "Corporate Loans as an Asset Class," *Journal of Portfolio Management* (Summer 1996), pp. 92-103; and Edward Altman and Joseph Bencivenga, "A Yield Premium Model for the High-Yield Debt Market," *Financial Analysts Journal* (September-October 1995), pp. 49-56.

[4] See Asarnow, "Corporate Loans as an Asset Class," p. 96, and Altman and Bencivenga, "A Yield Premium Model for the High-Yield Debt Market," p. 51.

[5] See Asarnow, "Corporate Loans as an Asset Class," p. 94, and Keith, Miller, and Rushmore, "The New Leveraged Loan Syndication Market," p. 85.

[6] See Asarnow, "Corporate Loans as an Asset Class," p. 95.

[7] See Asarnow, "Corporate Loans as an Asset Class."

The lower total return to B rated loans was due to a negative price return of −10.26%. Simply put, changes in credit quality reduced the total return to lower rated bank loans despite their higher coupon rates.

Credit risk, however, is not one-sided. Over the same time period, the cumulative total return to BB rated bank loans exceeded that of BBB bank loans by 11.6%.[8] Part of this higher return was due to higher interest payments offered to induce investors to purchase the lower rated BB bank loans, but a significant portion, over 5%, was due to enhanced credit quality. Consequently, over this time period, portfolio managers had ample opportunity to target specific credit risks and improve portfolio returns.

In their simplest form, credit derivatives may be nothing more than the purchase of credit protection. The ability to isolate credit risk and manage it independently of underlying investment positions is the key benefit of credit derivatives. Prior to the introduction of credit derivatives, the only way to manage credit exposure was to buy and sell bank loans or restrict lending policies. Because of transaction costs, tax issues, and client relationships this was an inefficient way to hedge or gain exposure.

Furthermore, credit derivatives offer an attractive method for hedging credit risk in lieu of liquidating the underlying collateral in a bank loan. Despite the security interest of a fully collateralized bank loan, there may be several reasons why a bank manager or portfolio manager may be reluctant to liquidate the collateral.

From a bank manager's perspective, the decision to liquidate the collateral will undoubtedly sour the customer relationship. Most banks consider loans as part of a broader client relationship that includes other non-credit business. Preserving the broader relationship may make a bank reluctant to foreclose.

Conversely, institutional investors focus on commercial loans as stand-alone investments and consider the economic risks and benefits of foreclosure. From their perspective, seizure of collateral may provoke a litigation defense by the debtor. The attempt to foreclose on collateral may result in dragging the investor into protracted litigation on issues and in forums which the institutional investor may wish to avoid. Additionally, foreclosure by one creditor/investor may trigger similar responses from other investors leading to a feeding frenzy on the debtor's assets. The debtor may have no choice but to seek the protection of the bankruptcy laws which would effectively stop all seizures of collateral and extend the time for collateral liquidation. Lastly, there may be possible collateral deficiencies such as unperfected security interests which could make collateral liquidation problematic.[9]

The seizure, holding, and liquidation of collateral is also an expensive course of action. The most obvious costs are the legal fees incurred in seizing and liquidating the collateral. Additional costs include storage costs, appraisal fees, brokerage or auc-

---

[8] See Asarnow, "Corporate Loans as an Asset Class."

[9] A security interest is effective between a lender and a borrower without any perfection. Perfection is the legal term for properly identifying an asset as collateral for a bank loan such that other lenders and creditors will not attach their security interests to the identified collateral except in a subordinated role.

tion costs, insurance, and property taxes. Hidden costs include the time spent by the investor and its personnel in managing and monitoring the liquidation process.

In sum, there are many reasons why the seizure and liquidation of collateral may not be a feasible solution for bank loan credit protection. Credit derivatives, therefore, represent a natural extension of the financial markets to unbundle the risk and return buckets associated with a commercial loan investment. They offer an important method for investment managers to hedge their exposure to credit risk because they permit the transfer of the exposure from one party to another. Credit derivatives allow for an efficient exchange of credit exposure in return for credit protection.

CREDIT OPTIONS

Credit options are different from standard debt options because while the latter is designed to protect against market risk (i.e., interest rate risk), credit options are constructed to protect against credit risk. Thus, the purpose of credit options is to price credit risk independently of market risk. Credit options may be written on an underlying asset or on a spread over a referenced riskless asset. These two type of options — one triggered by a decline in the value of an asset and one triggered by the change in the asset's spread over a comparable risk-free rate — have different payout structures.[10]

Credit Options Written on an Underlying Asset

In its simplest form, a credit option can be a binary option. With a binary credit option, the option seller will pay out a fixed sum if and when a default event occurs with respect to a referenced credit (e.g. the underlying borrower is unable to pay its obligations as they become due). Therefore, a binary option represents two states of the world: default or no default; it is the clearest example of credit protection. At maturity of the option, if the referenced credit has defaulted the option holder receives a predetermined payout. If there is no default at maturity of the option, the option buyer receives nothing and forgoes the option premium. A binary credit option could also be triggered by a rating downgrade.

A European binary credit option pays out a fixed sum only at maturity if the referenced credit is in default. An American binary option can be exercised at any time during its life. Consequently, if an American binary credit option is in the money (a default event has occurred), it will be exercised immediately because delaying exercise will reduce the present value of the fixed payment.

---

[10] Note that credit options are different from options on credit risky assets. In the latter case, these options are on the outright asset, but the asset is subject to credit risk, i.e., the issuer may default on the security. Conversely, credit options recognize the possibility of default and construct the payoff on the option to be a function of the decline in asset value due to default. For a thorough analysis of options on credit risky assets, *see* Robert Jarrow and Stuart Turnbull, "Pricing Derivatives on Financial Assets Subject to Credit Risk," *Journal of Finance* (March 1995), pp. 53-85.

Exhibit 1: Binary Credit Default Option

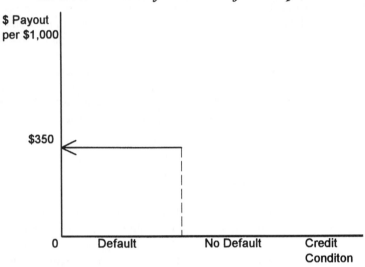

Exhibit 1 presents a binary credit option where the payout is dependent upon whether the referenced credit is in default. As previously discussed, the expected loss on a defaulted commercial loan is about 35 cents on every dollar. Therefore, a binary credit option can be structured to pay $350 for every $1,000 of loan value in the event of default.

Mathematically, the payoff to a binary put option is stated as:

$$P[\text{Loan}(T); \$1,000] = \begin{cases} \$350 \text{ if default} \\ \$0 \text{ if no default} \end{cases} \tag{1}$$

where Loan(T) is the value of the commercial loan at maturity of the option and $350 is a fixed payment per $1,000 of loan value if a default has occurred.

Equation (1) demonstrates the payoff for a put option. The option pays a fixed sum of $350 per $1,000 of loan value if the borrower defaults at any time, and nothing if the borrower remains solvent. Note that this type of option does not have to depend on the borrower defaulting on a specific loan; it can be established such that any default on any fixed obligation of the borrower triggers the option value.

An alternative to binary options is an option where the option writer agrees to compensate the option buyer for a decline in the value of a financial asset below a specified strike price. This type of credit option has two advantages over the binary option discussed above. First, the expected loss of 35 cents for every $1 is an average loss rate. Depending on the remaining credit strength of the borrower, the default loss may be more or less than 35 cents. Second, a credit option with a specified strike price does not have to wait for a default event to be in the money.

Credit options written on a commercial loan work differently than a credit option written on a traditional fixed income asset such as a high-yield bond. The reason is the amortization of loan principal. Most bank loans typically have an amortization schedule, established at the outset of the loan, which determines how much interest and principal is paid each period. Instead of a bullet payment at maturity, the principal is paid back over time according to the amortization schedule.

The amortization of principal over time reduces the default risk to the investor. With the passage of time, as more and more of the principal is repaid, the potential loss to the investor is reduced. This is in contrast to a bond where the repayment of principal is deferred until maturity. The declining principal at risk of a commercial loan has important implications for determining the strike price for a credit option.

We consider two cases, one where the investor is concerned about a credit deterioration, and one where the investor is concerned about default. In the first case, a credit deterioration can come about as a result of general financial market turmoil leading to a widening of credit spreads after the loan is issued (a macroeconomic event), or it can result from a credit rating downgrade due to the weakening of the financial status of the underlying borrower (a microeconomic event). The borrower continues to make its scheduled payments, but now its credit spread has increased, reducing the value of the amortizing cash flows. In the second case, the borrower defaults on the commercial loan, essentially canceling further payments. Both situations will reduce the value of a commercial loan, with a credit deterioration being the less severe example.

Taking the example of a credit deterioration option, assume an institutional investor has purchased a $1,000, 5-year BB rated bank loan priced at 150 basis points over LIBOR. With 5-year LIBOR at about 6%, and with annual amortization, each yearly payment of principal and interest would be $247 ($172 principal and $75 interest for the first year). At the end of the first year, the amortized value of the bank loan would be $1,000 − $172 = $828.

If the investor wishes to protect himself from credit deterioration by the end of the first year, he should purchase a 1-year credit put option struck at $828. This is demonstrated in Exhibit 2. Assume that the borrower is, in fact, downgraded to single B by the end of the first year of the bank loan. The value of the bank loan would decline from $828 to $800. The market price of $800 is determined by taking the remaining four amortization payments of $247 and discounting them at LIBOR + 300, the average rate for single B bank loans. Mathematically, the strike price for the credit put option at the end of the first year is determined as:

$$K_1 = \$1,000 - (A - I_1) \tag{2}$$

where

K_1 = the strike price for the option at the end of the first year of the bank loan

A = the periodic (annual) amortization payment

I_1 = the accrued interest payable at the end of the first year

Exhibit 2: Credit Deterioration Put Option on BB Rated Bank Loan

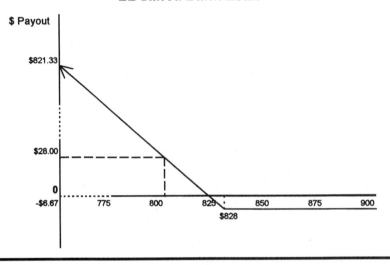

What equation (2) and the simple example above demonstrate is that the strike price for a credit put option on a commercial loan is *time dependent*.[11] Over time, as the borrower pays its obligations and the loan is amortized, the amount that can be lost by the investor declines. Consequently, the strike price for the credit put option must be adjusted over time to reflect the amortization of the principal balance of the loan; the exercise price declines with the passage of time.

More generally, to protect against credit deterioration for any time t, the strike price on a credit put option for an amortizing commercial loan is determined by:

$$K_t = P_{t-1} - (A - I_t) \tag{3}$$

where

$\begin{aligned}
K_t &= \text{the strike price at time } t \\
P_{t-1} &= \$1,000 - \Sigma \, (A - I_j) \\
A &= \text{the constant amortization amount} \\
I_j &= \text{the interest payments over the time interval 1 to } t-1 \\
\Sigma &= \text{the summation sign over the time period } j = 1 \text{ to } j = t-1 \\
I_t &= \text{the interest payment for period } t \\
\$1,000 &= \text{the principal borrowed by the debtor}
\end{aligned}$

---

[11] The time dependency of the strike price for credit options has been noted with respect to coupon paying bonds with a bullet payment at maturity. See Yiannos A. Pierides, "Valuation of Credit Risk Derivatives," Chapter 13 in Frank J. Fabozzi (ed.), *The Handbook of Fixed Income Options* (Burr Ridge, IL: Irwin Profession Publishing, 1996).

Additionally, based on our definition of P_{t-1} in equation (3), the above formulation of the strike price may be reduced to:

$$K_t = \$1,000 - \Sigma\,(A - I_j) \tag{4}$$

where the other terms are as defined as before and Σ is the summation over the time period $j = 1$ to $j = t$.

How will the credit deterioration put option be priced? While a full blown discussion of credit option pricing models is beyond the scope of this chapter, a simple example should help.[12] The essential question to answer is what is the probability of a credit downgrade for the borrower from BB to B?

This probability can be determined through the formation of transition credit matrices which use historical data to determine the statistical likelihood of credit downgrades and upgrades.[13] By using these transition matrices, and the term structure of credit spreads for different credit rating levels, a distribution of returns can be derived for the underlying bank loan.[14] From this distribution, the probability of a downgrade to a single B rating can be determined. Denoting this probability π, the investor can then use a simple 1-period binomial pricing tree to determine the current price of the option.

Assume that $\pi = 0.25$. That is, with a 25% probability, the investor expects the credit rating of the borrower to be downgraded from BB to B, and with a $1 - \pi = 75\%$ probability, the borrower's credit rating will remain at BB or better. If we assume a 1-year risk neutral rate of 5%, a the strike price of $828, and that the value of the bank loan declines to $800 if the borrower is downgraded to single B, then the price of a credit deterioration put option on the BB bank loan is $6.67:

$$P[\text{Loan}(T); \$828] = [(0.25) \times (\$828 - \$800) + (0.75) \times (\$0)] \div (1 + 0.05)$$
$$= \$6.67$$

This binomial pricing is demonstrated in Exhibit 3.

---

[12] In the sophisticated financial practice of the trading houses, the pricing of credit options can be quite complicated. For instance, one author has developed a model for credit options that incorporates firm value as an underlying stochastic variable as well as random strike prices. See Sanjiv R. Das, "Credit Risk Derivatives," *Journal of Derivatives* (Spring 1995), pp. 7-23. Another paper uses mean reverting credit spreads and interest rates to determine the value of credit spread options. See Francis A. Longstaff and Eduardo S. Schwartz, "Valuing Credit Derivatives," *Journal of Fixed Income* (June 1995), pp. 6-12. Still another author values credit derivatives as barrier options. See Pierides, "Valuation of Credit Risk Derivatives." For a complete discussion and comparison of these pricing models, see Mark J. P. Anson, "Risks and Rewards of Credit Derivatives," OppenheimerFunds working paper (1997).

[13] For a demonstration of a transition credit matrix, see Gailen Hite and Arthur Warga, "The Effect of Bond-Rating Changes on Bond Price Performance," *Financial Analysts Journal* (May-June 1997), pp. 35-51.

[14] If the investor assumes a normal distribution, then all that is needed to derive the distribution is the expected return on the bank loan and its variance. In practice, normal distributions are not observed for bank loans and other investment securities. Consequently, simulation techniques such as Monte Carlo Simulation are used to model the hypothetical distribution of returns.

Exhibit 3: Binomial Pricing for a
Credit Deterioration Put Option

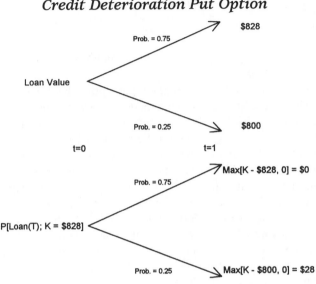

The above credit option assumes that there is a risk of widening credit spreads or a credit downgrade, but no default. That is, the borrower continues to make its amortization payments, but the value of the loan has decreased because either credit spreads have generally increased (a macroeconomic event) or the borrower's credit situation has deteriorated (a microeconomic event).

If the investor considers the possibility of default, the determination of the strike price is different. Unlike zero-coupon bonds, default on a commercial loan can occur prior to maturity at any scheduled payment date. Default occurs on a payment date if the borrower fails to meet its amortization payment. In the event of default, the ex-amortization price of the loan (market price of the loan after an amortization payment) is not defined on the payment date because the borrower has effectively canceled all future payments. Consequently, the exercise price for a credit default option must be based on the loan value plus its scheduled amortization payment.[15]

Stated another way, it is to the advantage of the borrower to default right before the scheduled date of an amortization payment. Consider the same $1,000, 5-year BB rated term loan with annual amortization payments of $247. At the end of the first year, the borrower is scheduled to pay $247, with four remaining payments of $247 for each of the next four years. If, in fact, the borrower defaults just before the first payment date, the present value of the investor's loss at the time of the first amortization payment is

---

[15] This point has been noted by Pierides ("Valuation of Credit Risk Derivatives") with respect to coupon paying bonds.

Exhibit 4: Credit Default Put Option on BB Rated Bank Loan

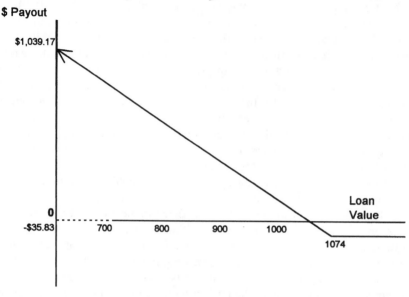

$247 + $247/(1.075) + $247/(1.075)^2 + $247/(1.075)^3 + $247/(1.075)^4$
= $1,075

To fully protect against default risk at the end of the first year, the strike price for a credit option must be set at $1,075. As indicated above, the exercise price is equal to the loan value at the end of year 1 ($828) plus the scheduled amortization payment ($247). It may seem odd that the strike price at the end of the first year is higher than the initial market value of the loan ($1,000), but this is because the time value of the amortization payments has increased by the time the investor gets to the end of the first year. (Note, for example, that the first amortization payment is no longer discounted because it is currently due and payable.)

If we assume a probability of default of 10%, a decline in loan value by 35 cents on the dollar right after default, a 1-year risk neutral rate of 5%, and a strike price of $1,075, then the price of the option may be determine using the simple binomial model discussed above. The credit option value may be determined by

$$P[\text{Loan}(T); K = \$1,075] = [(0.10) \times (\$1,075 - \{0.65\}(\$1,075\})) + (0.90)$$
$$\times (\$0)] \div (1.05) = \$35.83$$

This credit default option is demonstrated in Exhibit 4.

As in the case of credit deterioration, the strike price for a credit default option is time dependent. Over time, the strike price will decline as more and more of the outstanding principal is paid back by the borrower. Two points should be noted with respect to the difference in strike prices at time $t = 1$ between the credit deterioration option (K_1 = $828) and the credit default option (K_1 = $1,075).

First, it makes intuitive sense that the strike price for the credit default option is higher than that for the credit deterioration option because in the former case the investor is concerned with loss of principal, while in the latter case the investor is concerned not with loss of principal but with earning an appropriate credit spread given the borrower's current credit situation. Therefore, the level of credit protection is higher for the default case and a higher strike price must be established to protect against default risk. Second, because of its higher strike price, the cost of the credit default option will be greater than that for the credit deterioration option. Once again, this makes common sense: the greater the credit protection, the more expensive the credit option.

On a general note, it can be observed that credit put options will be a decreasing function of firm value. As the value of the firm increases, the credit rating on the outstanding bank loan is also expected to increase and the value of the put option decreases. In fact, the credit option becomes almost worthless when firm value is high enough because the outstanding debt becomes almost credit risk free. However, credit put options are increasing in the volatility of firm value for two reasons. As the volatility of the firm assets increases, the value of outstanding debt decreases and the value of the put option increases. Additionally, an increase in volatility has the same value enhancing impact in option pricing models as higher volatility has on the value of a put option on the firm's common stock.

Credit derivatives may be used to exploit inefficiencies in the market when there is imperfect correlation between stock prices and interest rates. For instance, when interest rates and stock prices are negatively correlated, commercial loan values may be higher than when the correlation is positive. Credit spreads in the market may not correctly reflect the correlations between stocks and the term structure of interest rates. As a result, investors may hold a portfolio of commercial loans and credit derivatives, which may cost less than equivalent riskless debt yet offer the same risk and return characteristics.

Credit Spread Options

The second type of credit option is a call option on the level of the credit spread over a referenced benchmark such as LIBOR. If the credit spread widens, the referenced asset will decline in value. This type of credit option is structured so that the option is in-the-money when the credit spread exceeds the specified strike level.

An example may clarify. We continue with our $1,000, 5-year BB rated term loan with annual amortization payments of $247. At the initiation of the loan, its fair value is determined by:

$$\text{Loan}(t_0) = \$247/(1+L+s) + \$247/(1+L+s)^2 + \$247/(1+L+s)^3$$
$$+ \$247/(1+L+s)^4 + \$247/(1+L+s)^5 = \$1,000 \tag{5}$$

where

L = the 5-year LIBOR
s = the market credit spread for BB rated loans

Plugging in a 5-year LIBOR of 6% for L, we can solve for the value of the credit spread (s) which will equate the present value of the amortization payments to the value of the Loan at $t = 0$ of $1,000. From our discussion above, we already know that this value is 1.5%. What equation (5) illustrates is that the value of the loan is dependent on the credit spread (s). As the credit spread increases, the value of the loan decreases. Therefore, a call option struck on the credit spread qualifies as a credit derivative because its value increases as the credit quality of the borrower decreases. Consequently, a call option on the credit spread can offer the same credit protection as a credit put option on the loan's market value.

The payoff on a credit spread option is determined by taking the difference in the credit spreads multiplied by a specified notional amount and by a risk factor. In a mathematical format, the payoff at maturity of the option may be specified as

$$C[\text{spread}(T); K] = (\text{spread}(T) - K) \times \text{notional amount} \times \text{risk factor} \qquad (6)$$

where

spread(T)	=	the spread for the financial asset over the riskless rate at the maturity of the option
K	=	the specified strike spread over LIBOR for the loan
notional amount	=	a contractually specified dollar amount equal to the amount
risk factor	=	quantity based on measures of duration and convexity

Assume the portfolio manager purchases a $1,000 notional call option with a strike price equal to the current credit spread over LIBOR for a BB rated bank loan. The tenor of the option is one year and the risk factor for the bank loan is 1.867. At maturity, the portfolio manager will receive the following payout: (change in credit spread) × (notional amount) × (risk factor). If the borrower is downgraded to single B and the credit spread widens to 300 basis points, at maturity of the option the portfolio manager will earn: $[(3\% - 1.5\%) \times \$1000 \times 1.867] = \$28$. Note that the credit spread option payout compensates the portfolio manager for the decline in amortized loan value from $828 to $800. This is demonstrated in Exhibit 5.

Credit spreads can be reviewed from either a macroeconomic or microeconomic analysis. Under a macroeconomic view, a slowdown in the economy can lead to a flight of capital to more secure investments such as U.S. Treasury securities, resulting in wider credit spreads across all non-Treasury investments. Under a microeconomic analysis, a buyer of a credit spread option can express the view that the credit quality of the underlying referenced issuer will decline due to poor operating performance. In either scenario, the price of the referenced asset "cheapens" relative to a benchmark interest rate.

Exhibit 5: Credit Call Option
Credit Spread Option Struck at 150 Basis Points

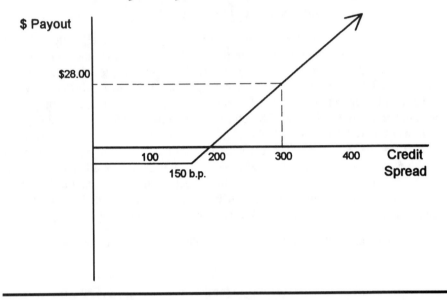

Alternatively, credit spread options may be used as income enhancement tools. A portfolio manager may believe that the credit spread for the borrower will not exceed 300 basis points. To monetize this view, she can sell a put option on the credit spread with the strike set at 300 basis points. Additionally, the portfolio manager can agree to physically settle the option. In effect, the portfolio manager has agreed to buy the bank loan at a spread to LIBOR of 300 basis points — her targeted purchase price — and she can use the premium received from the sale of the credit option to finance the purchase price should the put be exercised.

Furthermore, by selling a put option on a credit spread an investor can capitalize on a higher credit spread volatility than on a sale of the yield volatility for the same loan.[16] Higher spread volatility is the result of the less than perfect correlation between the yield on the referenced bank loan and LIBOR. Therefore, an investor can receive a higher put premium by selling richer spread volatility than by selling a put on the underlying debt.

Credit spread options are relative value options. Their value is not derived from the absolute price change of the underlying referenced asset, but rather from the price change of the referenced asset relative to LIBOR. By purchasing a call option on the credit spread between the referenced loan and LIBOR, the option is in the money only if the price of the referenced asset declines more than would be warranted by an increase in LIBOR (i.e., the credit spread widens).

[16] See Bjorn Flesaker, Lane Hughston, Laurence Schreiber, and Lloyd Sprung, "Taking All the Credit," *Risk* (September 1994), pp. 104-108.

Credit spread options are, therefore, underperformance options. Similar to outperformance options where the payoff is contingent on the relative outperformance of one referenced asset over a second referenced asset, the payoff of a credit spread call option is contingent upon the relative underperformance of a bank loan measured by its yield compared to LIBOR.

Credit spread options are not designed to protect against market risk such as interest rate spikes where LIBOR increases but the credit spread does not. Instead, credit options are another form of insurance against a credit decline in the referenced asset or issuer. This strategy can be used to protect the value of an existing portfolio position should its spread relative to LIBOR increase. However, this type of option will not protect against an absolute decline in value of the referenced asset if LIBOR increases.

Credit spread options may also be used by corporate treasurers to hedge the credit risk embedded in future borrowing requirements. Typically, the spread paid by corporations based on different rating levels compared to LIBOR tends to widen during periods of economic downturns. Credit call options on the spread over LIBOR can protect against an overall rise in the risk premiums for different rating levels. The payoff from the option can be used to offset the increased funding costs.

CREDIT FORWARDS

Credit forward contracts, like credit options, are an essential building block in the derivatives market. They may be contracted either on loan values or on credit spreads. They can be used by corporations that wish to lock in their funding costs, or by portfolio managers who wish to purchase credit exposure. In particular, corporations can purchase credit forwards referenced to their own credit ratings to hedge their cost of capital.

Consider the example of a corporate treasurer who in June 1997 intends to seek a 5-year commercial loan within the next six months, but is concerned that over this time period his firm's credit rating may decline from BB to B. Macroeconomic events such as the turmoil that occurred in the worldwide financial markets in October 1997 could result in credit downgrades. Alternatively, the treasurer may expect poor future operating performance for his firm, which may increase the company's credit spread to that of a single B credit risk.

To hedge this risk, the treasurer can purchase a 6-month credit spread forward contract at the company's current commercial loan spread of 150 basis points. If the credit spread for the company's debt widens above 150 basis points, the treasurer will receive a positive payment. However, if the credit spread declines below 150 basis points, the treasurer must make a payment to the credit forward seller.

The exact payment amount at maturity of the credit forward is determined by the following equation:

Exhibit 6: Credit Forward

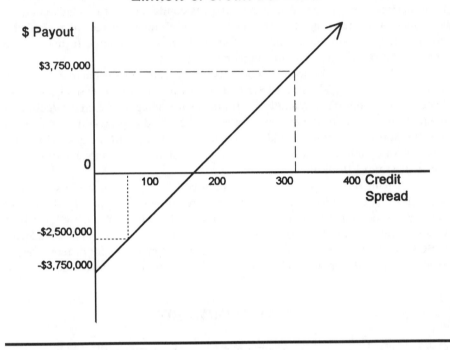

$$[\text{credit spread at maturity} - \text{contracted credit spread}] \times \text{duration} \\ \times \text{notional value} \qquad (7)$$

where the credit spread at maturity is the observable market spread at maturity of the credit forward, the contracted credit spread is the spread established at the outset of the forward agreement, the duration is the duration of the referenced credit asset, and notional value is the dollar amount of economic exposure.

Assume that, in fact, the credit rating of the borrower declines to single B by December 1997 and its commercial loan rate rises to 300 basis points over LIBOR. Additionally, assume that the duration on the commercial loan is about 2.5 and the amount to be financed is $100 million. At maturity of the credit forward contract, the treasurer will receive

$$[3\% - 1.5\%] \times 2.5 \times \$100,000,000 = \$3,750,000$$

However, if the credit spread declined to 50 basis points at maturity of the credit forward, the treasurer must pay

$$[0.5\% - 1.5\%] \times 2.5 \times \$100,000,000 = -\$2,500,000$$

Exhibit 6 demonstrates the payout for a credit forward.

This example of credit forwards highlights an essential difference between all forward and option contracts. The purchaser of a forward contract receives the upside appreciation of the underlying asset, but also shares in its depreciation. In the example above, the treasurer is required to make a payment to the credit forward seller if the credit spread declines in value. In the unlikely event that the credit spread narrowed to zero, the maximum the treasurer would have to pay is $3,750,000. In contrast, the purchase of an option allows the investor to profit from his position but limits his downside loss to the option premium paid.

How effective is this credit forward protection? Consider the commercial financing case of $100 million dollars over 5 years at a BB spread of 1.5% over LIBOR. If we assume 5-year LIBOR equals 6%, then the annual amortization payments for the commercial loan will be $24,716,417. Now suppose that by the time the corporate treasurer comes to the capital markets, his company's credit rating has declined to single B, and the appropriate credit spread is 3% over LIBOR. The 5-year annual amortization payments of $24,716,417 discounted at 9% would equal $96,138,242. In other words, at a credit spread of 3% over LIBOR, and with 5 annual payments of $24,716,417, investors would be willing to lend only $96,138,242 to the corporate treasurer instead of $100 million. In sum, the treasurer would have a financing shortfall of $3,861,757. However, if the corporate treasure had purchased the credit forward at a credit spread price of 1.5%, he would have recovered $3,750,000 of the financing shortfall and effectively hedged his company's credit exposure.

In addition to hedging financing costs, credit forwards are a useful tool to forecast future default premiums. By constructing zero-coupon yield curves for commercial loans and Treasury securities and subtracting these curves to obtain their difference, it is possible to derive a zero credit spread curve. From the zero credit curve it is then a simple matter to derive forward credit spreads.[17]

Deriving forward credit spreads has two important implications. First, these derived spreads represent the market's unbiased expectation regarding future credit spreads. Consequently, they reflect the credit market's best guess as to future default probabilities. Second, implied forward credit spreads can be compared to current market spreads for possible arbitrage opportunities. In fact, existing credit spreads should be priced close to the implied forward credit spreads to limit such arbitrage opportunities. A large discrepancy between implied and existing spreads would reflect a fundamental mispricing of credit risk, and offer an opportunity to profit from credit exposure.

CREDIT SWAPS

Credit swaps come in two flavors: credit default swaps and total return swaps. Credit default swaps are used to shift credit exposure to a credit protection seller.

---

[17] For a demonstration of this process, see Charles Smithson and Hal Holappa, "Credit Derivatives," *Risk* (December 1995), pp. 38-39.

They have a similar economic effect to credit options discussed above. Total return credit swaps are a way to increase an investor's exposure to credit risk and the returns commensurate with that risk.

Credit Default Swaps

A credit default swap is similar to a credit option in that its primary purpose is to hedge the credit exposure to a referenced asset or issuer. In this sense, credit default swaps operate much like a standby letter of credit. A credit default swap is the simplest form of credit insurance among all credit derivatives.

There are two main types of credit default swaps. In the first type, the credit protection buyer pays a fee to the credit protection seller in return for the right to receive a payment conditional upon the default of a referenced credit. The referenced credit can be a single asset, such as a commercial loan, or a basket of bank loans. The credit protection buyer continues to receive the total return on the referenced asset. However, should this total return be negative, i.e., the referenced basket of assets has declined in value (either through defaults or downgrades), the total return receiver will receive a payment from the credit protection seller. This type of swap is presented in Exhibit 7.

Mechanically, the contractual documentation for a one period credit default swap will identify the referenced asset, its initial value (V_0), the time to maturity of the swap (T), and a referenced payment rate (R). The payment R may be a single bullet payment or can be a floating rate benchmarked to LIBOR. At maturity, if the value of the asset has declined, the credit protection buyer receives a payment of $V_0 - V_T$ from the credit protection seller and pays the referenced payment rate R. If the value of the referenced asset has increased in value, the credit protection buyer receives the value $V_T - V_0$ from the underlying asset and pays R. In this simple one period example, the credit default swap acts very much like a credit put option described above. However, for multi-period transactions, there are two differences between a credit default swap and a put option.

First, the credit protection buyer can pay for the protection premium over several settlement dates, t_1 through time T instead of paying an option premium up front. Second, the credit protection buyer can receive payments $V_{t2} - V_{t1}$ at intermediate settlement dates where $t2 \leq T$ and $0 \leq t1 < t2$. Therefore, if the value of the referenced asset continues to deteriorate, the credit protection buyer may receive several payments.

Exhibit 7: Credit Default Swap

Exhibit 8: Credit Default Swap

Alternatively, the credit protection buyer can pay the total return on a referenced loan to the credit protection seller in return for receiving a periodic payment. The credit protection buyer keeps the referenced loan on its balance sheet but receives a known payment on the scheduled payment dates for the bank loan. In return, it pays to the credit protection seller on each cash flow date the total return from the referenced asset. Additionally, depending on how the swap agreement is structured, the credit protection buyer may be reimbursed for the decline in value of the referenced credit. This credit default swap is presented in Exhibit 8.

Default swaps usually contain a minimum threshold or materiality clause requiring that the decline in the referenced credit be significant and confirmed by an objective source. This can be as simple as a credit downgrade by a nationally recognized statistical rating organization or a percentage decline in market value of the asset. Additionally, the payment by the credit protection seller can be set to incorporate a recovery rate on the referenced asset. This is particularly applicable to the bank loan market where recovery rates are much higher than the junk bond market. This value may be determined by the market price of the defaulted asset several months after the actual default.

Large banks are the natural dealers for credit default swaps because it is consistent with their letter of credit business. On the one hand, banks may sell credit default swaps as a natural extension of their credit protection business. Alternatively, a bank may use a credit swap to hedge its exposure to a referenced credit who is a customer of the bank. In this way the bank can limit its exposure to the client without physically transferring the client's loans off its balance sheet. Therefore the bank can protect its exposure without disturbing its relationship with its client.

The methods used to determine the amount of the payment obligated of the credit protection seller under the swap agreement can vary greatly. For instance, a credit default swap can specify at contract date the exact amount of payment that will be made by the swap seller should the referenced credit party default. Conversely, the default swap can be structured so that the amount of the swap payment by the seller is determined after the default event. Under these circumstances, the amount payable by the swap seller is determined based upon the observed prices of debt obligations or equal seniority and security of the borrower in the capital markets. Lastly, the swap can be documented much like a credit put option where the amount to be paid by the credit protection seller is an established strike price less the current market value of the referenced asset.

Exhibit 9: Total Return Credit Swaps

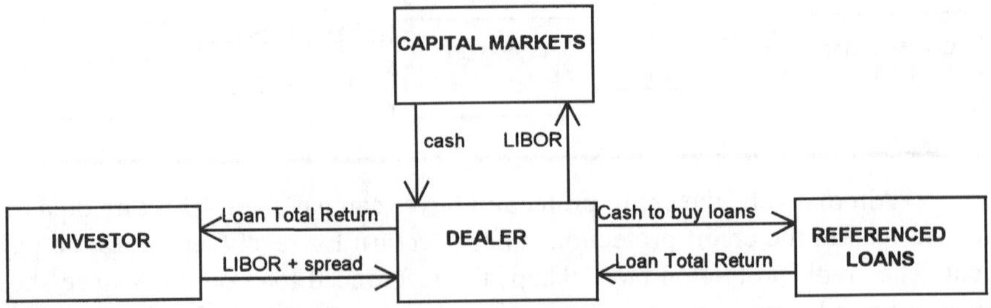

Total Return Credit Swap

A total return credit swap is different from a credit default swap in that the latter is used to hedge a credit exposure while the former is used to increase credit exposure. A total return credit swap transfers all of the economic exposure of a reference asset or a referenced basket of assets to the credit swap purchaser. A total return credit swap includes all cash flows that flow from the referenced assets as well as the capital appreciation or depreciation of those assets. In return for receiving this exposure to an underlying asset, the credit swap purchaser pays a floating rate plus any depreciation of the referenced asset to the credit swap seller.

If the total return payer owns the underlying referenced assets, it has transferred its economic exposure to the total return receiver. Effectively then, the total return payer has a neutral position which typically will earn a spread over LIBOR. However, the total return payer has only transferred the economic exposure to the total return receiver; it has not transferred the actual assets. The total return payer must continue to fund the underlying assets at its marginal cost of borrowing or at the opportunity cost of investing elsewhere the capital tied up by the referenced assets.

The underlying asset basket may be composed of any type of referenced credit to which the total return receiver wishes to become exposed. This may include loan participation interests, junk bonds, accounts receivable, or other high-yielding debt. It is usually the case that the total return receiver chooses the exact credit risks to be incorporated into the referenced asset basket.

The total return payer may not initially own the referenced bank loans before the swap is transacted. Instead, after the swap is negotiated, the total return payer will purchase the bank loans to hedge its obligations to pay the total return to the total return receiver. In order to purchase the referenced assets, the total return payer must borrow from the capital markets. This borrowing cost is factored into the floating rate that the total return receiver must pay to the swap seller. Exhibit 9 diagrams how a total return credit swap works.

In some cases, a total return credit swap may be transacted through a special purpose entity such as a corporation or a trust. Some counterparties, such as mutual funds, often have restrictions on the type of transactions they may enter.

For instance, a mutual fund may be limited by the terms of its prospectus from transacting in swaps or from investing in bank loans directly. Additionally, under the Internal Revenue Code, income from swap contracts is generally not considered "good income" for tax purposes.[18]

In these circumstances, a trust or a corporation is established as a conduit between the mutual fund and the total return payer where the trust or corporation enters into the credit swap with the total return payer and passes through the credit swap payments to the mutual fund. The trust/corporation accomplishes the pass through by selling private securities to the mutual fund which incorporate the swap payments paid to the trust.[19] Exhibit 10 demonstrates this pass through structure.

There are several benefits in purchasing a total return credit swap as opposed to purchasing the bank loans themselves. First, the total return receiver does not have to finance the purchase of the loans. Instead, it pays a fee to the total return payer in return for receiving the total return on the bank loans. In effect, the total return receiver has rented the balance sheet of the total return payer: the referenced loans remain on the balance sheet of the total return payer, but the total return receiver receives the economic exposure to the bank loans as if they were on its balance sheet.

Exhibit 10: Leveraged Credit Swap

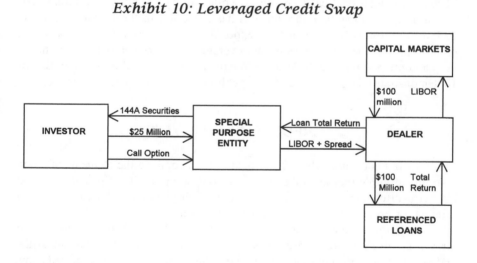

---

[18] See Internal Revenue Code, 1986 Code--Subchapter M, Sec. 851(b)(2) (Chicago, IL: Commerce Clearing House, 1993).

[19] These private securities are typically in the form of Securities and Exchange Commission (SEC) Rule 144A securities which are not required to be registered with the SEC but which may be sold only to Qualified Institutional Buyers. See SEC Release No. 33-6862, CCH par. 84,523, April 30, 1990, amended in SEC Release No. 33-6963, CCH par. 85,052, effective October 28, 1992. Additionally, a third-party investor usually invests in the special purpose vehicle (SPV) as an equity investor. This prevents the SPV from being consolidated on the balance sheet of the mutual fund.

Second, the total return receiver can achieve the same economic exposure in one swap transaction that would otherwise take several cash market transactions to achieve. In this way a total return swap is much more efficient than the cash market. For example, if a total return receiver wanted to gain exposure to the commercial loan market, it could purchase loan participation interests through various loan syndications. However, it would take several syndication transactions to achieve the same economic exposure that a total return credit swap can offer in one transaction. Furthermore, a total return credit swap can offer a diversified basket of bank loans.

Third, the total return receiver can take advantage of the natural expertise of the total return payer. Large money center banks are natural dealers in the total return credit swap market. Their core business is the credit analysis of customers and the lending of money. To the extent the total return receiver is not as experienced in credit analysis as a large money center bank, it can rely on the bank's expertise to choose appropriate credit risks for the underlying basket of bank loans.

Fourth, a total return swap can incorporate leverage. Leverage is the ability to achieve a greater economic exposure than capital invested. With a total return credit swap, a total return swap receiver can specify a leverage percentage (e.g., 400%) to increase its exposure to a referenced basket of assets. For instance, a total return payer can contract to receive the total return on a reference basket of $100 million loan syndication interests, while putting up only $25 million as collateral. In effect, the total return receiver has a leverage factor of 4: it has invested $25 million to receive an economic exposure worth $100 million. However, in order to protect the total return payer, leveraged swaps typically have an embedded call option to unwind the swap before the invested capital is depleted. Exhibit 10 demonstrates the use of swap leverage through a special purpose vehicle.

CREDIT LINKED NOTES

Credit linked notes are hybrid instruments which combine the elements of a debt instrument with either an embedded credit option or credit swap. They are cash market instruments but represent a synthetic high-yield bond, loan participation interest, or credit investment. Credit linked notes may have a maturity of anywhere from three months to several years, with 1 to 3 years being the most likely term of credit exposure. These notes are often issued as 144A private securities and may be issued through special purpose vehicles such as those described above for total return credit swaps. Like credit options, forwards, and swaps, credit linked notes allow an investor to take a tailored view towards credit risk.

Credit linked notes may contain embedded options, embedded forward contracts, or both. Credit linked notes with embedded options can effect a credit view of the investor with respect to declining or improving credit spreads of an underlying borrower. For example, an investor may be willing to sell a put option on the commercial loan borrowing rate of a corporate debtor in return for a higher coupon payment on the credit linked note. Under normal market conditions, an investor might expect to receive a coupon of 7% on a "plain vanilla" medium-term note. However, if the investor believes that the commercial lending rate for a referenced borrower is priced fairly, he can monetize this view by selling a binary put option against the lending rate and receiving the put premium in the form of a higher coupon paid on the note.

This is demonstrated in Exhibit 11 where the investor buys a note and simultaneously sells to the issuer of the note a binary put option on the credit rating of a chosen BBB borrower and receives 25 basis points of premium. The notional amount of the option is the same as the face value of the note ($10,000,000), and the binary payout is set at 100 basis points — the difference between the average BBB and BB commercial lending rates.[20] If the option expires out of the money, the option premium provides incremental coupon income up to 7.25%. However, if the credit rating on the referenced creditor declines to BB, then the short put will expire in the money and the note buyer will receive a lower coupon payment of 6%.

Credit linked notes with an embedded call option have the advantage of principal protection. At maturity of the note, the noteholder is promised at least a return of his principal, or face value, of the note with a chance for additional appreciation if the credit option matures in the money. Credit linked notes with embedded forwards, however, do not have the advantage of principal protection. Depending on the ending value of the embedded credit forward, the noteholder may receive more or less than the face value of the credit note. Credit notes linked to forward contracts, therefore, entail greater risk to the noteholder than credit notes linked to option contracts. The tradeoff for the greater risk is usually in the form of a higher coupon payment.

Exhibit 11: Credit Linked Note with a Short Binary Put Option

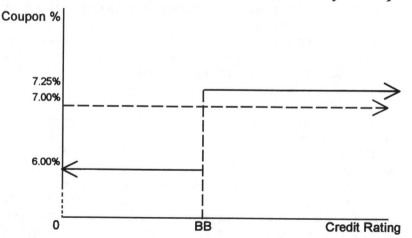

Exhibit 12: Credit Linked Note with an Embedded Forward, an Embedded Short Credit Call, and an Embedded Long Credit Put

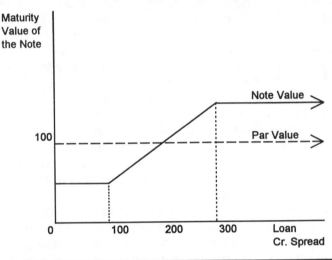

In practice, the cost of a credit linked note to the investor (in terms of lower coupon payments) can be quite high. Unlike the more common equity linked note, for example, where there is a large options and futures market for equity indices, there is no exchange traded market for credit options. Without a deep, liquid market for credit options, the issuer of the credit linked note may not be able to effectively hedge the credit exposure embedded in the note. The only way for the issuer to accurately hedge its short credit exposure is to buy the underlying bank loan at its financing cost. This financing cost, in turn, is passed on to the investor in terms of a lower coupon payment.

Just like total return swaps, credit linked notes may contain leverage which can enhance return, but only at the increased risk of loss of principal to the noteholders. For instance, a credit linked note with a leverage factor of 2 will increase in value by 2 basis points for every 1 basis point decline in value of the referenced credit spread. However, if the referenced credit spread increased by 1 basis point by the maturity of the note, the credit investor would receive back only 99.98 of its invested principal.

Credit linked notes can become quite complicated, combining both embedded options and embedded forwards. Consider the credit linked note in Exhibit 12 which is short a call option on a referenced loan spread struck at 300 basis points, long a put option on the loan spread struck at 100 basis points, and long a credit spread forward contract priced at a current loan spread of 200 basis points. If the loan spread remains at 200 basis, the investor will receive the par value of the note at maturity. If the loan spread widens, the credit investor will receive at maturity a payment in excess of the par value. However, the appreciation of the note is capped at a loan spread of 300 basis points by the short credit call option. Conversely, if the loan spread narrows, the principal value of the note returned at maturity will decline. The depreciation of the note is stopped by the long credit put option struck at a loan spread of 100 basis points.

In Exhibit 12, the long protective credit put option can be financed by the sale of the credit call option. Some upside potential is sacrificed to pay for downside protection. Between the loan spread range of 100 and 300 basis points, the principal value of the note is allowed to fluctuate.

RISKS OF CREDIT DERIVATIVES

The recent history of losses associated with derivative instruments have highlighted their risky nature. Significant losses at Barings, Plc., Orange County, Gibson Greetings, Procter & Gamble, Pier 1 Imports, Daiwa Bank in New York, the Wisconsin Investment Board, and the Sumitomo Corporation have ushered in a new age of risk consciousness.[21] Although derivatives are essential tools for income enhancement and hedging exposure, there are many risks associated with their use. Below, we highlight those risks most pertinent to credit derivatives.

Credit Risk

Credit risk is defined as the risk to cash flows as a result of an obligor's failure to honor its commitments under a transaction or contractual agreement. Although credit derivatives are designed to effectively hedge the credit risk of a borrower, another type of credit risk is introduced through their use: counterparty credit risk. Credit derivatives are not exchange traded; they are transacted in the over-the-counter financial markets as privately negotiated contracts between two parties. Consequently, a purchaser of a credit derivative assumes the credit risk of the seller's performance under the contractual agreement documenting the credit derivative.

Conversely, for the seller of the credit derivative, the primary credit risk is that of the referenced asset. That is, the seller of the credit derivative will be required to make a payment when the credit quality of the referenced borrower has deteriorated. The credit derivative seller bears the credit risk of the referenced borrower just as if that borrower's loans were on its balance sheet instead of the balance sheet of the credit derivative purchaser. However, with respect to a total

---

[21] See "Top Managers at Barings Face Fresh Criticism," *The Financial Times Limited* (July 20, 1996), p. 4; "Orange County Seeks Protective Order Vacating Depositions," *Derivatives Litigation Reporter* (April 22, 1996), p. 12; "Gibson Files Lawsuit over Derivatives," *The New York Times* (September 13, 1994), sec. D, p.1; "Procter & Gamble Reaches Accord with Bankers Trust," *Los Angeles Times* (May 10, 1996), part D, p.2; "Pier 1 Shareholders Fault Board for $20M Derivatives Loss," *Derivatives Litigation Reporter* (May 27, 1996), p.3; "Lack of Care Costs Funds; Wisconsin Audit Cites 'Excessive Risk' in Derivatives Losses," *Pensions & Investments* (July 24, 1995), p. 32; "Daiwa Debacle Shows Flaws in High-Voltage Finance," *Asahi News Service* (September 29, 1995); "How Copper Lost its Luster for Sumitomo," *The New York Times* (June 15, 1996), p. 31.

return credit swap, because the total return may be positive or negative, both the total return receiver and the total return payer have exposure to the referenced borrower.

For the credit derivative purchaser, the credit risk is the same as that for swaps, forwards and other over-the-counter derivative contracts. Therefore, the same type of credit analysis applies as to that of a swap counterparty. Before purchasing a credit derivative, a buyer of credit protection should evaluate the financial condition of the seller of the credit derivative. Additionally, during the term of the credit derivative, the purchaser should continually monitor the financial condition of its counterparty.

For the buyer to incur a loss, both the referenced borrower must suffer a credit deterioration and the credit derivative seller must fail to honor its obligations under the credit derivative agreement. Therefore, the credit derivative purchaser should consider the joint probability distribution of a referenced borrower and counterparty default. The best way to minimize this joint probability is to seek sellers of credit protection whose business operations have a low correlation with the potential default cycle of the referenced debtor.

For instance, consider an insurance company that wishes to hedge the credit risk associated with a commercial loan issued by Company Y. Company Y is an industrial producer of heavy machinery with a current credit rating of BB. The seller of the credit derivative is a large money center bank with a large commercial loan department. Under the analysis discussed above, the insurance company should consider the operating cycle of Company Y as compared to that of the bank to determine whether a significant deterioration of Company Y's performance would occur at the same time as a downturn in the bank's performance. Unless the bank has a significant loan portfolio concentrated in the same heavy machinery industry as Company Y, it is unlikely that there is a high correlation between the bank's performance and that of Company Y. Even so, after the purchase of the credit derivative from the bank, the insurance company should continue to monitor the bank's performance for any signs of deterioration in its operations separate and distinct from those of Company Y.

Documentation Risk

Credit derivatives are a relatively new form of financial derivative instrument. Unlike swaps, forwards, and stock options, uniform documentation for credit derivatives does not exist. Although, the International Swap Dealers Association (ISDA) has established standardized documentation which is used by the financial industry to document financial swaps, it has not developed contracts for credit derivatives.[22] Consequently, two dealers offering similar credit derivative transactions, may present different documentation. To the extent that total rate of return swaps and default swaps resemble other swap transactions, ISDA documentation

---

[22] ISDA is currently working on documentation for credit swaps within a Master Schedule. However, standard language is still being developed.

may suffice. However, other credit derivatives such as credit options are typically subject to the individual documentation of the option seller.

For credit linked notes and default swaps, the criteria for default and the manner of calculating cash flows after a default are key issues to define. Without standardized contract forms, each term and definition of the credit derivative must be individually negotiated. Not only is this time consuming and expensive, it can be risky if the contractual terms are not well understood by both parties. Legal counsel for a credit protection buyer must play an integral role before a credit derivative is purchased.

For instance, when conducting a credit swap through a special purpose vehicle such as a trust, the following documentation will need to be negotiated: the trust document, the master swap agreement and supplementary schedule, swap confirmations, a note indenture, and a private placement memorandum. Negotiating these documents is time consuming as well as legally intensive, and considerable expense may be incurred by inside and outside legal counsel.

To the extent possible, a buyer of credit derivatives should strive to have the contractual terms consistent across all counterparties. Given the relative newness of these type of derivatives, the best way to ensure consistency is to develop a standard contract form in-house by the credit protection buyer. This will provide a starting point when negotiating the terms of the credit derivative with the dealer community, and subject the buyer less to the individuality of dealer contract forms.

Pricing Risk

Pricing risk is common to all derivative transactions, including credit derivatives. As the derivative markets have matured, the mathematical models used to price derivatives have become more complex. These models are increasingly dependent upon sophisticated assumptions regarding underlying economic parameters. Consequently, the prices of credit derivatives are very sensitive to the assumptions of the models.

Consider, for instance, the pricing of a credit default swap. The credit protection seller receives the total return on a referenced basket of assets in return for paying to the credit protection buyer a floating interest rate which is reset quarterly. To determine the present value of the credit swap, it is necessary to forecast the forward value of the quarterly credit payments, discount the individual forward values back to the present, and then take the summation of the present values.

However, the large and infrequent nature of credit payments required under a credit swap makes it difficult to accurately forecast the future payment amounts. Furthermore, the credit payments are dependent on a credit downgrade or default, which are discrete events as opposed to a risk neutral appreciation of value under standard forward pricing models.

Pricing models for credit options may involve stochastic strike prices, path dependent barrier options, mean reverting random credit spreads, or compound option modeling. Which model to choose depends on the structure of the transaction and the assumptions of the credit protection buyer and seller. If the term of the option is short and interest rates are assumed to be relatively constant, stochastic strike prices may not be necessary. Alternatively, if the referenced asset has a single coupon payment over the term of the option, path dependent pricing may not be needed. Further, if mean reverting credit spreads are used, their correlation with the term structure must be determined. Lastly, compound option pricing is only practical with European options — those exercisable at maturity.[23]

Given the relative immaturity of the credit derivative market, price discovery is one of the key issues facing credit derivatives. The complexity of the option models discussed above indicates that very sophisticated proprietary models must be used to properly value credit derivatives. However, until consistent valuation technology is developed, credit derivative purchasers must rely on the pricing of the credit dealer. The lack of uniform technology makes the pricing of credit derivatives less transparent and increases the pricing risk.

The complexity of pricing credit derivatives is compounded by the difficulty in hedging such transactions. Consider a default swap where the seller of the credit default swap will most likely make infrequent, but large, payments. The lack of continuity in payments, and the large, random cash outflows are in direct contrast to other financial derivatives, such as forwards and options, which have a continuous pricing function. The lack of a continuous pricing function makes it difficult to find an effective hedge which will match both the infrequent nature, and the size, of the cash outflows which the seller of the default swap must make under the credit derivative agreement. Yet a well developed derivative market depends on the ability to offset the risk of the derivative instruments. Without this hedging ability, a risk neutral position cannot be established which is a crucial element in determining derivative prices.

Liquidity Risk

Currently, there are no exchange-traded credit derivatives. Instead, they are traded over-the- counter as customized transactions designed to hedge or expose a specific risk for the credit derivative buyer. The very nature of this customization makes credit derivatives illiquid. Credit derivatives will not suit all parties in the financial market and therefore a party to a tailored credit derivative contract may be unable to obtain a "fair value" should he wish to exit his position before maturity.

Furthermore, with a relatively new market for credit derivatives, the dealer market for transacting in these instruments is still thin. Consequently, participants in this market may find it difficult to price transactions and to hedge cash flow exposures in an efficient manner. As a result, credit derivative participants may find themselves more vulnerable to a higher volatility of cash flows than other more developed derivative instruments. This is all the more compounded by the lack of an exchange-traded product.

---

[23] For a more detailed discussion on pricing credit derivatives, see the bibliography provided in footnote 12.

Lack of marketability, or liquidity risk, is hard to quantify. One way to manage this risk would be to take a "haircut" from the model or quoted price of the credit derivative. This haircutted price would incorporate the cost to the credit derivative seller to liquidate the credit derivative (or to repurchase it from the credit derivative buyer) before its maturity as well as the cost of unwinding the seller's hedge position for the derivative instrument. Consequently, a "fair exit price" may be a more accurate reflection of the true market value of the credit derivative rather than a theoretical or model value.

Regulatory Risk

With the relative youth of credit derivatives, regulators have not had time to formulate policies with respect to these instruments. Currently, banking regulations require a bank that hedges a loan via a credit swap to reserve capital against both the loan and the swap contract, rather than netting the two positions. However, bank regulators are beginning to address the issue of capital requirements for credit derivatives.

For instance, the Office of the Comptroller of the Currency (OCC) recently noted that national banks must ensure that credit derivatives are incorporated into their risk-based capital computations.[24] However, over the near term, the OCC has decided that risk-based capital calculations for credit derivatives will be determined on a case-by-case basis through a review of the specific characteristics of each transaction. Absent further guidance, it is up to the banks to determine whether the credit derivative resembles more, for instance, a standby letter of credit or an interest rate linked instrument in computing their capital requirements. There is a risk that inconsistent capital treatment for these derivatives may result in over exposed financial institutions with insufficient capital to cover potential defaults.

A similar lack of guidance exists with respect to risk-based capital requirements for federally-chartered banks. According to the Federal Reserve Board of Governors if a bank provides an unrestricted credit derivative to protect an entity from a credit default of a referenced asset or issuer, the bank must take a full capital charge based on the creditworthiness of the referenced asset or issuer.[25] However, if the bank provides a restrictive credit derivative such that the transfer of credit risk to the bank is limited, then the bank is directed to hold only "appropriate capital" while it is exposed to the credit risk of the referenced asset. What capital allocation constitutes an appropriate amount is left to the bank's discretion.

CONCLUSION

Credit derivatives are a relatively new addition to the financial markets. They provide an additional filter by which financial managers may isolate, price, and trade

---

[24] See Comptroller of the Currency, Release OCC NR 96-84, August 12, 1996.

[25] See Board of Governors of the Federal Reserve System, Division of Banking Supervision and Regulation, SR 96-17, August 12, 1996.

the fundamental credit risk associated with a commercial bank loan. Consequently, credit derivatives offer an efficient way to gain, or hedge, exposure to the credit markets through options, forwards, swaps, or credit linked notes.

However, credit derivatives are not without risks. The relative infancy of the market raises issues of pricing, liquidity, documentation, and regulation. Until these transactions become more uniform, participants in the high-yield and credit markets should use proper risk due diligence before entering into a credit derivative transaction.

Index